BAPTISTS THROUGH THE CENTURIES

BAPTISTS THROUGH THE CENTURIES
A History of a Global People

David W. Bebbington

BAYLOR UNIVERSITY PRESS

Cover design by Andrew Broyzna, AJB Design, Inc.
Cover image: The Jordan River, © Roman Sigaev / Shutterstock

Library of Congress Cataloging-in-Publication Data

Bebbington, D. W. (David William), 1949-
 Baptists through the Centuries : a history of a global people /
David W. Bebbington.
 p. cm.
 Includes bibliographical references (p.) and index.
 ISBN 978-1-60258-204-0 (pbk. : alk. paper)
 1. Baptists--History. I. Title.
 BX6231.B39 2010
 286.09--dc22
 2010004524

Printed in the United States of America on acid-free paper with a
minimum of 30% pcw recycled content.

To the President, Faculty, Staff, and Students
of Baylor University, Waco, Texas

CONTENTS

List of Illustrations

Acknowledgments

This book is the printed equivalent of a course I have taught at Truett Seminary, Baylor University, in Texas on four occasions since 2003. The students who took the course taught me a great deal about American Baptist history by their questions as well as their answers. Some of them generously allowed me to draw on the evidence contained in their written work. My graduate assistants, Tim Sisson and Lauren Tapley, began collecting the illustrations, and another, Ben Wetzel, has been particularly assiduous in preparing them for publication.

Many historians of the Baptists have contributed to the project. Bill Brackney, Bill Leonard, and Bill Pitts provided orientation in American Baptist history. The anonymous reviewers for the press helped reshape the argument of several chapters. Others gave guidance on a variety of points: Boone Aldridge, Cullen Clark, Michael Collis, Anthony Cross, Sébastien Fath, Gord Heath, Ken Manley, Ian Randall, Brian Stanley, Brian Talbot, Valdis Terauldkalns, and Linda Wilson. Friends from the Baptist Historical Society and the Scottish Baptist History Project laid many foundations and the contributors to the International Conferences on Baptist History over the years did much to erect the superstructure on global developments.

Several readers took pains to go through the text as it was completed during 2009. Ian Randall and Brian Stanley each commented on a chapter at very short notice. Eileen Bebbington, Barry Hankins, and Tommy Kidd undertook the task of examining the whole text. None of them is responsible for the views expressed here, but I appreciate how much their reactions have improved the book.

I am extremely grateful to all these people, named and unnamed, but the dedication expresses my particular thanks for generous institutional hospitality given me while preparing this book.

David W. Bebbington
23 January 2010
University of Stirling and Baylor University

Chapter 1

INTRODUCTION

In 1864 a congregation in the English East Midlands that was planning a baptism decided, according to the minutes of its church meeting, "that a pair of waterproof boots be purchased by the Church
for the occasion and for future Baptisms."[1] The congregation was
clearly not envisaging that the baptismal ceremonies would be conducted, as in most Christian churches, by sprinkling water on the
brow of an infant. So much water would be used that the minister in
charge would need boots to keep himself dry. The volume of water
shows that the candidates were to be submerged, and were evidently
to be large people. The mode of baptism was immersion; the subjects were to be those capable of conscious faith. This was a Baptist
church, one belonging to the New Connexion of General Baptists
in Castle Donington, Leicestershire. The type of baptism reveals
something central about the identity of the congregation. But the
entry in the minutes tells us more. Previously the minister had been
content to enter the water without protection when conducting baptisms, but now the church wanted him to escape the experience of
having his trousers soaked. The boots were designed to protect his
dignity—an indication of the growing respectability of the Castle

Donington Baptists. They no longer wished to see their minister facing the congregation after a baptism while dripping wet. Instead, they wished him to show a new measure of decorum and so reflect their rising status in the world. The New Connexion, once a fervent revival movement, was becoming more staid in its ways, and being wet in public no longer accorded with its members' self-image. The Castle Donington Baptists were accommodating themselves to their times and circumstances. The adjustment symbolized by the boots was as much a part of their identity as was the act of baptism itself.

This book attempts to address the question of who Baptists have been over the four centuries of their existence. It tries to take account of ways in which they adapted to the societies in which they lived as well as their central practices. The Castle Donington minister's waterproof boots are as much a part of the Baptists' story as the baptismal ceremonies themselves. Even the core attributes of the Baptists, however, are not simple matters to report. They were Protestants, and yet many in their ranks would have denied this suggestion, claiming an ancestry older than the Protestant Reformation. From the eighteenth century onwards most of them were Evangelicals, but some hotly repudiated the label. They practiced believer's baptism, and yet a number of Baptist churches allowed people to become full members without baptism of any kind. So it must not be assumed that Baptists possessed a single, consistent identity. There were, after all, many types of Baptists. The General Baptists of Castle Donington, for example, entirely repudiated the Calvinism that most Baptists then professed. The variety of Christian bodies called "Baptist" has to be taken into account. So does the consideration that there was great deal of change over time. The circumstances of the early seventeenth century, when Baptists first arose, were very different from those of the early twenty-first century. It was a hallmark of the denomination to be strongly attached to the Bible, but ways of understanding the place of scripture in ordering church life altered over the centuries. Again, there was much variation over space. Baptists soon spread from their origins in England to the New World and eventually planted churches in most countries on earth. There was great scope for adaptation in distinct ways to different cultural settings. The investigation of Baptist identity entails exploration of diversity.

The coverage of this book extends not just over England in the period from 1609 to the present but also over the world at large. It is true that Baptists first flourished among the English and, over the next two centuries, England remained the center of Baptist life, but the United States subsequently took over that role. A large majority of Baptists—roughly two-thirds—still live in the United States. In 2008 America could claim over 37 million Baptist church members, with more than 16 million in a single denomination, the Southern Baptist Convention. In the rest of the world the churches affiliated with the Baptist World Alliance could muster only about the same number of members as America's Southern Baptist Convention alone. A great deal of this book, therefore, focuses on England and America. Yet sizeable communities of Baptists have grown up elsewhere as well. Nigeria claims over 2 million members, while Congo, India, Myanmar (Burma), and Brazil all report between 1 and 2 million. There is, therefore, a need for Baptist history to have an international

A Russian Baptism (c. 1960)

dimension. Because research on many countries (including some of the nations just mentioned) is at a very preliminary stage, there are all too many gaps in the coverage of the present volume. The aim here is not to deal with every country where Baptists have existed, but to discuss broad trends with representative instances. It has been possible to draw on an increasing number of articles with international themes that have been published in recent years. The Baptist World Alliance has encouraged historical work, and since 1997 there have been International Conferences on Baptist Studies, held every three years, that have generated papers on many parts of the world. This book is heavily indebted to those studies. A valuable compendium of information about Baptists in every land has also appeared, *Baptists around the World* (1995), edited by Albert W. Wardin. There have also been some outstanding monographs on Baptist history. Brian Stanley's *History of the Baptist Missionary Society, 1792–1992* (1992) is a model account of the planting of churches in every continent by the main British Baptist missions agency. Ken R. Manley's *From Woolloomooloo to "Eternity"* (2006) is a comprehensive analysis of Baptist life in Australia. These books show something of what can be achieved by detailed research.

This volume can claim much less, for it relies heavily on the research of others. It is primarily a work of synthesis that attempts to put the pieces of the puzzle into an intelligible framework. Its approach is, in the first place, topical. In accordance with the maxim that it is better to study problems rather than periods, each chapter addresses an issue in Baptist history. Some topics are limited in time, but others extend over the whole length of the denomination's existence. In each case, a single theme occupies the entire chapter. A second feature of the book is its effort to set the problems at hand in a wider context than Baptist history. Baptists did not exist alone, and so the analysis gives space to the broader influences—intellectual, social, and political—that played on religious developments. In addition, other Christians are not forgotten, because their stories often interwove with that of the Baptists. The third aspect worth mentioning is the principle of organization. Countries are not kept apart, for that misrepresents the reality of the past. For all the contrasts between different nations, Baptists traveled between them, read each other's writings, and corresponded across oceans. What happened in one part of the world was often duplicated elsewhere. The studies of a particular theme, therefore, draw together evidence from different countries. In the early chapters dealing with periods when Baptists lived almost exclusively in Britain and America, the discussion covers only those lands. In later chapters, which cover the years in which Baptists reached other parts of the world, developments elsewhere are taken into account. This is especially true of the two chapters on missions and global spread, but there, too, the examination concentrates on factors that impinged on more than one land at a time. By dealing with issues in their contexts and by weaving together accounts of different countries, this study offers a portrait of the Baptists that may, in some respects, look new.

The chapters are arranged so as to begin with a roughly chronological view of the main developments in Baptist life down to the twentieth century. Chapter 2 considers what preceded the emergence of the Baptists, the Protestant Reformation. The next chapter addresses the vexed question of the relationship between the continental Anabaptists and English Baptist origins. Then, in chapters 4 and 5, there is discussion of the Particular and General Baptists in the seventeenth century and of the Evangelical Awakening in the eighteenth. The internal frictions of the nineteenth century are treated in chapter 6, before two parallel chapters take the story into the twentieth century by covering debates over liberal trends in theology and pressing problems in society. The four following chapters turn to examine issues over the entire period of Baptist existence. Chapter 9 considers the evolution of Baptist attitudes on race, and chapter 10 the place of women in Baptist life. Chapter 11 examines Baptist doctrines of the church, ministry, and sacraments, and chapter 12 the Baptist record on religious liberty. Two further chapters broaden the coverage to the world at large during the nineteenth and twentieth centuries. In chapter 13 the theme is Baptist missions to non-Christian peoples; and then chapter 14 discusses the means by which Baptists advanced in nominally Christian lands. The fifteenth chapter takes up the question of Baptist identity itself, a subject of acute controversy in the later twentieth century, and carries the analysis down into the twenty-first century. Finally, the conclusion pulls together the themes of the book as a whole. The aim is to review what Baptists were like down the generations and across the globe. This book is about their efforts to propagate the faith and so to have baptisms to conduct. It is also about the boots that the Castle Donington minister needed for a baptism in order to look respectable.

Chapter 2

Roots in the Reformation

The origins of the Baptists lie in the maelstrom of the sixteenth-
century Reformation. The medieval Catholic Church in the West
had preserved, for the most part, the substance of unity. It had
been far from monolithic, with a plethora of secular and regular
clergy, monks and friars, confraternities and guilds. Dominicans
and Franciscans, though both were orders of friars, had an intense
rivalry that at times degenerated into buffets and blows. The notion
of an age of faith, single in practice and uniform in observance, is
far from the reality of western Christianity during the later Middle
Ages. Even the papacy, in theory a focus of unity, had been riven
by schism in the later fourteenth and early fifteenth centuries. For
nearly a century there were two popes—and for a while there were
three—bidding against each other for international support and
anathematizing each other in unmeasured terms. Yet the sense that
the church was a single entity had triumphed, not least through the
conciliar movement that saw councils of the whole church as the
remedies for the ecclesiastical shortcomings of the times. Worship
formed a common bond. Although there were many eucharistic lit-
urgies in use in different places, there was an awareness that they

were all variants of one pattern of the mass. The central sacramental act of the faith united Christians, even if they were more often observers than participants. Catholicity, the principle that all believers were in communion with one another, was a visible reality. But the Reformation was to alter all that.

In the two centuries beginning around 1500 all semblance of unity was shattered. There had been local anticipations beforehand. During the fifteenth century the followers of Jan Hus in Bohemia broke away from the structures of the church to create their own congregations. But only after the start of the sixteenth century were there divisions within Europe as a whole, divisions as acute as the rift that had long subsisted between the Eastern Orthodox and the Western Catholics. Christians ceased to be in communion with one another. The Catholic Church continued under the authority of the popes and gained the allegiance of southern Europe, a proportion that grew rather than shrank over the decades. Protestants, however, took over large stretches of the north. Lutherans dominated much of northern Germany and Scandinavia. The Reformed, whose leading figure was John Calvin, initially made strong advances in France, but fell back on their bastions in Geneva, the Netherlands, Scotland, and parts of Germany and Hungary. The Church of England, firmly Protestant but nevertheless distinctive, became the established form of the faith in its land. In regions of eastern Europe such as Transylvania, Unitarianism put down deep roots. Scattered around many areas were Anabaptists of various kinds, Mennonites and others, who testified to the ideal of a gathered church and so differed from the predominant expressions of Christianity. England was the place where, by the middle years of the seventeenth century, the greatest diversity was to be found. Alongside the Anglicans were Presbyterians, Independents, Quakers, and a number of other bodies. Among them were the Particular Baptists, the General Baptists, the Seventh Day Baptists, and those who, with John Bunyan, the author of *Pilgrim's Progress* (1678), believed that Baptists and Independents should worship together. The Baptists, themselves divided into groupings that were not in communion with each other, were part of a new pattern of religious allegiance in the West. The age of the denomination had been born.

At the opening of the sixteenth century the subsequent fragmentation would have seemed unlikely. The Catholic Church was not, as later Protestant apologists often depicted it, hopelessly corrupt, alienated from the sympathies of the people and so ripe for reformation. The monasteries of Europe, though sometimes marked by abuses, were often being reformed already. The bishops were, on average, more rather than less responsible than in the past. Anticlericalism among the laity was weak, as evidenced by relatively few complaints about the inadequacy of pastoral care. In England the kings were on good terms with the papacy, prosperous folk gave generously to the church, and ordinary people participated in religious affairs with gusto. At Morebath in Devon, a parish that has been examined particularly closely, organizations for different age and gender groups ensured general involvement in church activities by most people in the village. There were regular fund-raising efforts, annual elections of lay officials, and a pervasive sense of responsibility for ensuring that the parish church was properly equipped for worship.[1] The faith was closely integrated with popular culture. Saints were venerated, often because of their reputation as healers of the sick who called on their aid. The fear of death was mitigated by the belief that prayers for the departed could reduce the period in purgatory before the dead could enjoy the repose of heaven. Ceremonies that reformers would subsequently denounce as lacking biblical warrant, such as pilgrimages and street processions, provided genuine enjoyment. The late medieval church was strong in the affections of the people.

Furthermore, there were powerful currents of spiritual change that were independent of the Reformation. Although they often flowed into the demands for doctrinal alteration made by the reformers, these developments were originally distinct and had the effect of revitalizing the enduring Catholic Church. There were places where preaching was invested with fresh importance and informal elements were inserted into the liturgy in the language of the people. A tide of *devotio moderna* ("modern devotion") swept through parts of Europe, especially in the Low Countries, enabling laypeople, female as well as male, to follow a style of spirituality that had once been confined to the monasteries. Its most influential product, Thomas à Kempis' *The Imitation of Christ* (c. 1418), was a manual that encouraged many to adopt a disciplined life of Christ-centered piety. The gathering intellectual forces of the Renaissance were also impinging on Christian thought. Its chief dimension, the rediscovery of classical works containing treasures of human knowledge, gave rise to the label "humanism" for the higher standards of scholarship that many adopted. Far from implying any disparagement of divine revelation, humanist learning fostered the study of the text of the Bible. The greatest of the humanist scholars, Desiderius Erasmus, published in 1516 an edition of the New Testament that established its authentic contents with unprecedented authority. Theologians of the past with a message for the present were also in fashion. In particular, Augustine, the most trenchant critic among the early fathers of the notion that salvation can be achieved by merit, was read with renewed interest. Many of these stirrings were to be taken up by those who, from the middle years of the sixteenth century, were to mount a Counter-Reformation within Catholicism, but they also prepared the way for the revolution that was the Reformation itself.

THE CONTINENTAL REFORMATION

The leader of the revolution was Martin Luther. As a cloistered monk (significantly, in the order named after Augustine) and biblical scholar, Luther reached the conclusion that salvation was the gift of God to those who put their faith in Christ. Hence he was angered by the declarations of Johann Tetzel, a preaching friar, that the kingdom of heaven was open to those who bought indulgences, freeing them from their sins and so shortening their time in purgatory. Luther denounced the system of indulgences in 1517, reputedly by posting a list of ninety-five academic theses on the door of the castle church in Wittenberg. His message electrified Europe, especially the northern half, where purgatory was a greater preoccupation. As Luther developed his teaching over subsequent years, he came into collision with the papacy for refusing its authority and turned to the princes of Germany for support. He insisted that justification, the way in which a person is put right with God, is by faith alone. The authority for that good news is the Bible, which Luther translated into German, more clearly in some parts of scripture than others. The letter of James, with its teaching that salvation is by works as well as faith, seemed highly dubious. Luther's principle was "scripture alone" (*sola scriptura*) rather than "scripture by itself" (*nuda scriptura*), for he still respected the tradition of the church, embracing the creeds. He approved infant baptism and found fault with aspects of worship and church organization only if they were clearly condemned by the Bible. Lutherans often continued to observe Catholic saints' days and to call their communion service "mass." Reformation in Luther's idiom was more drastic in its doctrine than in its practice.

Other reformers took the process of change further. In the Swiss city of Zurich during the 1520s, Huldrych Zwingli led one of many civic reformations. Breaking with Luther's typically moderate teaching that the bread and wine in the eucharist, though still remaining bread and wine, coexist with the actual body and blood of Christ, Zwingli contended that there is no change in the elements whatsoever. Instead, the Lord's supper is a way in which the Christian community reaffirms its identity by remembering the sacrifice of Christ that brought it into being. In 1529 there was an attempt at reconciling the two sides, sponsored by Philip of Hesse, the most energetic princely protector of the rising Protestant cause, but it failed through Luther's intransigence. To him, those who adopted Zwingli's position were fanatics.

In Geneva, another Swiss city, John Calvin exercised his powerful ministry from 1541, particularly among his fellow Frenchmen, who flocked to what became a model Reformed community. As early as 1536 Calvin, who was a humanist and lawyer by training, had written his *Institutes*, in which he outlined his theology systematically. The Almighty, he held, had chosen those who would be saved. This is the kernel of the doctrine of predestination for which Calvin is best known, but it was not the center of his system. Rather,

John Calvin (1509–1564)
Protestant Reformer

he stressed that salvation came by grace as the undeserved gift of God. On the communion service, he adopted a position midway between those of Luther and Zwingli: the elements do not convey Christ's body and blood, but they do bring a special grace unique to the sacrament. There was a conservative streak in Calvin's thought that led him, for example, to retain belief in the perpetual virginity of Mary the mother of Jesus. He retained infant baptism on the supposed analogy of circumcision in the Old Testament. Yet those who thought like Calvin, who became known as the Reformed, adopted a radical approach to discipline and worship. Discipline of church members for moral or doctrinal offenses was treated as a defining quality of a true church. In worship, instead of merely rejecting, like Luther, whatever scripture condemned, the Reformed asserted a firm regulative principle: the only legitimate features were what could be shown to have biblical support, "scripture warrant." Thus musical instruments had no New Testament sanction and so must disappear from worship. Here was the application of a root-and-branch biblicism.

THE REFORMATION IN ENGLAND

Baptists were to be influenced by the major reformers on the continent, Luther, Zwingli, and Calvin, but their own traditions were to emerge from developments in England. The English Reformation of the sixteenth century had a partial precedent in the Lollard movement. Lollards were inspired by the teachings of John Wyclif, a fourteenth-century Oxford scholar who denounced unsparingly the materialism of the church. His view was that the people should have the Bible in their own tongue so that they could compare contemporary ecclesiastical practice with what it ought to be. Copies of a translation made by his disciples circulated during subsequent years among the common people, particularly in certain areas such as the Chiltern Hills of Buckinghamshire. Periodically the trials of Lollards for heresy before the church courts revealed the opinions they commonly held. They appealed to the Bible as the charter of their beliefs; rejected images, pilgrimages, and prayers to saints; and showed a contempt for the clergy that led them to dismiss the medieval sacrament of confession to a priest. They did not, however, show any trace of the doctrine of justification by faith alone that was to energize the Reformation. Nor did Lollards start separate churches with their own pattern of ministry. Yet, when Luther's ideas began to filter into England, some of them seem to have merged fairly rapidly into the rising tide of Protestant feeling. It is probably significant that the Chilterns were to become an area of strength for the General Baptists in the seventeenth century. Lollardy did provide a program of diffuse religious dissent that anticipated aspects of the Reformation.

The process of religious change in England, however, was strongly associated with affairs of state. In the 1520s Henry VIII needed a male heir to ensure the continuity of good government, and became convinced that his wife, Catherine of Aragon, had given him only a daughter because he had infringed church teaching by marrying someone who had previously been the wife of his older brother. The pope disagreed and so refused to nullify the marriage. The masterful Henry broke with the papacy over the issue, ended his marriage with Catherine, and took Anne Boleyn, a patron of the Protestant cause, as his new wife. The corollary was that, in 1534, the church in Henry's dominions declared its independence under his headship. His first minister, Thomas Cromwell, and his Archbishop of Canterbury, Thomas Cranmer, pressed forward with church reform. The monasteries were dissolved and the Bible was made available in English in the parish churches. Although official change came to a standstill during Henry's later years, and in a few respects the clock turned back, the pace of transformation in a Protestant direction quickened in the short reign of his son, Edward VI. For six years from 1547, the government run for the boy king by his Lord Protectors welcomed leading Protestant theologians from the continent, pushed through the dissolution of the chantries where mass had been said for souls in purgatory, and issued two successive Books of Common Prayer designed by Cranmer. The second, published in 1552, was firmly Protestant in its teaching. It seemed that England would act as the leading champion of the Reformation in Europe.

The early death of Edward VI in 1553, however, put the process into reverse. His successor, Queen Mary I, was the daughter of Catherine of Aragon, and, like her, was a devout Catholic. Mary embarked on a policy of Catholic restoration. The leading figures in the church under Edward were removed from office. Two bishops, Latimer and Ridley, were burned for heresy in Oxford. Cranmer, who handed the Catholic regime a propaganda victory by recanting his views as archbishop, then won a greater triumph at his own burning by returning to his Protestant faith, famously putting the hand that wrote the recantation first into the flames. These scenes, and many judicial killings of lesser figures, earned Mary an unenviable reputation for cruelty. Although, at her accession, Protestant commitment was relatively weak in the population at large except in the southeast near London, she managed to alienate many more of her subjects. Meanwhile, those who fled to the continent to escape persecution made common cause with the more advanced personalities of the Reformed world. In Frankfurt and elsewhere they hammered out plans for further change in a Protestant direction, should Mary ever pass from the scene. In Geneva from 1557 they translated the Bible into English, a version that was to become the standard form of the scriptures for half a century and more. The marginal notes encouraged readers to see the text through Reformed eyes. The reign of Mary, if it had lasted, might have managed to marginalize Protestantism. It ended, however, with the queen's death in 1558, when refugees flocked back to provide leadership for the Church of England. By creating martyrs and exiles, Mary did almost as much as her half-brother Edward had done to advance the Protestant cause.

The accession of Elizabeth I, Mary's younger half-sister, the daughter of Anne Boleyn, and a resolute Protestant, led to a consolidation of the Reformed faith in England. The settlement of religion in the early years of her reign was not a compromise between Catholicism and Protestantism, but a Protestant triumph carried against Catholic opposition. "We have searched out of the Holy Bible, which we are sure cannot deceive," declared John Jewel, Bishop of Salisbury, in his *Apology of the Church of England* (1562), "one sure form of religion, and have returned again unto the primitive church of the ancient fathers and apostles."[2] The Thirty-Nine Articles of 1563, which constituted the standard of orthodoxy under the new regime, were emphatically Reformed in their contents. Elizabeth as the Supreme Governor of the church and her chief minister, William Cecil, Lord Burghley, ensured that ecclesiastical affairs were firmly under their control. A symbol of the new state of affairs was the replacement of the depiction of the crucifixion over the screen in many parish churches by the royal coat of arms. Catholics were excluded from office and, after the queen was excommunicated and declared deposed by the pope in 1570, they were subject to persecution. The reason, the government insisted, was not because they were Catholics but because they were traitors to the crown. Yet Elizabeth retained features of medieval religion in her settlement. Bishops still administered the church and cathedrals retained their distinctive place. It was fully expected that, after the interim arrangements made in 1559, there would be further reform. Four years later, the bishops, mostly ex-Marian exiles, supported extensive change, but the queen wanted no rocking of the boat. Although the country was firmly Protestant, there was considerable scope for restiveness among the more fervent reformers.

THE RISE OF PURITANISM

That was the context in which Puritanism arose. The term, first heard in 1565, applied to those who considered the process of Reformation in England incomplete. Their aim was to purify the church of the remains of Catholic superstition. In the past there has been a tendency among historians to see the period beginning with the Elizabethan settlement and culminating in the Civil Wars of the 1640s as a struggle between Anglicans and Puritans, the defenders of the Church of England against those wishing to replace it with a more Reformed institution. In light of the work of Patrick Collinson, that perception of the era is no longer tenable.[3] At this time the Church of England had not forged a distinct theological identity, a *via media* ("middle way") between Protestantism and Catholicism. Rather, despite its retention of bishops, cathedrals, and the like, it was emphatically Protestant, a part of the international Reformed community. Its bishops, and increasingly its clergy and people, were attached to the doctrines that Calvin and his fellow reformers had crystallized on the continent. Puritans shared these beliefs with the bulk of their Christian contemporaries in England. The difference that marked off Puritans, or "precisionists" as they were sometimes called, was how far they wanted to go, and how far they were prepared to go, in changing the arrangements that Elizabeth had introduced. Whereas many others were prepared to tolerate what the government had set up and maintained, Puritans held that loyalty to scripture required additional steps of ecclesiastical change. The line between Puritans and others was therefore much more fluid than was once supposed, with self-restraint varying from time to time and place to place among the hotter sort of Protestants. There were many, however, who believed that the Reformation was not yet over.

The Puritan impulse cannot be fully understood unless its ideological mainspring is appreciated. Behind it lay a powerful detestation of idolatry. In the Ten Commandments as used by the Western church in the Middle Ages, the prohibition of graven images was incorporated in the first commandment against having any other gods before the Lord. First in Zurich, and then in England from 1535, there was a renumbering so that the denunciation of graven images became the second commandment and so stood in its own right. The Reformed community in general, though not Catholics or Lutherans, therefore saw the erection of idolatrous substitutes for the Almighty as a cardinal sin. Indeed, according to a late Elizabethan Puritan, Abdias Ashton, "under idolatry and vain confidence in men all other sins are contained."[4] Anything that obscured the single-minded honor that was due to God alone came under the censure of Puritans. They objected to the wedding service in the Book of Common Prayer introduced by the Elizabethan regime for making the groom say that he offered "worship" to his bride; they whitewashed over medieval pictures of saints on church walls, smashed their images, and considered whether it was a duty to pull down churches named after saints altogether. Worship in particular, they thought, must be purified lest the Almighty should be mocked. Because, as Puritans increasingly believed, the validity of their faith needed to be tested by their behavior, they asked whether their services were clear of the taint of idolatry. If there was any trace of disrespect for the divine will, their worship might be insulting to God. In that case their faith might be vain and their salvation imperiled. There was the strongest of reasons for ensuring that the public services of the church conformed to scriptural principles. At all costs idolatry had to be banished.

The first clash between Puritans and the Elizabethan authorities took place over vestments, the clothes in which clergy dressed in church. The Prayer Book, as officially interpreted, required them to wear white surplices to conduct services. This distinctive form of dress, according to Puritans, had no scripture warrant. Furthermore, it marked off its wearers, the clergy, as different from the laity, and so formed a visible rejection of the priesthood of all believers that Protestants had held dear since Luther. Some Puritan ministers simply discarded the surplice, but in 1566, on the orders of the government, Archbishop Parker demanded that all should observe the church's rules. Thirty-seven clergy in the diocese of London were suspended and those who remained firm were expelled from the ministry. The result was the first wave of separations from the Church of England. A group led by ministers deprived of their duties assembled regularly for worship in Plumbers' Hall until it was broken up in 1567. The members of another "privy church," led by Richard Fitz, made the grounds of their secession explicit. "These Popish garments. &c," ran the statement that they subscribed, "are now become very Idolles in deede, because they are exalted aboue the worde of the almightie."[5] There must, they insisted, be no toying with soul-destroying idolatry. These people, who seem to have been confined to London, were not rejecting the authority of the state to require religious conformity. Rather, they were so scandalized by the form of public worship expected of them that they felt bound to withdraw from the church. They were the most extreme of the Puritans of their day.

A more intellectual Puritan case emerged at Cambridge shortly afterwards. Thomas Cartwright, Lady Margaret Professor of Divinity, argued in 1570 for the equality of all ministers and so for the abolition of bishops. This contention was to extend the Puritan critique from the conduct of worship to the organization of the church. The continental Reformed churches, the Stranger Church for foreign Protestants in London, and increasingly the Scottish kirk acted as models of how reform could be carried further than in the Church of England. The pattern urged by Cartwright approximated to later Presbyterianism, though there was still much more fluidity about ideals of the church than in later centuries. Others took up Cartwright's call. In 1572 an address to parliment called not only for the purification of the Prayer Book from abuses "picked out of that popish dunghill, the mass book," but also censured the bishops as "antichristian and devilish."[6] By 1586 Puritans were asking parliament to introduce a new system of discipline based on the Scottish example. At Dedham in Suffolk an embryonic Presbyterian synod brought together representatives of several Puritan congregations to consider matters of joint concern. Down to about 1590 there was a growing impetus to press forward with structural reform in the Church of England. From then onwards, however, the government showed clearly that it intended to be inflexible. The Puritan case was answered more vigorously by defenders of the established order. Bishops, they now claimed, were not only allowable but actually a required element of the church. The Church of England as Elizabeth had created it was becoming an immutable feature of the landscape.

THE EMERGENCE OF SEPARATISM

The persistent rigidity of the authorities induced increasing frustration among the most dedicated Puritans. The existing church was, in their view, palpably unreformed, and yet they despaired of being able to persuade the government to eliminate its remaining Catholic characteristics. Some began to consider setting up churches that were properly ordered outside the Church of England. In 1582 Robert Browne, a Cambridge graduate who had been influenced by Cartwright, published *A Treatise of Reformation without Tarrying for Any*. If the state would not complete the Reformation, he argued, the task must be taken up by individuals who recognized the obligation to obey God fully, so creating gathered churches of those who were willing to join. Although Browne subsequently submitted to the authorities and accepted livings in the Church of England, his views persisted. John Greenwood, Henry Barrow, and John Penry were arrested for propagating similar opinions and executed in 1593 for treason against the royal supremacy. In a sense the government was right to perceive the separatists as challenging the authority of the crown. Francis Johnson, a clergyman who became pastor of a London separatist church in 1592, insisted that, because Christ was not just prophet and priest but also "king of his church," the godly must obey all Christ's commandments for governing the church.[7] In effect, Johnson was erecting a form of monarchy in the religious sphere in competition with the royal supremacy. Johnson, like the other separatist leaders, was arrested, but was allowed his freedom in 1597 on condition of his leaving the country. He joined his own congregation in exile at Amsterdam, where greater religious tolerance allowed its members to worship unmolested. This church, though racked by disputes over cases of discipline, maintained a principled separatism in exile.

The new century seemed to offer new hope for the Puritan cause when, in 1603, Elizabeth died. Her successor, James VI of Scotland (who became James I of England), had accepted the Presbyterian form of church government north of the border and so might be expected to introduce fresh measures of reform in his new realm. Some thousand of the Puritan clergy requested changes and the king agreed to meet their representatives at Hampton Court Palace in January 1604. There were high hopes that, at the least, the sign of the cross in infant baptism would be abolished. The king, however, would make no concessions that might undermine episcopacy. James had reached the conclusion that submission in the church was a prerequisite for submission in the state. His principle, as he famously put it, was "No bishop, no king." The one significant result of the conference was agreement to begin a new official translation of the Bible, which led, in 1610, to the publication of the Authorized or King James Version. But the Puritans were bitterly disappointed. With no prospect of official progress toward completion of the Reformation, many of their more fervent spirits reached the conclusion that, if change was to come, they had to accomplish it themselves. In the wake of the Hampton Court conference, therefore, there was a fresh upsurge of radical and separatist sentiment. Those who had previously hoped for something like a Presbyterian order in the state church began to believe that it would never be enacted and so only independent congregations could expect to introduce a rigorously pure worship. Henry Jacob, who was to gather a church that eventually reached Baptist conclusions, decided at this time that the way in which churches are ordered is not optional but a matter of obedience to God's word. This was also the point at which John Smyth, afterwards the first to embrace believer's baptism, moved into separatism. Those who believed, by the early seventeenth century, that the national Reformation had failed were at the heart of the circles in which Baptist convictions first appeared.

The Puritans within the Church of England continued their preaching and teaching, recruiting a steadily higher proportion of the population to their cause over the next quarter of a century. In 1612 a moderate Puritan, George Abbot, was appointed Archbishop of Canterbury. At the same time, however, there was a counter-movement within the established church. Even in the reign of Elizabeth there had existed a small body of clergy, especially at Westminster Abbey, who wanted more elaborate ceremonial in worship. Under James I, Lancelot Andrewes, Bishop of Ely from 1609 and of Winchester from 1618, gave spiritual and intellectual leadership to this party. Drawing directly on the thought of the early church, he fashioned a style of doctrine and devotion that was definitely anti-Calvinist. This grouping gained the ascendancy in the Church of England when, in 1629, James' son and successor, Charles I, appointed William Laud as Bishop of London. Four years later Laud followed Abbot as Archbishop of Canterbury. He pursued a single-minded policy of promoting the standing of the church and of introducing beauty into worship. To the horror of Puritans, he called for communion tables to be removed from the body of the church, where they had normally been sited since the Elizabethan settlement, and put against the east wall of the chancel, where they could be aligned on the pattern of Catholic altars. In 1640 new regulations required the communion tables to be railed off from the people; they also encouraged bowing toward the altar as a devotional practice. Such policies made many feel that the government wanted to roll back the Reformation entirely. They noticed with alarm that Charles' queen, Henrietta Maria, did not trouble to hide her Catholic allegiance. Alongside Charles' arbitrary rule and refusal to call parliament, these measures fostered the discontent that led to the Civil Wars of the 1640s.

The trend in the affairs of the Church of England also fostered a renewal of the separatist tendency. It was at this juncture that several of the early churches that were to adopt a Baptist identity came into being. At Bristol, for example, a group who worshiped in a parish church had been meeting regularly to pray and, in common Puritan style, to repeat sermons to each other. The policies of Laud deeply troubled them, but in 1639 one of their number named Matthew Hazzard was appointed to the living of St. Ewin's, a church in the town center. The members of the group were initially able to attend the church without violating their consciences, but then began to entertain scruples about attending Prayer Book services at all. They covenanted together to worship God "more purely," although they allowed themselves to slip into church in time for Hazzard's sermon. Next, however, a Baptist from London named John Cann spoke to them of "ye Duty of Separation from ye Worship of Antichrist, Cleaveing close to ye Doctrine of our Lord Jesus and his instituted worship."[8] Accordingly, they ceased hearing sermons in the parish church and became outright separatists. At first they were simply Independents, or Congregationalists, maintaining a church for believers only but retaining infant baptism. They went on to adopt believer's baptism as an option, and, though continuing to allow members to join without baptism, the congregation became known as Broadmead Baptist Church.

The seventeenth-century chronicler of Broadmead recorded the twelve steps they had passed through to reach the stage of gathering as a fully separated church. The nation had thrown off the "false Doctrine of ye church of Rome" about the sacrament of the Lord's supper and salvation by merit; the authorities had done away with monks, friars, abbots, and priests, "the Nest of Idollaters"; then, as "a step further in Reformation," feast days and saints' days had been abolished. The godly had gone on to reject carnal preachers, to become attached to "lively and powerful preachers," and to abandon listening to written pulpit homilies. They stopped bowing at the name of Jesus and to the altar, "a direct and visible breach of ye Second commandment"; they ceased to make the sign of the cross in infant baptism (which, the chronicler remarked, was good, though not as good as dropping infant baptism altogether); and they no longer used pictures and images. They refused to kneel to receive the bread and wine because even a "decency that God hath not commanded must not be observed"; they broke with the Prayer Book, "that *Nurse of Formality*"; and, finally, they declined to hear sermons by any ministers who conducted Prayer Book worship. It was a catalogue of steady illumination, as "ye Lord led them by Degrees, and brought them out of Popish Darknesse into his Marvellous light of ye Gospell."[9] The list shows how the earliest Baptists were preoccupied with ensuring that they should flee from all residual traces of Catholic influence, including those recently reintroduced by Archbishop Laud into the Church of England. Worship was their central concern. To purify their services of all hints of idolatry was their overriding aim.

The early Baptists were the products of their times. They were conscious of the broad outlines of the Reformation that had preceded their emergence. There had been protests by Luther, Zwingli, and Calvin against doctrines and practices that obscured the centrality of personal faith in the Christian life. In England the Lollards had long criticized the existing church. There had been tentative official moves toward change under Henry VIII, rapid developments in the same direction under Edward VI, and a sudden and cruel reversal under Mary. The Church of England under Elizabeth had established Protestantism, but there seemed to be much more scope for reform. Puritans wanted to press on with the task, objecting in particular to the idolatry that seemed bound up with the existing form of worship. The failure of demands for further change, especially at the Hampton Court conference, led to the creation of separatist congregations whose members would not tarry for the authorities. When, in the 1630s, the Church of England turned back toward Roman Catholic ceremonies, the undercurrent of hostility to false worship surfaced even more powerfully. Churches such as Broadmead arose in the middle years of the seventeenth century in order to bring the process of religious reform to its consummation. Like the Independents, Baptists were the heirs of the Reformation, Puritanism, and separatism. They adopted the same principles of punctilious loyalty to the word of God, of passionate desire to worship the Almighty correctly, and of willingness to restructure the church in accordance with God's precepts. Their biblical, liturgical, and ecclesiastical priorities drove them through Puritan loyalties into separatism and, eventually, to the further step of repudiating infant baptism. Baptists were the people who took Reformation principles to their ultimate conclusion.

FURTHER READING

Collinson, Patrick. *The Elizabethan Puritan Movement*. London: Cape, 1967.

Duffy, Eamon. *The Voices of Morebath: Reformation and Rebellion in an English Village*. New Haven, Conn.: Yale University Press, 2001.

George, Timothy. *Theology of the Reformers*. Nashville: Broadman, 1990.

MacCulloch, Diarmaid. *The Reformation: Europe's House Divided*. London: Penguin, 2004.

Marshall, Peter. *Reformation England, 1480–1642*. London: Arnold, 2003.

McGrath, Alister E. *Reformation Thought: An Introduction*. 3rd ed. Oxford: Blackwell, 2000.

Chapter 3

ANABAPTISTS AND BAPTISTS

The most developed historiographical controversy concerning the Baptists surrounds their relationship with the Anabaptists. Are the origins of the Baptists solely to be found in their evolution from Puritan separatism in the way the last chapter has outlined? Or were they also indebted to the Anabaptist movement on the continent? The Anabaptists, who had existed for much of the sixteenth century, practiced believer's baptism, their name, given by their opponents, meaning that they upheld "again baptizing" adults who had already been taken to the font as infants. The idea that there was a bond between Baptists and Anabaptists was popular in the nineteenth century with those who wanted to argue that believer's baptism had never died out since the apostles' time. The Anabaptists, on this understanding, were those who in the early sixteenth century passed on to the Baptists a perennial witness. When it became clearer that there was no such succession of true baptismal practice down through the centuries, those Baptists in the twentieth century who wished to forge links with features of the Anabaptist testimony such as pacifism were still predisposed to see connections between the two movements in the past. But the advocates of the case for a legacy to the Baptists from the Anabaptists are by no means confined to the ranks of those who have contemporary rather than historical reasons for their standpoint. In England the mid-twentieth-century Baptist historian and ecclesiastical statesman Ernest Payne, though admittedly swayed by his ecumenical sympathies for the Mennonites, argued for indebtedness; and in America the influential William R. Estep made a persuasive case for the same point of view.[1] Against them, however, are ranged, in England, the most authoritative expert on seventeenth-century Baptists, Barrie White, and, in America, the distinguished scholar Winthrop S. Hudson.[2] Other historians have played a prominent part in the same debate. It is one that is particularly worth exploring.

THE ANABAPTISTS

The Anabaptists arose from the first stirrings of the Reformation. They were part of its more radical expression that grew up alongside the so-called magisterial Reformation of Luther, Zwingli, and Calvin that was considered in the last chapter. The radicals were a diverse set of people, often but by no means always humble and unlearned, who pushed the process of change much further than other reformers. In many cases they believed that the true church had been lost on earth since the time when Christian organizations had succumbed to worldly forces, often identified as the reign of Constantine. The church had fallen away, and so needed to be restored rather than reformed. Radicals were prepared to start again from scratch in a way the better-known reformers deplored. The radicals might strike out in a direction that emphasized the inward role of the Holy Spirit and so properly be labeled "Spiritualists"; or they might apply reason to matters of religion, so becoming what have been called "Evangelical Rationalists." The Anabaptists, however, were a loose amalgam of those who turned with fresh eyes to the New Testament, examining its pages for new insight into the divine will. By contrast with the magisterial reformers who upheld the essential continuity of the Testaments, Anabaptists believed that there was a significant difference: the Old Testament, though fully inspired, was only the background to the New, which gave unique guidance to believers in the era of the church. Hence the teaching of Jesus about putting up the sword took precedence over the legitimation of war in the Old Testament, leading many Anabaptists to a pacifist position. Anabaptists were willing to reach unpopular conclusions and stick by them.

Anabaptist beliefs first sprang up at Zurich among the more extreme disciples of Zwingli. The earliest baptisms of believers were conducted there by Conrad Grebel in 1525. Two years later, the movement had matured sufficiently to issue the Schleitheim Confession. In this statement the members of the new grouping repudiated not just war but also lawsuits and oaths, so turning their backs on the ordinary customs of the day. The Anabaptists were withdrawing from society as it was known at the time to create a counter-culture of their own. In the early 1530s the movement spread to the Low Countries under the leadership of Melchior Hoffmann, who combined believer's baptism with a fiery millenarian message that the world was about to end. The Anabaptists of the Netherlands, though not those of Switzerland, followed Hoffmann in his distinctive views on the doctrine of the incarnation. He contended that Christ came to earth through his mother Mary, but did not take flesh from her. The infant Savior passed through her in the way that water flows through a pipe, so that his manhood, like his divinity, came from heaven. This view differed from received Christian orthodoxy, which insisted that, for Jesus to be fully human as well as fully divine, his flesh had to be derived from his mother. So the Melchiorite position further distanced some of the Anabaptists from other Christians. In 1534–1535 there took place a notorious episode that branded the Anabaptists as even more sinister. In the German city of Münster a fresh outburst of millenarian fervor led to the seizure of the city by militant Anabaptists who were expecting the imminent end of the age. Under siege by Catholic and Lutheran troops, the leader of the controlling Anabaptist faction, Jan of Leiden, abolished private property, promoted polygamy, and proclaimed himself the messianic king. The city was captured, Jan was executed, and the events became a by word for the horrific consequences of breaking up the traditional bonds of society by adopting Anabaptist opinions. Anabaptists were saddled with an unenviable reputation for destroying all that was sacred.

The aim of rehabilitating the movement was one of the overriding goals of the most influential Anabaptist writer, Menno Simons. Originally a Catholic priest in the northern Netherlands, he became a traveling preacher for the Anabaptists in 1536. He insisted that the congregations he nurtured must entirely disavow the use of force and so clear themselves of part of the ignominy of Münster. Non-resistance, even in the face of persecution, was the rule among Menno's followers. Inevitably they became the victims of intermittent bouts of official repression over the years, and they developed

Menno Simons (1496–1561)
Anabaptist Leader

the view that the true church of Christ must always suffer. Menno pleaded for their toleration by the rulers of the states where they were scattered abroad, arguing that it was not for magistrates to interfere at all in the affairs of the church. Although Menno declaimed against vain learning as a diversion from the path of following Christ, in 1540 he compiled a work called *The Foundation of Christian Doctrine.* His starting point was the conviction that salvation must be personally experienced in the new birth. He rejected the doctrine of predestination that the magisterial reformers were embracing, since he held that belief in the divine decrees could be an excuse for refusing to take responsibility for one's behavior. Menno claimed instead that the human will could freely choose to follow Christ, with the corollary that true Christians might abandon the faith and so fall away to perdition. The cross of Christ had abolished the guilt of sin on behalf of everybody, which was why there was no need to baptize infants, so that those who were eternally condemned suffered for their voluntary sinful acts. Those who repented and were baptized, however, constituted churches with a strong sense of brotherhood. Any serious breach of the moral law was ground for the exercise of church discipline, with offenders being put under the ban of excommunication. Right behavior was of the essence of following Christ. For Menno, the church was the place where radical disciples gave each other mutual support.

POSSIBLE ANABAPTIST INFLUENCE OVER THE BAPTISTS

Distinctive Anabaptist ideas soon seeped into England. In 1550 a woman named Joan Bocher was burned at the stake in Kent for denying that Christ took flesh from Mary. In 1575 two Anabaptists suffered in the same way for refusing to recognize the spiritual authority of the queen and Privy Council. The Forty-Two Articles drawn up by Archbishop Cranmer in King Edward's reign, largely reissued as the Thirty-Nine Articles to define the beliefs of the Elizabethan Church of England, contained stern denunciations of Anabaptist views. It has been argued that the early separatists showed signs of Anabaptist influence. The congregation of Richard Fitz saw itself in Anabaptist fashion as a suffering church; Mennonites were known to exist in Norwich, where Robert Browne gathered his separatist congregation; and some members of Francis Johnson's church seceded to the Anabaptists soon after going into exile in the Netherlands. The idea of a self-governing community free from state tutelage, it is suggested, was a continental import. From the separatists, it has been proposed, it was transmitted to those who established Baptist witness in the seventeenth century, and so there was a form of indirect but powerful influence flowing from the Anabaptists to the Baptists.[3] This hypothesis, however, will not stand scrutiny. The separatists were not crypto-Mennonites. Believer's baptism was unknown among them; they were uniformly Reformed in their theology and so differed from the Anabaptist endorsement of the freedom of the will; and the separatists continued to presume a role for the civil authorities in regulating religious affairs. The vision of the separatists, as we have seen, was an extension of the campaign of the Puritans for the reform of the church, not a scheme for restoring the church after its total dissolution. So the case of those who have claimed that Anabaptist ideals were transmitted to the Baptists through the channel of separatism fails to carry conviction.

A different theory connecting the Anabaptists to the Baptists has been put forward by Glen Stassen. The argument here is much more specific, concerning the use of the intellectual legacy of the Mennonites by the Particular Baptists, the largest denomination practicing believer's baptism in the seventeenth century. The Particulars upheld the Calvinist belief in particular redemption, that is, the doctrine that Christ died not for all but for the elect alone. Stassen examined their first communal statement of faith, the 1644 London Confession, in order to identify its sources. Much of it was based on the 1596 True Confession drawn up by the exiled church of Francis Johnson, and reflected the lineage of the subscribing churches among the separatists. There had to be alterations, however, to reflect the arrival of the churches endorsing the document at baptistic convictions. The clause expounding the meaning of baptism described it as representing "the death, burial, and resurrection" of Christ, and other changes, Stassen contended, flowed from that. The differences cannot be accounted for by any influence from the

General Baptists or elsewhere, but the motif of death, burial, and resurrection is present in Menno Simons' *Foundation of Christian Doctrine*. Hence, Stassen concluded, there was an indebtedness to the chief Anabaptist theologian. On this account, the Mennonites were at the headwaters of the Baptist mainstream.[4]

In evaluating this theory, the possibility must be acknowledged that the framers of the 1644 confession were aware of the motif of death, burial, and resurrection in Simons' work. A much greater debt, however, was undoubtedly to William Ames, who was recognized by Stassen as exerting a major influence on the confession. Ames had been associated in the Netherlands with one of the churches that subscribed the 1644 confession before it reached a baptistic position, and his treatise *The Marrow of Theology* (Latin 1623, English 1638) was a leading theological work of the age. All the novelties in the confession, it has been concluded, were available from Ames or else from scripture, which discusses baptism in terms of death, burial, and resurrection in Romans 6.[5] Even if the motif was indeed drawn from Simons, there are problems about the theory if it is taken to imply more than that. The Particulars, casting around for apologetic for their new stance, may possibly have pinned on Mennonite language, but that does not mean that they were inspired by Anabaptists to reach baptistic views. The words about the motif, furthermore, are used by the 1644 confession to explain the significance of "dipping or plunging the whole body under water,"[6] whereas the Mennonites normally observed baptism by pouring water over the head, not by immersion. So the phrase is given fresh significance in the Baptist document. And the theological difference between the Calvinistic Baptists and the freewill Mennonites remained a gulf of which they were profoundly conscious. So, while there may perhaps be some verbal connection, there is no sign of any more substantial bond between the Anabaptists and the Particular Baptists.

JOHN SMYTH AND BAPTIST ORIGINS

There is greater scope for positing a link between the Anabaptists and the General Baptists. This was the denominational body maintaining the belief that redemption was general, so that anybody who believed could be saved. The Generals began before the Particulars, in the exiled church initially led by John Smyth in the Netherlands. In 1609 Smyth baptized himself and created the earliest Baptist church. Because Smyth is recognized as the first Baptist, much of the debate surrounds the details of his trajectory and so he must be the focus of much of the discussion. Smyth (whose surname should be pronounced as though it were written in its alternative form "Smith") was swayed at Christ's College, Cambridge, in the late 1580s by Francis Johnson, who subsequently became the separatist leader. The mind of Smyth was marked for life by the tight methods of syllogistic reasoning he learned at Cambridge. Entering the ministry of the Church of England as an advanced Puritan, Smyth objected to surplices but was chosen lecturer in the city of Lincoln in 1600, only to be dismissed two years later for "enormous doctrine and undue teaching of matters of religion."[7] In the wake of the abortive Hampton Court conference and harried by the church authorities, he felt increasing sympathy for outright separatism, and early in 1607, while practicing as a physician in Gainsborough, not far from Lincoln, he took the decisive step of leaving the Church of England and gathering a church as its pastor. To avoid official harassment, the congregation soon left for Amsterdam. Smyth was now free to work out the implications of separation from the national church. With his strong mind and eagerness to follow out the ramifications of the intellectual positions he adopted, he could continue his quest for the true ecclesiastical order.

In Amsterdam, Smyth made contact with Johnson's exiled church, now led by his successor, Henry Ainsworth. Smyth's congregation, however, remained distinct, and in *The Differences of the Churches of the Seperation* (1608) he expressed disagreement with the other church on three points. In worship, according to Smyth, there should be no use of books whatsoever. The written word, he contended, constituted a type of image and so, if, in radical Puritan fashion, images were to be banished from public worship as idolatrous, all books must disappear. This rigorist position, derived from scrupulous exegesis of the scriptures, had the paradoxical effect of eliminating the Bible itself from Christian services. It was legitimate to read the scriptures before the formal service began, but "the Holy Scriptures are not reteyned as helps before the eye in tyme of Spirituall worship."[8] In finance, Smyth held that money should be accepted by the church from members only and that the gifts should be dedicated with prayer and thanksgiving. The aim of these provisions, which were similar to measures adopted by many twentieth-century Fundamentalists, was to ensure that, in financial matters as in every other respect, church affairs should be free from all worldly taint. In polity, Smyth rejected the pattern of ministry inherited from Calvin, dismissing the threefold eldership of pastors, teachers, and rulers as "none of Gods Ordinance but mans devise." Instead, he believed, there should be only one type of elder, and the eldership should be subordinate to the collectivity of the church. "The Saynts as Kings," he declared, "rule the visible Church."[9] This principle, the kingship of all believers, is perhaps Smyth's most enduring legacy. He accepted the general Reformation conviction of the priesthood of all believers, the status that gives access to the Father, but he added an entirely different point. Christians, he held, share in the kingly role of Christ as much as in his priestly role. Together they possess the authority of their ascended Lord to rule each local congregation. That, for Smyth, was the true foundation of church government.

Smyth's capacity to reach drastic and novel conclusions was soon demonstrated by an act that caused astonishment among his contemporaries. In leaving the Church of England, Smyth had decided that it was not a true church. Hence, like other separatists before him, Smyth had gone on to reject the baptisms carried out by the church. Others had simply refused to have their children baptized in the Church of England but had not doubted the general axiom that infants should be baptized. Smyth, however, with his characteristic single-mindedness, would not leave the issue there. If the baptism of the Church of England was invalid, then his own church members, including himself, were not baptized. Because baptism is the scriptural way of entering the church, Smyth concluded that his own congregation, despite being separate from the Church of England, had been improperly constituted. Baptism, not the covenant that the separatists had adopted, was what created a church. The members must begin their corporate life anew. Smyth and his friends, according to another separatist in the Netherlands, "having utterly dissolved and disclaimed their former church state and ministry, came together to erect a new church by baptism."[10] The question facing Smyth was how to do it. His solution, reached early in 1609,[11] was to baptize himself and then to baptize the others, so establishing a fresh church according to the pattern he had discerned in the New Testament. The repudiation of their earlier infant baptisms by all the members of the congregation was audacious enough, but the act of self-baptism seemed particularly scandalous. There was no scripture warrant for it, and it savored of the despised and hated Anabaptists. Contemporaries wondered whether the Anabaptists were actually responsible for Smyth's aberration. It is a question for historians as well.

There was an Anabaptist church belonging to the section called the Waterlanders in Amsterdam at the time of Smyth's action. They formed the broad-minded part of the Mennonite community that had been brought together on the basis of a confession composed in 1577 by Hans de Ries. The confession tried to mediate between different views on the birth of Christ and the role of the magistrate, and so to encourage forbearance over points of detail. Smyth must have known that a group of secessionists from Francis Johnson's church had joined the Waterlanders in the 1590s, shortly after arriving in the Netherlands, and must have seen their viewpoint as a possible resting place for English separatists of advanced opinions. The mode of baptism might also be considered evidence pointing toward Anabaptist influence over Smyth's decision. He performed his act of self-baptism using a basin to pour the water, and so was adopting the same method that Mennonites employed during his lifetime. The whole process of dissolving the former church and constituting a fresh congregation could also reflect the model favored by the Anabaptists. They believed that existing Christian bodies were corrupt and so needed replacing. In the same spirit, Smyth was going beyond reforming the contemporary church to restoring the primitive church according to the New Testament blueprint. It was as radical a step as the Anabaptists urged.

Smyth's subsequent career gives further evidence of Mennonite influence over him. In 1610, with the larger part of his congregation, he actually applied to join the Waterlander church. Smyth had decided that, since there was a church practicing believer's baptism in the vicinity, he should not have baptized himself but ought instead to have sought the rite from its elders. He spent the remaining months of his life expounding the theological position he had come to share with the Waterlanders. Hans de Ries, the author of the earlier Waterlander confession, composed a shorter version with a member of the Amsterdam congregation so that the English party could understand their views. Smyth and his friends duly signed the document. Smyth next wrote *Corde Credimus*, a statement in Latin of the doctrines held by his congregation for the reassurance of the Waterlanders. Then he produced a work called *Defence of Ries' Confession* in Latin to vindicate the common ground that he and de Ries occupied. Other Waterlanders were suspicious of Smyth and his compatriots, but the Amsterdam church wrote to a sister congregation that, having investigated the opinions of the English brethren, "we have not found that there was any difference at all."[12] Smyth did not live to see the eventual admission of his congregation to the Waterlanders' fellowship in 1615, because he died in 1612. It is clear, however, that in his final years his mind was at one with the Anabaptists.

In the last period of his life, this identification with the Waterlanders extended to embracing their view of salvation. Whereas Smyth, like all the Separatists before him, had previously upheld the teachings of Calvin about limited atonement, he went over to the belief that Christ's sacrifice was designed for the whole of humanity. Redemption was not particular but general. Smyth and his friends professed that "God has created and redeemed the human race to his own image, and has ordained all men (no one being reprobated) to life."[13] Any sin of which individuals are guilty is the result of their free personal choice and they may repent or resist the Spirit according to their own will. These statements show a firm anti-Calvinist character. It has been suggested that Smyth may have derived them from the Dutch context, because the Leiden theologian Jacobus

Arminius had been canvassing such views in the years since the Englishman arrived in Amsterdam. The Reformed tradition, according to Arminius, had to be revised by the admission that human beings were not irresistibly predestined to eternal life or death but, on the contrary, possessed the freedom to choose their own destiny. In 1610, at the time when Smyth was defending similar opinions, the followers of Arminius issued a Remonstrance to the States General of the Netherlands claiming the right to maintain his doctrines within the Dutch state church. The idea that Smyth's Arminianism was derived directly from Arminius has apparent plausibility. If so, his source was not the Waterlanders.

Yet the view of indebtedness to Arminius cannot be sustained. There are no known links between Smyth and Arminius or his followers. The phrasing of Smyth's exposition of his teachings about general redemption does not correspond to the way in which the Remonstrance of 1610 expressed its Arminian views. Crucially, there is a point of difference between Smyth and the Dutch Arminians of his day. Whereas they continued to believe in the prevalence of original sin, he did not. Smyth's doctrinal position therefore coincided with that of the Mennonites rather than with that of the followers of Arminius. It is not surprising that the structure of *Corde Credimus*, Smyth's statement of his congregation's convictions, was similar to that of de Ries' short confession. So it must be concluded that Smyth and his fellow believers derived their rejection of the Calvinist position from de Ries. The contemporary debate over the same issue within the Dutch Reformed Church may have encouraged them in their intellectual trajectory, but it was the Waterlanders' theologian who injected his view of the resistibility of grace into the life of the Baptists at the very start of their existence. In the year or so between Smyth's self-baptism and his application to join the Waterlanders, the church that he led, reconstituted on a baptistic basis, went over from a Calvinist to an anti-Calvinist theology of salvation. This church, the first General Baptist body, drew its doctrine of general redemption from the Anabaptists.

It is commonly held that Smyth went further with many Anabaptists in accepting the Melchiorite theology of the incarnation. He does, at one point, assert that Mary did not generate Christ, which looks remarkably like the teaching of Melchior Hoffmann and Menno Simons. It has recently been argued, however, that the remark may mean merely that the ultimate origin of the incarnate Savior was from the Father and so not from Mary. Elsewhere Smyth claims to believe that Christ's first flesh was taken from Mary, the orthodox teaching, but that he would not refuse fellowship to those who denied this point of detail. His point of view looks as though it conforms to de Ries' formula of mutual tolerance between those who accepted and those who rejected the taking of flesh from his mother by the Son of God.[14] Again, the closeness of Smyth's final position to that of de Ries is evident. The same influence seems to have been decisive in producing Smyth's latest attitude to the secular power. De Ries contended that, though rulers held office by the will of God, Christians should not wield worldly power. Likewise, in his final years, Smyth rejected the idea of a Christian magistracy. He had previously shared the common separatist view that secular authorities should not interfere in internal church affairs, but the exclusion of believers from public office was novel. The Waterlanders of Amsterdam managed to transmit their distinctive views to the Englishman.

That does not mean, however, that the adoption of believer's baptism can be attributed to the same source. The evidence in favor of a connection with the Mennonites before Smyth's act of self-baptism has seemed strong because the English congregation is known to have taken up accommodation and employment at Amsterdam in the bakehouse owned by Jan Munter, a merchant who was a Mennonite. It now appears much more likely, however, that the English group did not move there until, at the earliest, February 1609, just after the baptism and reconstitution of the church. So the Mennonite link would probably be a consequence rather than a cause of the taking up of believer's baptism. On the first arrival of the exiles in the city, the language barrier would have inhibited close ties. In any case, their separatist convictions would have driven the members of Smyth's church toward fresh light. Their church covenant, drawn up in Gainsborough, had committed them "to walke in all his wayes, made known, or to be made known unto them . . . whatsoever it should cost them."[15] As Smyth's fertile brain worked through the implications of their repudiation of the Church of England, the move to believer's baptism seemed the logical, though costly, conclusion of their quest for true churchmanship. There is important evidence about Smyth's attitude to the Waterlanders in his own apology for performing the self-baptism. He undertook it because, he explained, "ther was no church to whome we could Joyne with a Good conscience to have baptisme from them."[16] If he had already been under the sway of the Waterlanders, he would surely have considered their church to be one he could conscientiously approach. There are no signs of Mennonite influence in Smyth's writings down to March 1609, after the baptism, but there are indications of familiarity with Menno immediately afterwards. It is far more likely that Smyth entered on his explorations of Mennonite thought after rather than before the crucial act. The Anabaptists, we may conclude, were the source of most of the mature convictions of John Smyth, but not of his creation of the first Baptist church.

ANABAPTISTS AND BAPTISTS AFTER JOHN SMYTH

Even before Smyth's death, the Baptist and Mennonite paths had started to diverge. The application to join the Waterlanders, though welcome to thirty-one of Smyth's fellow members, was resisted by another ten, led by Thomas Helwys, the man of highest social standing in the fledgling Baptist church. Helwys (the name should probably be pronounced "Ellis," a common variant), the man whom Smyth had baptized first after himself, was the owner of Broxtowe Hall in Nottinghamshire. His standing as a lay member of the gentry allowed him to be the chief organizer of the emigration of separatists in which Smyth had joined. Helwys concurred in Smyth's move away from Calvinism after the reconstitution of the church, endorsing the new profession of general redemption in a *Short and Plaine Proof* (1611). Helwys, however, could not agree with Smyth's decision to repudiate the church's new baptisms for the sake of joining the Waterlander community. When, in 1612–1613, Helwys' small group returned to England, he was promptly arrested for writing *A*

Short Declaration of the Mistery of Iniquity, which rejected the king's authority in religious affairs. Helwys died before 1616, but he had planted the first of the General Baptist churches in England. He had also set out the reasons why the continuing church remained aloof from the Waterlanders in a declaration of faith, published in 1611. He did not accept the Waterlanders' dismissal of original sin or their toleration of the Melchiorite view of the incarnation; he thought them too lax in their sabbath observance and too stringent in rejecting a Christian magistracy. Baptists, according to Helwys, were not Anabaptists.

Nevertheless, later General Baptists maintained some continuing connections with continental Mennonites. In 1624 a group that had been excluded from the church and led back to England by Helwys sought fellowship with the Waterlander church in Amsterdam. Its members seem to have been close to the Mennonites because, although they were willing to take oaths, they held an unorthodox view of the incarnation, refused to become magistrates, and would not bear arms. Two years later, the five known General Baptist churches in England again were in touch with the Mennonites, but, although they sent two representatives to the Netherlands, they could not reach sufficient common ground to justify reunion. In 1630 the widow of Helwys' successor as leader of the General Baptists, John Murton, was received as a member by the Waterlanders. It is clear that later General Baptists were very similar to the Anabaptists in their church polity, especially in their willingness to exercise church discipline. Both groups refused to recognize marriage with outsiders. Even foot washing, often an Anabaptist ordinance, took place in General Baptist churches. In the best known London congregation of the 1640s, at Whitechapel, members worked on Sunday, as was common among Anabaptists. They seem to have had an enduring affinity for their continental cousins.

Yet this affinity did not constitute identity. The later General Baptists, as Stephen Wright has shown, may not have been the direct descendants of Helwys' followers, who may have died out. The individuals who accepted a non-Calvinist view of salvation in the 1640s seem to have been feeling their way toward Arminianism rather

than upholding doctrines they had received from an earlier generation.[17] The probable discontinuity between the first General Baptists
and the later tradition means that, even if the body that arose in the
1640s showed similarities with the Anabaptists, there was no direct
link to the continental movement. In any case, the General Baptists
were resolute in denying that they should be called Anabaptists, no
doubt partly because of the enduring stigma of Münster, but also
because they were self-consciously different. Apart from the group
expelled for heresy in 1624 and Matthew Caffyn, a minister in the
late seventeenth century who veered in an anti-Trinitarian direction,
General Baptists did not embrace the Melchiorite Christology. Nor
did they follow the Anabaptists in opposing a Christian magistracy.
Although the first General Baptists owed a debt to the Waterlanders,
both that group and the later tradition constituted a distinct body
of believers.

The debate around the relationship between the Anabaptists
and the Baptists has had several dimensions. The case for indirect
Anabaptist influence through the separatists carries little weight,
and the suggestion of a debt to Menno Simons among the Particular
Baptists is not, in the end, convincing. The argument in favor of the
Anabaptists being the source for John Smyth's revival of believer's
baptism has much more to recommend it. Smyth's act was certainly
a step of radical discipleship in the Anabaptist spirit, there was a
Waterlander church in Amsterdam when the event took place,
and Smyth soon became convinced of all the other articles in the
Waterlander creed. Yet the available evidence points to the contacts
with the Waterlanders taking place after the baptisms rather than
before. Smyth had not yet fallen under the sway of the Dutch congregation when he performed the decisive rite. At most, the existence
of the Mennonites in the vicinity may have displayed an example of
believer's baptism that provided a solution to the intellectual problems posed by denying the legitimacy of the Church of England.
The early General Baptists under Thomas Helwys and his successors
were not aligned with them. What the first General Baptists did

draw from the Anabaptists, however, was their distinctive theology of salvation. The stimulus to break with Reformed teaching about predestination came from the Waterlanders. The Arminianism of Smyth, Helwys, and their disciples came not from Arminius himself but from the Anabaptists. Although the Baptists did not derive their practice of believer's baptism from the Anabaptists, the earliest General Baptists seem to have accepted the doctrine of general redemption from that source.

FURTHER READING

Coggins, James R. *John Smyth's Congregation: English Separatism, Mennonite Influence and the Elect Nation.* Scottsdale, Pa.: Herald, 1991.

Estep, William R. *The Anabaptist Story.* Nashville: Broadman, 1996.

Lee, Jason K. *The Theology of John Smyth: Puritan, Separatist, Baptist, Mennonite.* Macon, Ga.: Mercer University Press, 2003.

White, Barrington R. *The English Separatist Tradition: From the Marian Martyrs to the Pilgrim Fathers.* London: Oxford University Press, 1971.

Williams, George H. *The Radical Reformation.* Philadelphia: Westminster, 1962.

Wright, Stephen. *The Early English Baptists, 1603–1649.* Woodbridge, Suffolk: Boydell, 2006.

Chapter 4

PARTICULAR AND GENERAL BAPTISTS IN THE SEVENTEENTH CENTURY

The seventeenth century witnessed the emergence of permanent religious Dissent in England. We have already noticed in chapter 2 the alarm created by the ecclesiastical policies of Charles I during the 1630s. That epoch bred a greater willingness among Puritans to leave the Church of England, so that, by 1640, London had at least ten separatist congregations and New England was being settled by religious refugees. The Civil Wars that broke out in Scotland, in Ireland, and then in England created a volatile atmosphere in which apocalyptic speculation was rife and religious innovation was common. From 1643 the Westminster Assembly deliberated over a confession of the Reformed faith that would unite English-speaking believers. The more orderly Puritans began to organize a Presbyterian system of ecclesiastical government, with superior church courts on the Scottish and Dutch models supervising local congregations. The Independents, rejecting the idea that particular churches could be regulated from outside their ranks, developed a network of distinct congregations. Baptists of various kinds sprang up alongside the Independents. By 1646 there were some three dozen separatist congregations, whether Independent, Baptist, or mixed, in the capital.

After the execution of the king in 1649, there was even greater freedom to experiment. Under the Commonwealth of which Oliver Cromwell was Lord Protector, there was official toleration of all brands of Protestantism. New groups, amongst whom the Quakers were by far the most successful, entered the religious marketplace. Baptists, though still only small groupings, competed vigorously in the open environment. Religious pluralism had become rampant.

The restoration of the monarchy with the return of Charles II to England in 1660 put an end to freedom of conscience. The Church of England became once more the national establishment and the new regime tried to stamp out those who refused to conform. In 1662 some two thousand clergy left their pulpits because they would not accept the Prayer Book imposed by royal authority. Only a handful—perhaps eight in England and Wales—were Baptists, but the unintended effect was to create a movement outside the Church of England that was too large to suppress. Intermittent persecution followed for all Dissenters, whether Presbyterian, Independent, Quaker, or Baptist, but it did not outlast the reign of Charles II, who died in 1685. The next ruler, Charles' brother James II, was openly a Roman Catholic and, because he wanted to ensure freedom of worship for his coreligionists, allowed Dissenters the same liberty. The country, however, would not accept a Catholic king and so James was removed from the throne in the "Glorious Revolution" of 1688. The new joint monarchs, William and Mary, retained the established Church of England as a bulwark of Protestantism, but in 1689 parliament passed an Act of Toleration under which Dissenters were relieved from the penalties of most of the earlier legislation against them. Although they were still not allowed to take many public offices and various petty forms of discrimination survived, they were now allowed to worship freely. Never again was Protestant Dissent subject to outright persecution by the state.

THE EMERGENCE OF GENERAL AND PARTICULAR BAPTISTS

The Baptists who participated in this process did not constitute a single body. There were, in the first place, the General Baptists, who held roughly the same views as John Smyth and Thomas Helwys.

Most of them, exactly like Smyth and Helwys, were Arminian exponents of general redemption. Christ had died, they insisted, for the sins of all, so that the Almighty was by no means responsible for the damnation of sinners. All who heard the gospel had the opportunity to be saved. The first two prominent Baptists of the 1640s, Thomas Lambe and Edward Barber, however, were not simple Arminians. In 1642 Lambe upheld particular election as well as general redemption; and in the following year Barber rejected universal redemption, free will, and the possibility of falling away from faith. Neither man maintained the same opinions that Helwys had expressed thirty years before. In the past it has normally been assumed that the main General Baptist church in London during the early 1640s, in Bell Alley, Whitechapel, was the same congregation that Helwys had brought back to England. In light of the difference of belief, however, it is likely that there was no continuity between Helwys' church and the Bell Alley church, led by Lambe. Nevertheless, Bell Alley gradually evolved into a congregation professing a definite Arminianism, fostering likeminded churches outside the capital. All the General Baptist churches thereafter upheld the principle of closed membership. This requirement that every member must be baptized as a believer normally ensured a strong sense of commitment to each congregation. Although there were regional variations in faith and practice, the denomination developed a tight sense of corporate identity. The General Baptists were fewer in number than the Particular Baptists, but at the end of the seventeenth century they were not far behind in strength.

The evolution of the Particular Baptists calls for closer scrutiny. Many of their congregations, like the Broadmead church at Bristol discussed in chapter 2, emerged gradually from an earlier separatist phase. The chief congregation, the Jacob-Lathrop-Jessey church, named by historians after its successive pastors, long remained more separatist than Baptist but gave rise to a whole series of Baptist developments. Its first minister, Henry Jacob, as a Puritan clergyman, had been one of the prime movers in the petition for further reform in the Church of England presented to James I at the opening of his reign. Like John Smyth, Jacob was disillusioned with the inadequate royal response and, by 1610, also like Smyth, he had found refuge in the Netherlands. Just as Smyth did, Jacob stressed the kingly office of Christ in each local congregation. He refused, however, to break entirely with the established church of his own land, declaring in 1612 that "for my part I never was nor am separate from all publike communication with the congregations of England."[1] Jacob was a semi-separatist, worshiping apart from the national church but refusing to repudiate it as false. It was on this principle that, in 1616, he constituted a church in Southwark, south of the River Thames in London, with himself as pastor. In 1622 or 1623 he moved to the colony of Virginia, where he soon died, but he was succeeded as minister by John Lathrop, a former curate in Kent. The members of the church maintained their founding conviction that they should enjoy pure fellowship as believers but that they might, if they wished, attend the parish church when they desired.

This view was challenged in 1630 by a more rigorist attitude. When a member of Lathrop's church took an infant to the parish church for baptism, John Duppa challenged the legitimacy of recognizing the validity of the Church of England. Duppa's point of view, however, was not accepted by his church, and so he and about a dozen others left to establish a fully separatist congregation. There was a further division in 1633 under Samuel Eaton, who established another congregation that wholly rejected the Church of England. It has sometimes been thought that one or both of these congregations adopted the baptism of believers, but neither seems to have taken that further step. In 1638, however, six members left the original church, now pastored by Henry Jessey, another former Anglican clergyman, to join a church led by John Spilsbury on the grounds that baptism should be restricted to those already professing faith. Although evidence about it is extremely sparse, Spilsbury's church may have been an offshoot of Duppa's. Like John Smyth, it seems to have practiced baptism by pouring water from a bowl rather than by immersion. Because it nevertheless stood for believer's baptism, it appears to have been the first church that can properly be called Particular Baptist.

Henry Jessey's church continued to give rise to others. A member named Richard Blunt reached the conclusion that baptism ought to be observed by wholly plunging the candidate under water. For the first time, immersion began to be considered the correct mode of baptism. Having persuaded over fifty other members, Blunt induced them to withdraw from Jessey's church, but they did not form another because they were unsure of what procedure best accorded with scripture. A serious question was whether it was right to baptize anybody as a believer without a special divine commission such as that received by John the Baptist. Traveling to the Netherlands, Blunt made contact with Timothy Batte, a former military chaplain, who may have been drawn to immersion by the branch of the Anabaptists called the Collegiants.[2] Returning to London in 1642, Blunt immersed a teacher of his circle named Samuel Blakelocke, who, with Blunt, then baptized the other members of the group and constituted a church. It soon spawned another, and Spilsbury's church adopted immersion, so that, by the end of the year, there were three churches of this type in existence. Others followed in Blunt's wake. In 1642 William Kiffin, who soon emerged as a pastor, became convinced of the rightness of believer's baptism. Two years later, Hanserd Knollys, an ex-clergyman who had returned from Massachusetts and was a member of Jessey's church, raised doubts about the rightness of baptizing his own child and soon joined a fresh church that practiced the immersion of believers. Jessey himself was baptized by Knollys in the following year, though he remained pastor of a partly pedobaptist congregation down to his death in 1663. By 1644, however, there were seven churches in London that observed the immersion of none but those who could profess their faith. A network of Particular Baptist churches had come into being.

As a confession of faith issued by the seven churches in 1644 made plain, they were resolutely Calvinist. Like the Puritans and separatists from whom they were descended, they believed in particular redemption. They contended that Christ died not for all but solely for those who had been predestined by God for salvation. Thus the confession declared that "Christ Jesus by his death did bring forth salvation and reconciliation onely for the elect, which were those which God the Father gave him."[3] Alongside their Calvinism they maintained a strict policy in the observance of communion. Only those baptized as believers were allowed to receive the bread and wine at the Lord's Supper. One of those who signed a 1646 revision of the 1644 confession, Benjamin Coxe, explained that they "doe not admit any to the use of the Supper, nor communicate with any in the use of this ordinance but disciples baptised, lest we should have fellowship with them in their doeing contrary to order."[4] So the new churches were both particular in their doctrine of salvation and closed in their practice of communion.

The public alarm at the breach with ordinary rites of passage represented by the Baptists should not be underestimated. Daniel Featley, long an apologist for the Church of England, published, in 1645, an account of the Baptists based partly on notes of a disputation he had undertaken against William Kiffin three years earlier. Called *The Dippers Dipt*, the book identified the new body with the continental Anabaptists and tarred them all with the brush of the crimes of Münster. The volume was extremely popular, reaching a sixth edition by 1651. Likewise, Thomas Edwards, a Presbyterian spokesman, was severely critical of the Baptists in his work *Gangraena* (1646), an anatomy of contemporary sects. Kiffin, according to a correspondent whom Edwards quoted, "hath by his enticing words seduced and gathered a schismatical rabble of deluded children, servants and people without either parents' or masters' consent."[5] The Baptists, like their continental counterparts, seemed to be breaking the natural ties of human communities, turning those who ought to be subject to authority against their superiors. Baptists were taken to be social subversives.

Nevertheless, they spread. Baptist convictions became rooted in the parliamentary army that fought against the king. After the formation of the New Model Army, Sir Thomas Fairfax's regiment contained a number of Particular Baptists. The military units, often moving round the country, carried Baptist opinions wherever they went. They succeeded in planting Baptist churches in Ireland, where by 1653 there were at least ten churches, and in Scotland, where garrison towns held Baptist meetings. In Wales the growth of a Baptist presence was the result of a deliberate evangelistic strategy. In 1649 John Miles and Thomas Pound were dispatched from London to set up churches in Glamorgan, where three churches existed by the following year. The English provinces also established Particular Baptist causes. During the 1650s Particular Baptists were strong enough to create associations in Berkshire, Somerset, and Devon, the west midlands and the south midlands, as well as in London, Ireland, and south Wales. Although the coverage was not nationwide, it was widespread by 1660.

Furthermore, Baptist views, though not necessarily firm Particular Baptist views, had permeated beyond the British Isles. During the 1640s many of the separatist exiles in the Netherlands adopted believer's baptism. Those who had fled to the New World were also affected. The most celebrated early American Baptist, Roger Williams, proceeded from separatist views to create a Baptist church at Providence, south of the Massachusetts colony in what would become Rhode Island. Williams was baptized in 1639 by a man named Holyman, and baptized him in turn, then some ten others. After only about four months, however, Williams decided that he had acted precipitately and left the church he had founded. He concluded that it was wrong to set up a church by baptism without a special commission from God and so became a seeker, remaining outside the congregations of the day until such time as true churches should be restored by some special providence. During the 1640s, however, a separatist church at Newport, Rhode Island, under John Clarke, moved toward a Baptist position, which it attained by 1648. At first it contained both Calvinists and Arminians. In 1644 the Massachusetts legislature, fearing that the growth of Baptist views might subvert the commonwealth, made the denial of infant baptism a crime. The fear was partly vindicated when, in 1654, Henry Dunster, the president of Harvard College, the Puritan seminary established in the colony, decided not to have his infant baptized. He was summarily removed from office. Although Baptists long remained a weak force in America, they had established a foothold there.

Among the Calvinistic Baptists in England was a party that stood apart from the main body. Those who formed this grouping, like Henry Jessey and the Broadmead church in Bristol, continued to allow those who had been sprinkled as infants rather than baptized as believers to become full members and so to share in communion. The best known church holding this "mixed" or "open" position on communion was the one in Bedford, which was eventually to be called, after its most famous minister, Bunyan Meeting. The church covenant, adopted in 1650, specified as the conditions of membership "faith in Christ and holiness of life, without regard to this or that circumstance or opinion in outward or circumstantial things."[6] Baptism was relegated to a matter that must not divide

John Bunyan (1628–1688)
Baptist Pastor and Author

true Christians. John Bunyan, the author of *Pilgrim's Progress*, stoutly defended this point of view against William Kiffin when the Particular Baptist leader criticized the open-communion position. In *Differences in Judgment concerning Water Baptism No Bar to Communion* (1673), Bunyan argued that some might overvalue the ordinances of the gospel. "It is possible," he wrote, "to commit idolatry, even with God's own appointments."[7] There were often good relations between the closed- and the open-communion parties, and in 1657 the Berkshire Association decided that baptism performed by the minister of a church practicing mixed communion was valid. Nevertheless, it condemned the "errour in judgement and practice about mixt communion."[8] There was no doubt that those who welcomed the unbaptized to the Lord's table were distinct from the Particular Baptist mainstream.

Another group that took a separate path, though they maintained the baptism of believers, consisted of the Seventh Day Baptists. The idea that there was no warrant under the gospel for revoking the requirement to observe the seventh day of the week as the sabbath was sometimes canvassed among Puritans, with their high regard for the Ten Commandments. The first known advocacy of this point of view by a Baptist appeared in James Ockford's *The Doctrine of the Fourth Commandment, Deformed by Popery, Reformed & Restored to its Primitive Purity* (1650). "Happy," he wrote, "shall the Church be, that worshippeth God according to his Law, and giveth him his due, by placing on the Seventh day, the honour which God requireth to be performed on it."[9] The earliest evidence of a church meeting for worship on a Saturday rather than a Sunday is of a London congregation, later known as the Mill Yard church, and comes from about 1653. Its leader, Peter Chamberlen, who held an appointment to both Charles I and Charles II as physician-in-ordinary, was an inventive man who patented assorted schemes such as one for bath stoves and another for phonetic writing. A willingness to adopt the same sabbath as the Jews was a similar piece of independent-mindedness. Henry Jessey espoused seventh-day views around the same time, but he observed the Saturday sabbath in private, in parallel with leading Sunday worship in his church. Calvinistic and Arminian convictions were both found among the Seventh Day Baptists, sometimes in the same church. There were never more than sixteen congregations of this persuasion in England, but, after the creation of the first church in America in 1671, they became more numerous there. This strand of Baptist life remained a separate grouping down to the twenty-first century.

DIFFERENCES BETWEEN PARTICULAR AND GENERAL BAPTISTS

In the seventeenth century, however, the main bodies, the Particular and the General Baptists, can usefully be compared. How similar were they? They were both Baptist groupings, but it is fruitful to enquire how much they shared beyond the rite of immersion. It is clear, in the first place, that they differed sharply over the theology of salvation. The Particular Baptists were stoutly Reformed, whereas the General Baptists accepted the Arminian position. The international standard of Calvinist orthodoxy had been laid down by the Council of Dort in the Netherlands in 1619, when it was agreed that the proposals of Arminius for the modification of received theological opinion were unacceptable. The 1644 London Confession of the Particular Baptists reflected the conclusions drawn up at Dort. It specified, as we have seen, that Christ died only for the elect, not for all humanity. The confession was rather less explicit about the Dort principles of total depravity and unconditional election to salvation, but both were definitely implicit in its text. Two other articles spelled out crucial differences marking off the Reformed at Dort from their opponents. Grace was clearly irresistible, for faith was said to arise "without respect to any power or capacitie in the creature" and its reception was "wholly passive." The confession also taught the perseverance of the saints, for it declared that true believers "can never finally nor totally fall away."[10] The first statement of faith of the Particular Baptists therefore upheld a firmly Calvinist position.

That is not surprising, for their purpose in issuing the confession was to put away the accusation of their Puritan contemporaries that, like the General Baptists, they had lapsed into Arminianism. They were rebutting the charge, they explained in the preface, of "hold-

ing Free-will, Falling away from grace, denying Originall sinne."[11]
When the confession was reissued in revised form two years later,
it was rephrased so as to make its doctrinal articles even more obviously distinct from the views of the General Baptists. In 1677, when
another confession was drawn up to try to represent the overall position of the Particular Baptists, it was partly modeled on the Savoy
Declaration (1658) drawn up by the Independents, which was itself
a modified version of the Westminster Confession (1648), the standard exposition of Presbyterian beliefs. The Baptist document therefore reflected these two Reformed statements of faith. The same is
true of the 1689 confession, drawn up in London by a representative
assembly of Particular Baptists from all over the country. It is true
that the Baptists omitted two articles in the older documents upholding the so-called doctrine of double predestination, the teaching that
the Almighty is responsible for the fate of those suffering eternal
punishment. That was to profess a lower variety of Calvinism than
the other bodies, but the overall thrust was nevertheless to reaffirm
the attachment of the framers of the confession to Reformed teaching. The Particulars remained resolute Calvinists.

The General Baptists, by contrast, professed the faith in a form
that can be called Arminian, although this was not yet true in the ideological flux of the early 1640s, when Lambe, Barber, and others were
still edging toward Arminianism. As late as 1645, Lambe still dis-
avowed freewill while embracing a universal atonement. His position
can most accurately be labeled "Amyraldian," a version of Calvinism
that did not see grounds in the Bible for limiting the number of potential beneficiaries of Christ's work on the cross. Soon, however, the
General Baptists came to repudiate all the distinctive conclusions of
Dort. They rejected total depravity, unconditional election, limited
atonement, irresistible grace, and the perseverance of the saints—
the so-called five points of Calvinism. Because the teaching of the
General Baptists was formulated by men who normally had little or
no theological training, their views were often rather more homespun
than those of their Calvinist opponents. In 1660, however, representatives of the General Baptist churches of London and the adjacent
counties issued a Brief Confession that, though homely in style, was

a bit more systematic. It contended that "no man shall eternally suffer in Hell (that is, the second death) for want of a Christ that dyed for them." Hence, it continued, "it follows against all contradiction, that all men at one time or other, are put into such a capacity, as that (through the grace of God) they may be eternally saved."[12] This document, with its insistence on the universality of the offer of redemption, gradually became a standard confession of faith. The General Baptists were self-consciously anti-Calvinist.

Hence the Particular and the General Baptists were distinct communities. Far from uniting for the purpose of disseminating the baptismal practice that they shared, the two groupings were normally hostile to each other. To the Particulars, the General Baptist avowal of the idea that all might be saved was both blasphemous and pernicious. Arminianism appeared to be outright heresy, a defection from the orthodoxy that ought to be upheld in common with Independents, Presbyterians, and others. To the General Baptists, on the other hand, the Particulars seemed an alien body. The General Baptists (according to an opponent) even labeled the Particulars "the gates of Hell, their common enemy."[13] There was, therefore, no question of mutual recognition or intercommunion. When an adherent of the Calvinist body transferred to the General Baptists, the person had to be baptized as a believer for a second time, "*Because* (said they) *You were baptized into the wrong Faith, and so into another Gospel.*"[14] While the Particulars insisted on the five points of Calvinism, the General Baptists stressed the enduring obligation of the six principles described as the rudiments of religion in Hebrews 6:1-2. Apart from repentance, faith, resurrection, and judgment, the passage includes reference to baptism (which united them with other Baptists) but also the laying on of hands (which did not). The placing of hands on the heads of the newly baptized also arose in Particular Baptist churches during the 1640s, but only among the General Baptists did it become universal. For many, this divergence of practice became an insurmountable obstacle to convergence: "Where there is not a uniting in the rudiments of religion," wrote a General Baptist apologist in 1655, "there can be no safe communion."[15] On both sides, the common acceptance of the immersion of believers seemed much less weighty than the differences that separated the two bodies.

There was, furthermore, a contrasting approach to church polity. The Particular Baptists treated local churches as self-governing communities, free-standing under the authority of Christ. Their congregations were as independent as those of the Independents. It is true that, unlike the Independents of the seventeenth century, they formed associations for mutual advice, financial support, and joint work. They saw no contradiction between independency and this degree of interdependence. Yet Particular Baptist churches were, as the 1644 confession put it, "distinct and severall Bodies, every one a compact and knit Citie in it selfe."[16] The General Baptists, on the other hand, were not strictly upholders of independency. They were conscious of together forming a united entity, a single church of Christ. Thus a confession issued in 1678 by one of their leaders affirmed that "General councils or assemblies . . . make but one church."[17] Central decisions were binding for local churches in a way that Particulars would have found abhorrent. In accordance with this greater corporate sense, the General Baptists appointed church officers, the "messengers," whose authority extended beyond a single congregation. In the local churches of both bodies there were elders, the equivalent of later ministers or pastors, who took charge of the preaching and pastoral work, and deacons, who were normally responsible for the temporal affairs of the church. But the General Baptists possessed a threefold pattern of ministry, commissioning the messengers as church planters and superintendents of congregations within a given area. Although the Particulars chose messengers, they possessed no superior authority over the churches. For the Generals, however, the messengers were, in large measure, the counterparts of the apostles of New Testament times. The office of "apostle or messenger," according to an early apologist, "has not ceased."[18] Hence the two groupings of Baptists did not maintain a common model of the church.

An associated distinction was that the Particular and the General Baptists showed affinities with different contemporary Christian groups. The Particulars shared virtually every point of their faith and order, save baptism, with the Independents. Members of the two often acted together, the mixed communion churches formed a bridge between them, and there were people of baptistic conviction in Independent congregations. In 1646 the Independent Thomas Goodwin reported that when such members wanted believer's baptism, they received the rite as individuals from Particular Baptists. The Independents, in turn, were often close to the Presbyterians and many of them long cherished a semi-separatism that allowed them to attend congregations of the Church of England to hear godly ministers. Hence a respect for decency and order percolated through more traditional ecclesiastical channels into the practice of the Particulars. The General Baptists, by contrast, were much more like the Religious Society of Friends, the Quakers. Founded by George Fox, the Quakers repudiated outward forms, including the gospel ordinances, in order to worship and act as moved by the Spirit. They believed they were guided by an "inner light" that gave access to the divine will, and often took up a radical stance, refusing, for instance, to doff their hats to social superiors. The General Baptists and Quakers evinced a common primitivism that led them to search the New Testament for authoritative direction. Because they were so close in attitude, Quakers recruited extensively from General Baptist ranks. Consequently, the General Baptists frequently cautioned their flocks against Quaker errors, pointing out in 1659, for example, that "he will not be safe, who, neglecting the scripture, resteth upon some inward inspirations above them, which oftentimes are false, but always doubtful."[19] Such stout anti-Quaker polemic should not disguise the substantial common ground occupied by the two bodies and indeed is often testimony to its extent. There was a tendency among General Baptists, hinted at by the warning of 1659, to rely on impulse and so to exalt the Spirit above the written word. Such Quaker-like sensibility would have been rare among Particular Baptists.

The ethos of the two Baptist groupings differed accordingly. Among the Particular Baptists, as among the Independents, there was generally an adherence to the norms of Puritan worship. The style of public services conformed rigorously to perceived scriptural precedent, so that, for example, singing was undertaken by individuals in turn, not by the community together, for want of New Testament evidence of corporate song. The General Baptists, however, went in for more innovations. At the Whitechapel church there were several preachers during a single service, and which would take the next turn in the pulpit could be put to the vote. Running commentaries on biblical passages, which were to become popular outside their ranks, seem to have started amongst the General Baptists. A biblical literalism made foot washing and the holding of a meal before the Lord's supper common among them, though late in the century the General Baptist Assembly determined that foot washing was not compulsory since it did not figure among the six points of Hebrews 6. The same adherence to the text of the Bible rather than to traditional ways of thinking induced Richard Overton, a member of the Whitechapel congregation, to argue for the mortality of the soul. To the alarm of the House of Commons, his *Mans Mortalitie* (1644) rejected the standard teaching that the soul is eternal, a significant break with a mode of thought more sanctioned by ancient philosophy than by scripture. General Baptists were not afraid of being different.

This willingness to plow a separate furrow arose partly because the General Baptist leaders were more commonly drawn from the ranks of outsiders than their Particular contemporaries. Certain of the Particular Baptists were people of some eminence. William Kiffin was a wealthy man who, on one occasion, gave ten thousand pounds to Charles II. He was Member of Parliament for Middlesex under Cromwell, Master of the Leathersellers' Company of the City of London in 1671–1672, and an alderman of the city from 1687. In a different sphere, Hanserd Knollys, an ex-clergyman of the Church of England, was respected for his learning in Latin, Greek, and Hebrew. There was nobody with such attainments among the General Baptists, who were generally of low social origins and poor educational background. Thomas Lambe, their chief protagonist in the early years, was a soap-boiler; Andrew Debman, one of their leading preachers, was an illiterate cooper. The General Baptist congregations were usually led by men without ministerial training, and even women sometimes had their say. A woman was said to preach and baptize in Lincolnshire. In Lambe's congregation a Mrs. Attaway was a preacher, but then (it was reported) she ran away with another woman's husband to Jerusalem. The 1660 General Baptist statement of faith concluded by professing to differ from "the learned, the wise and prudent of this World."[20] The General Baptists lacked the status brought to the Particulars by their outstanding figures.

There was also a political contrast between the two groupings. The Particulars tended to avoid taking the initiative in public affairs, fearing identification with the Anabaptists, and sometimes dissociated themselves from radical causes. When, in 1647, the Levellers, an egalitarian pressure group with strength in the army, was about to present its case to parliament, the Particulars, acting together with the Independents, submitted a declaration stating that "it cannot but be very prejudicial to human society . . . to admit of a parity, or all to be equal in power."[21] Kiffin took care to stay in Cromwell's good graces during the 1650s. Some of the Particulars, it is true, were Fifth Monarchists, holding that the final reign of King Jesus was about to be set up to replace the secular authorities. Although people of these opinions were involved in revolutionary efforts immediately after the Restoration of 1660, Baptists took little part, preferring abstract apocalyptic speculation to the violent overthrow of the government. Several of the General Baptists, however, were active Levellers. Richard Overton, though he had possibly left the denomination at an earlier date, was one of the most prominent spokesmen of the movement. So threatening to military discipline were the Leveller activities of the soldier Henry Denne, a General Baptist preacher, that he was condemned to be shot, but he recanted and was reprieved. Subsequently the General Baptists distanced themselves further from political radicalism, with a section of them endorsing Cromwell's regime in 1654. Yet some still refused to take oaths or to bear arms. The greater willingness of the General Baptists to seek drastic political change, at least for a while, was part and parcel of their more innovative mindset.

Similarities of Particular and General Baptists

The evidence therefore points to the Particular and General Baptists' being distinct and contrasting bodies. They were divided on a wide range of issues. Yet, in the seedtime of both movements in the early 1640s, the main congregation that was to become General under Thomas Lambe was only inching its way toward an anti-Calvinist position. There were also later efforts to reduce the distance between the two groups. A leading advocate of greater comprehension was Thomas Collier, long the coordinator of Baptist activities in the west of England, from Gloucestershire to Cornwall. Collier stated impeccable Calvinist views in a book of 1645, though even at this time he was suspected by eagle-eyed Reformed polemicists of favoring Arminianism. The West Country Association that he fostered from 1653 issued a Somerset Confession three years later that was again definitely Calvinist in its avowal of the limitation of the atonement to the church and the perseverance of the saints, yet omitted some of the stronger Reformed phraseology of the 1644 and 1646 London Confessions. The association was willing in 1655 to determine the question of whether Christ died "for all and every man or for the elect only" by answering "for all." Although the answer was qualified by adding that "he died not intentionaly [*sic*] alike for all," the aim of the broad formula seems to have been to draw in those who were more attracted to an Arminian position.[22] Certainly during the 1670s Collier fell under the censure of the London Baptists for tending in an Arminian direction, and he in turn criticized the 1677 confession for being too restrictive. From the General Baptist side, there was a similar effort to minimize theological differences in the Orthodox Creed of 1678. Thomas Monck, the Buckinghamshire messenger, was probably trying to steel the General Baptists against christological heresy in the south of England, and so stressed the extent of common ground with other Christians, including the Reformed, going so far as to avow a version of the perseverance of the saints. So the theological gulf between the Calvinists and the Arminians was not impassable.

The common experience of persecution after the Restoration accentuated the tendency to bridge the chasm. The campaign against

Dissent, orchestrated locally by royalist justices of the peace bent on revenge for the upheavals of the Civil Wars and Commonwealth, had a popular dimension. Mobs broke up worship meetings, making life hazardous for Dissenters. Already in 1660, fearing retribution from the incoming regime, the Particulars and the General Baptists combined to submit a published apology that professed loyalty to the crown. During the persecution, when twelve General Baptists were arrested for attending a conventicle in Aylesbury, they were saved from possible execution by the intervention of William Kiffin, the Particular leader, with the Lord Chancellor. The sense of solidarity between Dissenters in a time of acute adversity provided more fertile ground for the theological accommodations proposed by Collier and Monck. By the end of the century, several churches had members of both persuasions and refused to align exclusively with one side or the other. The breach between the closed- and open-membership groupings of Particular Baptists was formally healed, with delegates from both parties attending the national assembly that drew up the 1689 confession of faith. Representatives of the open Broadmead church in Bristol and of its closed Fryers counterpart in the same city sat alongside each other. In the final decade of the century, when Presbyterians and Independents came together in a "Happy Union," the temper of the times encouraged greater solidarity. Even though Particular and General Baptists remained entirely separate bodies for well over a century afterwards, there was more of a sense of pursuing common ends in 1700 than in 1650.

The features that united the two sides during the seventeenth century were, in truth, substantial. Like their fellow Dissenters, they differed from the Church of England in repudiating bishops, abhorring portions of the Prayer Book, and maintaining that worship should not be regulated by the state. Going further than the Presbyterians, they insisted that each congregation had the duty of ordering its own affairs. Like the Independents, they carefully examined candidates for church membership. Churches, they held, were to consist of conscious believers only. Thus the Particulars of the West Country Association required that applicants were to be admitted not upon "bare confession" but only after "a declaration of an experimental work of the Spirit upon the heart . . . being attended with evident tokens of conversion."[23] The General Baptists were equally insistent that candidates must show, and continue to show after their reception, indications of personal faith. Thomas Grantham, their chief apologist in the later seventeenth century, recalled the divine command for "the faithful ones to withdraw from such as have a form of godliness, when they deny the power thereof."[24] The chief business of the church meeting in each body was to exercise church discipline over errant members. Baptists were conscious of their obligation to behave as visible saints before the watching world. Furthermore, the two parties (apart from the open-membership Particulars) went beyond the Independents in requiring members to be immersed as believers. "The Baptisme of Christ is dipping," explained the Particular Baptist Christopher Blackwood in 1644. "The Baptisme of infants," he went on, "is not dipping, therefore the Baptisme of infants is not the Baptisme of Christ."[25] The General Baptists would have heartily concurred. Such stringent claims about the nature of baptism set Baptists apart from all others. At the same time, however, they created a testimony shared between Particular and General Baptists.

Underlying the convictions of the two sections of Baptist opinion about a converted membership and believer's baptism was a common theological axiom. The two groups were obedient to Christ's command to baptize disciples because they equally believed in the kingship of Christ in his church. John Smyth, as we have seen, derived from that principle the teaching that the members of a gathered church should exercise authority on behalf of Christ. Smyth propounded the doctrine of the kingship of all believers, a conviction which his General Baptist successors put into practice by entrusting a share in church government to all members. The Calvinistic separatists were often eager to make out a similar case. Kiffin wrote in 1641, shortly before his baptism, of "this great truth, Christ the King of his church."[26] The Particular Baptists maintained the same principle, and worked out its implications more fully than the separatists by adopting believer's baptism. It was a formative idea, establishing the foundation of church government. Identification with Christ in baptism meant a participation in the roles of Christ as prophet, priest, and king. Every church member shared in the prophethood of Christ, and so was bound to bear public testimony; every member shared in his priesthood, and so enjoyed access to the Father; and equally every member shared in the kingship of Christ, and so was empowered to bear authority in his church. Responsibility for mutual spiritual welfare was not restricted to the leaders but was carried by every individual. Thomas Collier wrote in 1646 that "all the body ought to watch over each other, and to judge the actions of each other, thus the Elder is to watch over the body . . . and thus may, nay, and ought, the whole Church to watch over (and if occasion be) reprove, admonish &c. the Elder. Thus is the Kingly office of Christ, carried along sweetly in the church of Christ."[27] The powers of Christ were to be wielded by the church as a collectivity, "the body." Together, in Collier's view, Christians exercised the royal authority of their Lord. The early Baptists, Particular as well as General, were at one in their doctrine of the kingship of all believers.

The Baptists, though they formed a section of the substantial body of religious Dissent that emerged during the vicissitudes of the seventeenth century, were sharply divided amongst themselves. There was a small Seventh Day community that stood largely apart. The Particulars disagreed among themselves about whether to allow those not baptized as believers to enter their ranks. And there were fundamental differences between Particular and General Baptists. The theology of salvation, first and foremost, put Calvinists and Arminians in distinct and hostile camps. In addition, Particular Baptists were independent in church polity and therefore close to the Independents themselves, whereas General Baptists gave supervisory powers to messengers outside the local churches and had affinities with the Quakers. The General Baptists, whose leaders rarely enjoyed social standing or a liberal education, were in general more radical in their worship and, at times, their politics. Nevertheless, the two groups had sufficient in common for some individuals to minimize their theological differences, and the shared period of persecution brought them closer together. They both upheld the principle of the gathered church and both provided a rationale in terms of the kingship of all believers. The Particulars, and most of all those in the peaceable open-communion strand, were often very different from the more angular General Baptists. Yet their joint adoption of believer's baptism gave them a common badge that distinguished them from all their Christian contemporaries in England. Both groups were so committed to their religious convictions that they were prepared to be singular.

FURTHER READING

Nelson, Stanley A. "Reflecting on Baptist Origins: The London Confession of Faith of 1644." *Baptist History and Heritage* 29 (1994): 33–46.

Tolmie, Murray. *The Triumph of the Saints: The Separate Churches of London, 1616–1649.* Cambridge: Cambridge University Press, 1977.

Watts, Michael R. *The Dissenters: From the Reformation to the French Revolution.* Oxford: Clarendon, 1978.

White, Barrington R. *The English Baptists of the 17th Century.* Didcot, Oxfordshire: Baptist Historical Society, 1996.

———. "The Frontiers of Fellowship between British Baptists, 1609–1660." *Foundations* 11 (1968): 244–56.

Wright, Stephen. *The Early English Baptists, 1603–1649.* Woodbridge, Suffolk: Boydell, 2006.

Chapter 5

BAPTISTS AND REVIVAL
IN THE EIGHTEENTH CENTURY

The Baptists of the eighteenth century lived in a world conditioned by toleration and Enlightenment. The Church of England remained the established religious body in England and Wales, so that its adherents alone were regarded as fully loyal members of the body politic. Since the Act of Toleration of 1689, however, Baptists were rarely actively persecuted. It is true that they were sometimes treated as outsiders in the village communities and regarded with suspicion because they refused to attend the parish church. It is also true that there were occasional outbursts of hostility to Dissenters such as the Sacheverell riots of 1710, when a mob destroyed a number of their meeting houses in London. In the main, however, Dissenters of all descriptions—Presbyterians and Independents as well as Baptists— lived securely within the British dominions. In Lincolnshire, for example, members of the sizeable General Baptist community participated fully in village life, and sometimes held positions of responsibility within their parishes. In urban centers Baptists could prosper in commerce. Some even became rich, such as the London bookseller Thomas Guy, who was, shortly before his death in 1724, to endow a hospital that bore his name. In theory, the Test and

Corporation Acts of the previous century were still in operation, requiring holders of local office to show that they were faithful sons of the Church of England. Each year, however, parliament passed an indemnity act relieving Dissenters from the penalties of the law, and so, in practice, they could join the corporations that ran the towns, and in certain places, such as Nottingham, could dominate them. There was nothing to prevent those outside the Church of England from being elected to the House of Commons. At the start of the century, for example, Thomas Guy served as Member of Parliament for Tamworth. The Dissenting vote counted at many elections during the century. So the Baptists, though they were a small section of a Dissenting community that, in the early eighteenth century, accounted altogether for only some 6 percent of the population of England and Wales, were relatively safe from harassment for their faith and were able to achieve prosperity and respect.

Rational Theology

The Enlightenment was the great intellectual movement of the age. Beginning in the later years of the seventeenth century, this development was most marked by its elevation of the capacity of human reason. Exponents of the Enlightenment characteristically urged that modern knowledge was capable of giving humanity greater power over its destiny. By means of scientific enquiry in the manner of Sir Isaac Newton, the secrets of the universe could be uncovered. If philosophers adopted similar empirical methods, as had John Locke, they could explain the operations of the human mind and the nature of true knowledge. This broad current of thought is often portrayed as hostile to religion. In France the *philosophes* who admired Voltaire, with his jibes at the claims of Christianity, did indeed tend to show an aversion to revealed religion. It has increasingly been recognized, however, that many other lands, including the English-speaking world, produced a different style of Enlightenment that was much more sympathetic to the Christian faith. Many religious leaders were themselves exponents of enlightened views. John Tillotson, Archbishop of Canterbury down to 1694, expounded a reasonable form of faith in which natural and revealed religion were complementary. His views, which remained normative in the Church of England long into the eighteenth century, set the tone for later theologians to adopt a similar style of doctrinal expression. Religion was integrated with the scientific worldview propounded by Newton and the philosophical methods inaugurated by Locke. Such views were likely to lead toward a broader-minded understanding of doctrine, but it should not be supposed that all of those who were swayed by the Enlightenment became so liberal in their theology that they discarded a firm allegiance to the teachings of the Bible. John Wesley, for example, the founder of the Methodist movement, was as attached to the authority of reason in religion as any intellectual of the epoch. The whole Evangelical impulse was closely associated with the rise of enlightened attitudes. The Enlightenment was the context in which all Christian thinking was done. Some might react against its tendencies; others might follow its recommendations. None, however, could escape its impact on the theology of the times.

Hence Dissenters were swayed by enlightened patterns of thought. Reason seemed to suggest that the doctrinal debates of their Puritan past had been too subtle. Religion needed to be cleared of metaphysical lumber, which must be replaced by the clear and distinct ideas that Locke had urged. Simplicity must be the goal in theological statements. In particular, complex declarations of faith such as the Westminster Confession or the Baptists' own 1689 London Confession merely obscured the plain truths of the Bible. Leaders of Dissenting opinion increasingly felt that the scriptures alone were a satisfactory guide to truth. At Salters' Hall in London in 1719, a representative gathering of Dissenting ministers debated whether it was desirable to subscribe to the confessions of the previous century. A majority determined that, on the contrary, the bare text of scripture was sufficient. That decision was not necessarily a sign of unorthodoxy. Many of those in the majority were simply announcing their confidence in the Bible as God's revelation to humanity. Nevertheless, a few in the group who rejected subscription had already dismissed the doctrine of the Trinity as an unnecessary form of speculation. Many others, especially among the

Presbyterians, were beginning to doubt whether Jesus could properly be called God in the same sense as his Father. They were moving toward the position occupied by Arius in the fourth century that Jesus, though divine, was created by his Father and so inferior to him in status. Arianism steadily advanced during the rest of the century, and led toward the stronger type of heretical view known, after the sixteenth-century theologian Socinus, as Socinianism. For Socinians, Jesus had no existence before his birth at Bethlehem: he was merely human. Salters' Hall was a sign of an impending parting of the ways between those who, bolstered by the confessions, wanted to adhere to received orthodoxy and those who, inspired by the confidence of the Enlightenment in new knowledge, wished to strike out on fresh doctrinal paths.

The General Baptists were more affected by the trend toward Arianism than the Particular Baptists. There was less sympathy for the seventeenth-century confessions among the Generals. While all but two Particular Baptist ministers at Salters' Hall voted for subscription, only one of the General Baptists present took the same view. General Baptists, apart from having fewer educated ministers, were strongly attached to the six points of Hebrews 6:1-2 as the charter of their body. Having read in Hebrews that repentance, faith, baptism, the laying on of hands, resurrection, and judgment were the foundation of the Christian faith, many of them supposed that such a biblical summary of the faith was entirely adequate without elaborate creeds. They therefore tended to reject the need for subscription. Matthew Caffyn, their leader in the southeastern counties of Kent and Sussex, had already, in 1686, expounded an understanding of the person of Christ that had affinities not only with the Melchiorite denial of Christ's full humanity but also with the Arian rejection of his coequal divinity with the Father, leading to a breach in fellowship with Caffyn's coreligionists further north who remained orthodox. Although there was a healing of the schism in 1731 on the basis of the six principles, most of the General Baptists of the southeast gradually shifted in a more liberal direction as the century wore on. Several ministers of ability who adopted a similar viewpoint occupied General Baptist pulpits. James Foster had expressed the attitude of the open-minded in the denomination in his *Essay on Fundamentals* (1720), three years before he was selected as minister of the Barbican General Baptist church in London: "No doctrine is a fundamental and necessary article of a Christian's faith but what is so plainly and distinctly revealed as that an ordinary Christian in his enquiries can't miss the knowledge of."[1] Simplicity was no doubt appreciated by the respectable London congregation to which Foster preached. The message was at once molded by the presuppositions of the Enlightenment and welcome to the prosperous sector of the denomination. But sober rational teaching was less likely to stir ordinary people than a more full-blooded challenge based on the doctrines that had mobilized Baptists in the previous century. The intellectual trend, combined with rising social standing, meant that the impact of many of the General Baptists was blunted.

The Particular Baptists were still very conscious of being distinct from their General contemporaries. Although many of their churches composed their own confessions of faith, they normally retained a firm allegiance to the Reformed position set out in the 1689 London Confession. Thus the Philadelphia Association in America, which from 1707 united the colonial Particular or Regular Baptist Churches, adopted the London Confession as its own in 1742. Ten years later, it ruled that any who denied the Calvinist doctrines of unconditional election, original sin, or the final perseverance of the saints should not be a member of any of its constituent churches. The most influential of eighteenth-century Baptist theologians, John Gill, minister of the Horsleydown church in Southwark, south London, from 1719 to his death in 1771, was a stalwart defender of orthodoxy. He wrote *A Treatise on the Doctrine of the Trinity* (1731) as a rebuttal of deviations on that subject, and the four-volume work *The Cause of God and Truth* (1735–1738) as a statement of his own position. In defending the Calvinist convictions of the denomination, however, Gill expounded higher Reformed views than some of his Particular Baptist predecessors. In particular, he upheld double predestination, the belief that the Almighty had determined the eternal destiny of those going to hell as much as of those going to heaven. He went further by adopting the doctrine of eternal justification. He asserted that a person's justification by God took place in eternity, not, as most Reformed teachers held, at the time when the sinner turned to Christ. The implication of these convictions was that the fate of each individual was more entirely dependent on long-term divine planning than many other Calvinists supposed. He did not draw the practical conclusion that preachers should not invite sinners to receive the gospel, leaving the work entirely to the Almighty, but others of his contemporaries did. That teaching severely limited the motivation for evangelism. A circle of hyper-Calvinists holding such views gained the ascendancy in many congregations in London and some in other parts of the country. From time to time their fatalism had painful practical consequences. At Soham in Cambridgeshire in 1770, some of these extreme Calvinists, believing that no human action is possible without divine enabling, supposed that the drunkenness of a church member was unavoidable. The imperative to moral behavior was undercut and the peril of antinomianism that opponents had often ascribed to Calvinist teaching became a reality. Believers no longer felt obliged to keep the moral law of God. On the one hand, hyper-Calvinist churches felt no need to preach the gospel to the unconverted; on the other, their ideas could foster immorality. Many of the Particular Baptist churches suffered from a theological handicap that severely limited their appeal.

The increased respectability that marked many urban congregations of Dissenters also affected the Baptists, General as well as Particular. Some of those who became successful found it natural to gravitate to a parish church, which normally enjoyed more prestige than the despised meeting house. Dissent lost many of its natural leaders at the same time as it was failing to attract new converts. As a result, parts of both the Baptist bodies became torpid and introverted. "A sleepy frame of mind," wrote John Gill himself in 1750, "has seized us."[2] Early in the century there was still vigorous expansion in Lancashire, in the northwest of England, but thereafter there was a sharp decline. The number of Particular Baptist adherents in England for 1715–1718 was around 40,500; by 1750 it was thought to be about 16,500. The General Baptists, who had roughly half as many in their congregations as the Particulars, were losing attenders at approximately the same rate. The churches in the American colonies, largely General in New England but mostly Particular further south, were able to recruit from immigrants, but they too were conscious of decay. The Philadelphia Association circular letter for 1743 urged its churches to "hold fast the profession of your faith without wavering, in these shaking and wavering days. . . . We fear there are many among you who neglect prayer in and with your families. Oh sad! What life of religion can there be in such a Sardis-like state!"[3] So a combination of rational religion, together with its opposing high Calvinism, and increasing social pretensions, together with neglect of Christian standards, was sapping the foundations of Baptist life.

THE EVANGELICAL AWAKENING

The situation was to be transformed by revival. The Evangelical Revival in Britain and the Great Awakening in America were branches of the same vast movement. Its roots were not among the Baptists, who were affected by it later than several other bodies, but among other Christian communities. Part of the background lay in continental Europe, where Pietists had nurtured a warm spirituality in small fellowship groups from the later seventeenth century. From 1727 there existed the renewed Moravian movement, directed by Count Nicholas von Zinzendorf, which carried the message of justification by faith across the globe. Its example stirred other Protestants to emphasize its teaching about the new birth and to imitate its zeal for the spread of the gospel. Another stimulus to revival arose among the Puritans of New England. The original Puritan refugees from religious persecution in England were close to the Baptists in that, although they still accepted infant baptism, they believed as Congregationalists that people required conversion before they could be admitted to church membership. The sons and daughters of the original settlers, however, did not necessarily embrace their parents' faith, and yet remained closely associated with the churches they founded. Hence the ministers had a captive mission field within the walls of their meeting houses. They naturally preached sermons so as to arouse their hearers to spiritual commitment. Revivals of religion, mass turnings of whole congregations to authentic faith, were the result. Such events took place regularly, for instance, in the parish of Northampton, Massachusetts, where, in 1734, a sermon by Jonathan Edwards on justification provoked a revival. It was the starting point of a much more sustained movement, the Great Awakening.

The movement soon developed elsewhere. In Wales two young men, a schoolmaster named Howel Harris and an Anglican curate called Daniel Rowland, were converted in 1735, started preaching over large areas, and gradually gathered together local societies of awakened individuals. The network they pioneered turned into Calvinistic Methodism, which remained, during the eighteenth century, a network of revival converts within the Church of England. In the same year, an undergraduate at the University of Oxford, George Whitefield, also came to faith. Two years later, he stirred Bristol and London, which were to become his chief bases, with powerful sermons urging the new birth on his hearers. Whitefield soon made contact with the Welsh revivalists and took his message to America, crossing and recrossing the Atlantic repeatedly during his sustained preaching career. He possessed a powerful voice, marked histrionic gifts, and unusual characteristics, such as an obvious squint, that drew crowds to him. His oratory, which closely resembled the theatrical performances that he condemned, often had to be delivered in the open air because of the numbers eager to hear him. People, it was said, would swoon at his pronunciation of the word "Mesopotamia." Emotional outbursts were common in his audiences, but other revivalists were far more extreme than Whitefield. James Davenport, a Presbyterian minister originally serving in Long Island, New York, for example, was delighted when his hearers shouted because of their agony of soul. On one occasion when he preached there was "a Cry all over the Meeting-House."[4] On another he attempted to speak for twenty-four hours at a stretch. As outpourings of the Spirit multiplied, so did such phenomena. Reports of awakenings at a distance were lapped up, often stimulating fresh outbreaks of revival enthusiasm. The *Christian History*, the first religious newspaper in the colonies, was launched to bring accounts of revival elsewhere.

Circulating on both sides of the Atlantic, it helped to bind the burgeoning revival into a single entity.

Although Whitefield and the Welsh and American participants in the gathering awakening were overwhelmingly Calvinistic in doctrine, the outstanding figure in England was not. John Wesley, like Whitefield a clergyman of the Church of England, was entirely attached to its prevailing anti-Calvinistic interpretation of scripture even after his conversion experience in 1738. His Methodist followers, whom he encouraged to stay within the bounds of the established church, were directed to be resolute Arminians. Wesley exercised tight discipline in the societies that he organized, showing a skill in management that Whitefield lacked. He soon arranged for a set of helpers, mostly laymen, to itinerate in specified areas preaching the common message of justification by faith that unified the revival. As converts were gathered in, Methodist societies grew to as many as 22,410 members by 1767. Alongside Wesley, other Anglican clergy joined in the movement, often choosing, by contrast with Wesley and his men, to minister in particular parishes rather than travel about to preach. A few members of the aristocracy, among whom the Countess of Huntingdon became the most prominent, gave their patronage to the Evangelicals, in her case initiating a whole denomination, the Countess of Huntingdon's Connexion. As the century wore on, there was a steadily rising tide of commitment to the revival cause. The Evangelical movement had been born.

Baptists at first looked askance at the novelties around them. In 1740 the First Baptist Church of Boston in New England dismissed Whitefield as suffering from "enthusiasm," what a later age would have called fanaticism. The emotionalism of the awakening was foreign to the growing stress on reason in many a congregation. The Arminianism of Wesley was anathema to the Particular Baptists, while the Calvinism of Whitefield was equally repugnant to the General Baptists, including a majority of the Baptist congregations of New England. Furthermore, Methodists of both kinds seemed little better than sheep stealers. Wesley often attracted former General Baptists to his societies. The General Baptist church in Norwich resolved in 1753 that it was "unlawful for any so to attend upon the meetings of the Methodists."[5] Some Baptists, however, found the lure of the new style of religion irresistible. At the Little Prescot Street Particular Baptist Church in London, a woman announced in 1742 that if it came to a choice between her congregation and Whitefield's Tabernacle, she would leave the Baptists. For most of her coreligionists, however, the revival seemed at odds with their understanding of the faith. The awakening was not the result of careful imitation of New Testament church order, but an expression of a delusive attachment to what was called "New Light." The Old Light drawn from scripture sufficed most Baptists. Most crucially, none of the revivalists in the early years practiced believer's baptism, and so the fundamental testimony of the Baptists was imperiled. As a result, Baptists generally stood apart from the revival at first, discouraging participation and resisting any influence from its ways. Many churches of the denomination remained resolutely impervious long into the century and even beyond.

There were also, however, stirrings of sympathy for the new wave of spiritual life that was sweeping the English-speaking world. The revivalists were as committed to the Reformation principle of justification by faith as the Baptists. They believed that converts had to reveal personal experience of the grace of God in exactly the way that candidates for Baptist membership had to demonstrate their faith in the conversion narratives they delivered to the churches. And Methodists, unlike many Baptists, understood how to bring the gospel to the unheeding. At First Baptist, Boston, a group of those who had been stirred by Whitefield's ministry became dissatisfied with the Arminian teachings from the pulpit and especiallywith the denial of the doctrines surrounding the new birth. Accordingly, in 1742 they withdrew to worship separately, and eventually set up a Second Baptist Church in the city. In London, Andrew Gifford, the cultivated minister of Eagle Street Particular Baptist Church from 1735, became a friend of Whitefield and on at least one occasion entertained Wesley at dinner. The gulf between the Baptists and the revival was narrowing. A major bridge between the two was the Bristol Baptist Academy. Although only a small institution run by the minister of Broadmead Baptist Church, the academy was the sole Baptist denominational training institution in the world down to 1765. Its succession of tutors turned out a steady flow of ministers who maintained a form of Calvinism that was friendly to evangelistic work. From the 1750s it received a significant number of candidates, particularly from Wales, who were converts from the revival. At the academy, students added knowledge to their zeal without extinguishing it. In their subsequent ministries many Bristol men synthesized Baptist traditions with revival influences. The same was true of many individuals converted under Whitefield who found their way into Baptist pulpits by other routes. They included influential figures such as, in England, Robert Robinson of Cambridge and, in America, Oliver Hart of Charleston, South Carolina. Of the thirty-seven Particular Baptist ministers in London between 1760 and 1820 whose background is known, twenty-three came from non-Baptist origins. Baptist life was being revitalized by permeation from outside.

A striking instance of this phenomenon is the influence of the New England Congregationalist Jonathan Edwards on the Baptists. Edwards' weightiest work, *The Freedom of the Will* (1754), was a rigorous defense of the Reformed position tempered by ideas canvassed in the early Enlightenment. It made a crucial distinction between natural and moral inability to accept the gospel. Human beings, according to Edwards, had no natural inability imposed on them by the Almighty, but they did show a moral inability as a result of their own sin. Hence it was not God who was responsible for their perdition, but they themselves. This idea constituted a rejection of the fatalism inherent in the double predestination taught by high Calvinists such as Gill. Human beings, if only they turned from their sins to Christ, might enjoy eternal life. In practice, the fresh theological position swept away any inhibitions about preaching the gospel as widely as possible. Far from infringing on the divine prerogative, efforts to evangelize were the appointed means for fulfilling God's purposes. Those holding such views could align themselves, as Edwards himself had done, wholly with the revival. Members of the Northamptonshire Association of Particular Baptists in the English Midlands read and discussed Edwards' work with each other in the 1770s. Concluding that Edwards was correct, they redoubled their missionary efforts. In 1784 they reissued Edwards' prayer call, summoning Baptists to monthly prayer for the spread of the gospel throughout the world. One of the Northamptonshire ministers, Andrew Fuller, wrote *The Gospel Worthy of All Acceptation* (1785) to embody many of Edwards' convictions. It was a telling instance of the way in which outside influences turned the Baptists into a dynamic evangelistic denomination.

New Vigor

The transformation through external sources was most obvious in America. The revival converts of New England often felt uncomfortable in their Congregational churches. The minister might not preach the gospel clearly and might even oppose the revivalists who had brought them the message of salvation. Even where the minister befriended the awakening, the existing pattern of Congregational church life commonly did not satisfy its adherents. The membership usually included people who gave no evidence of conversion, but the New Lights wanted no fellowship with unbelievers. They demanded tighter requirements for membership that would divide the wheat from the chaff. From the 1740s onwards, there was therefore a steady hemorrhaging of New Lights out of the standing order of Congregational churches into congregations of "Separates." In the continuing quest for a purer church, many Separates began to question whether infant baptism was legitimate. Only believer's baptism, many concluded, would provide a solid bulwark against hypocrites creeping into church membership. Individuals adopted Baptist principles, groups within Separate churches left to form churches practicing believer's baptism, and even whole Separate congregations went over to the Baptists. Among those who followed the path toward Baptist convictions was Isaac Backus, who was to become the architect of denominational structures in New England. Converted in 1741 after hearing James Davenport and other revivalists, Backus helped to found a Separate church five years later. In 1748 he was called to the ministry of a newly formed Separate congregation in Middleborough, Massachusetts. After becoming convinced of

Isaac Backus (1724–1806)
Baptist Pastor and Statesman

believer's baptism, he was himself immersed in 1751 but remained
minister of the Separate church while its members included both
pedobaptists and antipedobaptists. Eventually he determined that
this compromise would not endure and, in 1756, founded a Baptist
church in Middleborough. It was one of a growing body of Separate
Baptist churches, organizationally distinct from the long-established
Regular Baptists. A whole new denomination was being created by
the revival.

It enjoyed enormous dynamism. Set free from the shackles of the standing order, Separate Baptists were free to itinerate in the manner of Whitefield. They carried their urgent message of the new birth around New England and then spilled over to the South. Shubal Stearns, minister of the Separate church at Tolland, Connecticut, was baptized in 1751 and set off to preach in Virginia, where he was joined by his brother-in-law, Daniel Marshall, who also became a Baptist preacher. The extended family settled at Sandy Creek, North Carolina, where the church they created in 1755 became the epicenter of missionary tours in the region. Growth was immediate and immense. By 1772 Sandy Creek had spawned 42 churches and 125 ministers. The style of Stearns' ministry is evident in an account by a young man named Elnathan Davis of a baptismal ceremony that Stearns conducted in a North Carolina creek in 1762 or 1763. Davis, at first merely a curious observer, was astonished when a man who was stricken in conscience wept on his shoulder. The young man ran to report to his friends that the crowd had been seized by a "crying and trembling spirit" and decided at first not to return, but then was drawn back by "the enchantment of Shubal Stearn[s'] voice."[6] Davis himself began to tremble, fell down in a trance, and woke up with alarm at the wrath of God against his sins. A few days later he reached an assured faith, received baptism from Stearns, and before long was serving as pastor of a Separate Baptist church in the colony. Through episodes such as this, the revival temper ensured rapid denominational expansion.

The approach of the Separate Baptists was so successful that it changed the ways of other Baptist groups. In many quarters Arminianism seemed a spent force and was discarded. Nearly all the General Baptists of North Carolina, for example, went over to the Calvinism of the revival by 1775. The Regular Baptists, who had been active in the colonies for over a century, were equally struck by the impact of the Separates. In South Carolina, by 1772, the Separates formed half the Baptists of the colony even though they had been active there for less than two decades. There was some cooperation between the two bodies of Baptists from an early date. Thus Oliver Hart, minister of the Regular church in

Charleston, encouraged preaching by the Separates from the 1750s. His work was consolidated by Richard Furman, converted among the Separates in the early 1770s but chosen as Hart's successor in Charleston in 1787. The Philadelphia Association that represented the Regulars, far from ignoring the awakening, sent out itinerants from 1755 and urged fervent prayer for revival in its annual pastoral address of 1770. Gradually, institutions merged. The pioneering agency was the Warren Association, founded by a circle of ministers in New England, including Backus. From its inception in 1767, the association blended Separate with Regular churches. The Rhode Island College, begun in 1765 by James Manning to train ministers, was attached to the Warren Association and so helped the distinction between the two groups to fade away. The expansionist Evangelical Calvinism of the Separates became dominant among the Baptists of America.

The revival spirit did not pass by the General or Free Will Baptists. In England, a church begun in 1745 at Barton in the Beans in Leicestershire fostered the growth of societies in the villages of the area by sending out preachers on Methodist lines. Its message was emphatically a revivalist version of Arminianism before its leaders adopted believer's baptism independently of Baptist influence. Likewise, Dan Taylor, originally a Methodist local preacher, retained his Arminian convictions after he was baptized in 1763. Taylor founded a New Connexion of General Baptists in 1770, drawing in the Barton group of churches and appealing to any existing General Baptist churches to join. He did not break entirely with the older General Baptists, being content for many years to act as the leader of a ginger group within their ranks, but forged a revival movement that grew rapidly in subsequent years, especially in the counties around Leicestershire. There was a close parallel in America, where Benjamin Randall, a sailmaker who had been converted under Whitefield, organized an entirely new Arminian movement. He set up a Free Will Baptist Church in New Durham, New Hampshire, in 1780. The movement spread over the northern parts of New England, again under the personal leadership of an individual. Randall was entrusted in 1792 with the "general supervision over the entire denomination."[7] The Free Will Baptists had connections with the followers of Henry Alline farther north in the Maritimes region of what later became Canada. Between 1776 and 1784 Alline preached a strongly experiential "New Light" message which, though not explicitly Arminian, again did not fit the Calvinist mold. Although Alline was not committed to believer's baptism, his followers adopted the practice and laid the foundations of the strong Baptist presence in the Maritimes. These three bodies, each deeply indebted to a strong revivalist leader, reinvigorated the tradition of the non-Calvinistic Baptists.

The result of the infusion of a new dynamic into the Baptists by the revival movement was a change of ethos. Because the spread of the gospel seemed the one great imperative, there was less concern to reproduce all the details of church order that the early Baptists had deduced from scripture. A case in point is the laying on of hands at baptism. The General Baptists had regarded this practice, one of their six points, as obligatory for gospel churches. Dan Taylor, however, saw it as optional, and refused to submit to pressure from the old General Baptists to require it of the churches in the New Connexion. The Philadelphia Association added a clause insisting on the same rite when it adopted the London Confession in 1742, but the laying on of hands among Particular Baptists faded on both sides of the Atlantic as revival influences spread in their churches. As old practices waned, new ones waxed. Corporate hymn singing, originally prohibited in the seventeenth century as having no scripture warrant, had found a place in Particular Baptist life at the start of the eighteenth century, but it was the revival that put hymnody at the center of worship. Many of the old General Baptists still would not countenance singing by the unregenerate in the later eighteenth century, but Dan Taylor asserted that singing was "binding on all men, converted and unconverted."[8] The full-throated rendering of a hymn, in fact, could move people toward conversion. Furthermore, experience of the revival brought Baptists closer to other Christian traditions. Evangelicals were sure that what united them, the gospel of salvation, was far more important than what divided them.

Interdenominational cooperation became common. Thus Oliver Hart in South Carolina was willing to share pulpits with likeminded Presbyterians and even Anglicans; and the London Baptist Itinerant Society, founded in 1797 to send out preachers to places surrounding the English capital, agreed from the start to work together with pedobaptists. There was a prevailing sense that the one essential task eclipsed all lesser matters.

The overriding result of the Baptist transformation by the revival was the increase in the priority of mission. The introspective, weakening bodies of the tolerant age of Enlightenment that had existed in the earlier eighteenth century were given an entirely new outlook. It is true that some of the churches refused to abandon their older ways. The English General Baptists who declined to align themselves with the New Connexion moved gradually further into a rational form of religion that eventually brought most of them into fellowship with Unitarians. The trajectory on which these churches had set out in the years around the Salters' Hall conference was continued and, consequently, their numbers rarely grew and often languished. When other Baptist churches overcame their initial hesitations about the revival movement, however, its influence, especially through its converts, turned Baptists in a fresh direction. Jonathan Edwards' theology, a form of Calvinism modified by enlightened ways of thinking, gave them a new rationale for preaching the gospel. Their numbers increased hugely. In Massachusetts the six churches of 1740 had become ninety-two by 1790. In England the Particular Baptists mushroomed from around four hundred churches in 1789 to over 1,000 by 1835. Whole new denominations were formed: the Separate Baptists, the New Connexion, and the Free Will Baptists. Home missionary agencies were multiplying by the end of the century, and the foreign missionary enterprise had been launched by William Carey, fired by the same theological convictions that his friend Andrew Fuller articulated. The global missionary impulse among Baptists, the subject of chapter 14, showed the extent of the change inaugurated by the revival.

FURTHER READING

Brown, Raymond. *The English Baptists of the Eighteenth Century.* London: Baptist Historical Society, 1986.

Goen, C. C. *Revivalism and Separatism in New England, 1740–1800: Strict Congregationalist and Separate Baptists in the Great Awakening.* New Haven, Conn.: Yale University Press, 1962.

Kidd, Thomas S. *The Great Awakening: The Roots of Evangelical Christianity in Colonial America.* New Haven, Conn.: Yale University Press, 2007.

Lumpkin, William L. *Baptist Foundations in the South: Tracing through the Separates the Influence of the Great Awakening, 1754–1787.* Nashville: Broadman, 1961.

Roberts, R. Philip. *Continuity and Change: London Calvinistic Baptists and the Evangelical Revival, 1760–1820.* Wheaton, Ill.: R. O. Roberts, 1989.

Watts, Michael R. *The Dissenters: From the Reformation to the French Revolution.* Oxford: Clarendon, 1978.

Chapter 6

DIVISIONS AMONG BAPTISTS IN THE NINETEENTH CENTURY

The awakening of the eighteenth century prepared the way for vast expansion during the nineteenth century by all the Evangelical denominations. In England, Anglicans who belonged to the Evangelical party grew markedly and Evangelical Dissenters of every kind made rapid advances. In Scotland Presbyterian numbers mushroomed, and in Wales Nonconformity, a newer term for Dissent, turned into something like a national faith. In America all types of Evangelicals hugely increased their numbers. The movement began to make an impact on Ireland, Canada, South Africa, Australia, and New Zealand. In the course of this global development, no body did better than the Methodists. In 1800 they had 96,000 members in England; by 1850, they had 518,000; and by 1900 membership numbered 770,000. Although the population grew markedly, Methodist membership outpaced its rise until the last quarter of the century. In America the denomination was even more successful. In 1800 there were 65,000 Methodists; in 1850, 1.25 million; and in 1900, a remarkable 5.5 million. Baptists also participated in the great tide of Evangelical religion that rolled over the English-speaking world. In England and Wales the number of their churches (membership figures are scanty) increased from 445 to 1,080 in mainstream associations during the first half of the nineteenth century; their membership rose from 100,000 to 516,000 during its second half. In America Baptist membership grew from some 100,000 to 313,000 during the first half of the century and climbed to over 3 million by its end. Although the advance of Baptists was nationwide, growth was disproportionately larger in the South. After the Methodists, Baptists were the second greatest gainers from the immense progress made by Evangelical religion in the nineteenth century.

Much of the growth, especially earlier in the century and especially in the United States, came from local revivals. A revival was a time when members of a whole community became anxious about the state of their souls and large numbers of conversions took place. A typical episode of this kind took place at Washington-on-the-Brazos in Texas, then a sovereign country, in 1841. Texas, newly conquered from Mexico and not yet annexed to the United States, was beginning to be occupied by Anglophone settlers. A small Baptist church was set up in Washington-on-the-Brazos in the late 1830s but collapsed for lack of support. An agent of the American Baptist Home Mission Society, William Tryon, refounded it in March 1841, and in July the baptism of the church's first candidate, a slave girl, precipitated a religious awakening. Tryon preached a gospel sermon, appealing for sinners to seek salvation. "Deep feeling pervaded the assembly," he reported afterwards; "and very many, with streaming eyes, manifested that their hearts were affected."[1] Two professed conversion before the day was over. The next evening, after nightfall, four candidates were baptized in the Brazos River by moonlight. The sight moved many more. A prominent freethinker in the town was converted, and meetings had to be held every night because the people of the area wanted to know how to be saved. After a week's services, thirty-one people had made professions of conversion, a remarkable impact on a town of only about a hundred permanent adult inhabitants. Such events were often the times when churches made substantial gains in numbers. Revivals were a major contributor to growth for much of the nineteenth century.

The process of expansion brought consequences in its wake. Nathan Hatch has propounded the influential thesis that, in the aftermath of the American Revolution, there was a democratization of the religion of the new republic. Leadership shifted from ordained ministers to ordinary laypeople of little or no theological training who devised their own forms of faith, energetically propagated their beliefs, and generated a populist style of spirituality. Hatch's theory encompasses Baptists alongside Methodists, Mormons, and others, and explains their success in terms of the distinctiveness of American religious culture.[2] What the thesis neglects, however, is that similar developments took place in the United Kingdom, where there were movements among the common people that broke entirely with received patterns of doctrine and traditional norms of propriety. The Primitive Methodists, for example, copied the American technique of camp meetings and, under the firm leadership of Hugh Bourne and William Clowes, set up an exuberant revivalistic movement in the early years of the century. There were equivalent happenings among the Baptists. The New Connexion of General Baptists, discussed in the last chapter, was very much the creation of a religious entrepreneur, Dan Taylor, who formulated his own statement of faith that differed from that of the old General Baptists. There were bivocational preachers of little education who undertook vigorous ministry among the Particular Baptists. Although there were also respectable ministers and laymen in and around London who were wary of popular provincial religion, the Baptists had their share of vivid dreams, wild ideas, and unorthodox methods. There was a democratization of religion in Britain as well as in America, because anyone could preach the gospel and gain a hearing. The process was not a consequence of forces unique to the United States, but the result of the egalitarian dynamic unleashed by the Evangelical Revival.

The result was a time of extraordinary divisiveness in the Evangelical world. Strong-minded souls who confidently carved out their own path in religion threatened the unity of denominational structures. Methodism in England suffered repeated schism, and Baptists, as we shall see, were drawn into conflict with each other.

Yet the Evangelical Revival simultaneously fostered an entirely different tendency, toward greater institutionalization. Agencies were needed to organize and finance the spread of the gospel, to coordinate local activities, and to promote benevolent efforts. Hence, from the 1790s onwards, the era witnessed a series of new ventures in denominational and interdenominational enterprise. There were overseas missions, domestic missions, city missions; Bible societies, book societies, tract societies; Sunday schools, ragged schools; organizations to help strangers, soldiers, sailors, widows, mothers, prostitutes, flower-sellers, orphans, and a host of other categories of the needy. The center of this benevolent empire in Britain was Exeter Hall in London, where the societies assembled for their annual meetings each May. America held equivalent events in New York, Boston, and elsewhere. The strength of this parachurch activity, however, was in the branch auxiliaries, which raised money in the localities and often expended it there too. The effect of these efforts was twofold: to bring members of different denominations together in common mission, whether Bible distribution, charitable giving, or whatever, and to combine the members of individual denominations into new agencies designed to advance the distinctive principles of each body. The result was therefore to promote Evangelical unity and also, often in some tension with the first consequence, to consolidate denominations. There was a trend toward cooperation that restrained the individualism of the age.

Among Baptists, the first step in the new phase of organization-building came with the foundation, in 1792, of the Baptist Missionary Society. Begun in order to express the fresh ambition of British Baptists to spread the gospel throughout the world, the society acted as a novel focus for unity in the denomination. The society's literature disseminated a vision of a global mission that bound Baptists together, drawing in a large number of British churches and even attracting support from the Philadelphia Association in the United States. The consolidating effect should not be exaggerated, for even at mid-century the society received financial backing from only about half the Baptist churches in England. Yet it prepared the way for the foundation, in 1813, of a Baptist Union as a national organization for the denomination in the United Kingdom. The Union was poorly supported and achieved little, but it was followed in 1832 by a more enterprising body of the same name. Gradually, as the Union developed over the course of the century, it came to be seen as the mouthpiece of the British denomination. An equivalent national body in America was formed in 1814, the General Missionary Convention of the Baptist Denomination in the United States, usually known, on account of its meeting every three years, as the Triennial Convention. Founded largely as a result of the efforts of Luther Rice, one of the earliest Baptist missionaries, its remit was primarily, as its formal title implied, the promotion of foreign missions, but in the early years it also toyed with home missions and educational activity before determining to concentrate on overseas work. A tract society followed in 1824, as did a home mission agency eight years later. State conventions, the first of which was established in South Carolina in 1821, were equally part of the process of creating organizations to increase effectiveness in gospel work. The same is true of the colleges, chiefly intended for the training of ministers, which were inaugurated across much of the Baptist world during the century. The denomination was self-consciously mobilizing for missionary enterprise.

THE ANTI-MISSIONARY CONTROVERSY

The problem was that by no means all Baptists considered these developments legitimate. An anti-missionary movement arose to resist the new institutions, and soon divided associations. The first split took place in 1828, when the Canoochee Association seceded from the Hephzibah Association in Georgia. In 1832 a summons to resist "modern inventions" was issued by "Old School" Particular Baptists at Black Rock in Maryland.[3] Struggles followed in Alabama and its adjacent states over the next couple of decades until the anti-missionaries formed a distinct set of associations, too decentralized to be termed a denomination but sometimes called Primitive or Hardshell Baptists. Part of the explanation for the schism lies in the considerable resentment that built up against the constant appeals for money made by advocates of missions at home and abroad. The

Kehukee Association of North Carolina, for instance, resolved that "no missionary preacher or beggar . . . shall be invited into our pulpits . . . to beg and cheat the people."[4] Another source of opposition to the new institutions was hostility to the degree of authority that was concentrated in a few hands. John Taylor, the author of *Thoughts on Missions* (1819), expressed dismay at the "mighty convention" run by men in quest of power as well as money. "I consider," he declared with an American flourish, "these great men as verging close on aristocracy, with an object to sap the foundation of Baptist republican government."[5] And there was also an element of anti-intellectualism about the movement. The anti-missionaries did not see why human wisdom was required to preach a divine message, and often maintained that college learning dampened the zeal of ministers by plucking them away from the people. The Primitives have been diagnosed as an expression of the frontier spirit among Baptists. Where there was little wealth, away from the centers of power on the East Coast, and where educational facilities were limited, resistance to the new structures of mission was likely to set in.

It is important, however, to recognize that the mainspring of the opposition was theological conviction. The missionary Baptists were motivated by the moderate Calvinistic outlook considered in the last chapter. Rejecting double predestination, Andrew Fuller and others who came after him held that the Almighty did not himself consign the unsaved to perdition. Sinners who refused the gospel offer were responsible for their own ruin. All human beings needed to hear the gospel so that they might have a chance to turn from their wicked ways. A missionary Baptist church, according to an apologist for their position in a four-day debate with anti-missionaries at Fulton, Kentucky, as late as 1887, "holds that the gospel should be preached to every creature, and that every sinner should be exhorted to repentance and faith." The speaker also urged that "repentance and faith are duties as well as graces."[6] Here was the key element in the moderate Calvinist position to which the anti-missionaries objected. They repudiated the idea of duty faith on the ground that sinners could not be commanded to do what they were unable to do. According to the Primitives, God had chosen certain people for

Andrew Fuller (1754–1815)
Baptist Theologian and Missionary Organizer

salvation but had passed over others. Those who were not elect were certainly unable to embrace faith and so were under no obligation to do so. The anti-missionaries were upholding a higher version of Calvinism that insisted on the absolute prerogative of the Almighty to determine the line between the unsaved and the saved. Theirs was the theology that had prevailed among Baptists before the onset of the eighteenth-century revival. They had strong claims to represent the authentic views of the Particular Baptists.

Likewise, there was a theological dispute about methods. For those who thought like Fuller, the spread of the gospel entailed using all the instruments that providence put into the hands of Christians. They could employ the techniques of money-raising pioneered by a commercial age since these were legitimate means to the end of the salvation of the world. The term "means" became a slogan among those who believed in missionary agencies such as Bible societies and denominational conventions. For the opponents of these institutions, however, such means were illegitimate, a brazen attempt to interfere in the ways of the Almighty. The societies purported to do what God would achieve by his own agency, the gathering of the elect. They were, according to the Kehukee Association, "only the inventions of men . . . without any warrant from the New Testament, or any example in the purest ages of the church."[7] They were a defection from true Baptist order, which saw the local church, and only the local church, as the divinely appointed agency for spreading the gospel. Hence the Apple Creek Association of Illinois, founded as an anti-mission body in 1830, announced in its constitution that "we declare an unfellowship with foreign and domestic missionary and bible societies, Sunday Schools and tract societies, and all other missionary institutions."[8] This was not mere prejudice. Rather, it was traditional Baptist attachment to the bare requirements of God's word as the determinants of church order as well as of Christian faith. The Primitives were strict on questions of polity as well as particular—in more senses than one—about matters of doctrine.

That theological issues were central to the division in America is confirmed by the existence of a parallel schism in England. During the nineteenth century there grew up a body of Strict and Particular Baptists who upheld a strict churchmanship and believed in particular redemption. The first split in an English association occurred in 1829, only a year after the first equivalent rupture in America, when a number of churches seceded from their existing affiliation to establish the Suffolk and Norfolk Association. The dissidents retained a high Calvinism that revealed its roots in the seventeenth century by its refusal to adopt recent doctrinal modifications. They rejected the theology of Fuller, who became their *bête noire*, and especially the axiom of duty faith. Exactly like the Primitive Baptists of Georgia, they recommended the works of William Huntington, an ebullient English popular preacher who set out an uncompromising theological system that magnified the absolute sovereignty of God. Strict and Particular Baptists initially refused to adopt such innovations as Sunday schools and missionary societies, and, though after a while many of their churches themselves adopted the novel techniques, there remained in some circles a dogged resistance to any agencies unwarranted by scripture. Naturally, they declined to associate with the Baptist Union, and instead rallied around a series of periodicals, *The Gospel Standard, The Earthen Vessel*, and *The Gospel Herald*. They eventually secured the support of as many as a third of the Baptist churches of England, but their proportion of the overall Baptist church membership was much lower. Except in London, where some of their churches were huge, they usually attracted only small congregations. Like their American counterparts, the Strict and Particulars often lived in rural and remote parts of the country. The Baptists of England suffered the same experience of division over how far to modify received faith and order as those in the United States.

THE COMMUNION CONTROVERSY

The issue that most troubled nineteenth-century English Baptists, however, was the communion controversy. Although all the Strict and Particulars were ranged on the conservative side in this dispute, the line of division over communion did not correspond to the separation between the Strict and Particulars and the other Baptists but instead ran through the Baptist Union, at times threatening its existence. The issue surrounded the question of who should be allowed to participate in the Lord's supper. The traditional answer of most Baptists was that only those who had been immersed on profession of their faith could receive communion. Abraham Booth, perhaps the leading Particular Baptist minister of his day, had set out the case for this "closed" position in *An Apology for the Baptists* (1778). In New Testament times, he argued, baptism was associated with entry to the church, whereas communion was a sign of subsequent membership. So participants in the Lord's supper must previously have been baptized. There was no question, therefore, of admitting those who had not been immersed. This position did not go unchallenged, however, for the open-membership tradition endorsed by John Bunyan had never died out. Two years after Booth's book, a

new church was established at Oxford on open communion principles. The members declared that differences over baptism would be
set aside because, as they put it, "we can find no warrant in the Word
of God to make such difference of sentiment any bar to communion
at the Lord's Table in particular, or to Church fellowship in particular; and because the Lord Jesus receiving and owning them on both
sides of the question, we think we ought to do so too."[9] Despite such
dissenting voices, the overwhelming majority of Baptists, General as
well as Particular, favored closed communion.

The temper of the age, however, provided powerful reinforcement to the minority position. The spirit of the Enlightenment,
which, as later chapters will show more fully, was closely allied
with the Evangelical Revival, was pragmatic. Inherited ways could
be modified by the requirements of a new age, as in the adoption
of means for the spread of the gospel. Should the New Testament
exclusion of the unbaptized from communion apply at a time when
most Christians did not practice believer's baptism? Robert Hall, the
formidably intellectual Baptist minister at Leicester, contended that
because times had changed, so should Baptists. In his treatise *On
Terms of Communion* (1815), he dealt powerfully with Booth's arguments from the previous century. If a believer failed to obey the command to be baptized, Hall argued, the obligation to sit at the Lord's
table nevertheless remained. Baptists should allow those whom they
acknowledged as fellow Christians to obey their Lord by receiving
the tokens of his body and blood. "It must appear surprising," Hall
wrote, "that the rite, which, of all others, is most adapted to cement
mutual attachment, and which is in a great measure appointed for
that purpose, should be fixed upon as the line of demarcation, the
impassable barrier, to separate and disjoin the followers of Christ."[10]
Although Hall was answered by his colleague from Norwich, Joseph
Kinghorn, the Leicester minister made an eloquent case for changing the prevailing Baptist practice.

As a result, the policy of British Baptists over admission to communion gradually altered. In 1824 it was estimated that, out of
roughly seven hundred Particular Baptist churches in England, only
about fifty had an open table. By the 1840s, however, the Baptist

Missionary Society was overwhelmingly open. The most celebrated conflict over the principle occurred at St. Mary's Baptist Church, Norwich, the church that had been, under Kinghorn, Hall's opponent, a bastion of the closed position. When, in 1857, the church resolved to open the Lord's table to all Christians, a closed-communionist trustee took the case to the law courts. The church, however, was able to demonstrate historically that there were different Baptist views on the subject, and so won the legal battle. Thereafter, opposition to the open-communion position among mainstream Baptists collapsed except in the north of England, Scotland, and Wales. A Welsh association still condemned open communion as "an unscriptural practice" in 1897.[11] The policy of opening the table to all believers, though not unknown in the United States, was extremely rare there. Consequently, Canada was a battleground between British and American attitudes, with the Montreal College founded in 1838 collapsing eleven years later because the institution's successive English principals advocated open communion but the bulk of its natural constituency preferred a closed stance. The matters under debate in the communion controversy were deeply felt in many parts of the Baptist world.

THE SECTIONAL CONTROVERSY IN AMERICA

The most explosive issue among American Baptists, by contrast, was the sectional question that divided North and South. The Triennial Convention and the related societies represented the whole country during the 1830s, but in 1845 the Southerners withdrew to form their own convention. The mode of organization differed from that previously adopted by the national bodies, which were separate societies run by committees that were elected by subscribers—essentially the structure of joint stock companies. The South preferred the method recommended by William B. Johnson of South Carolina, who became the first president of the new body. Johnson proposed having a single convention under which there would be boards for particular purposes, initially foreign and home missions. This structural approach, closer to the Methodist model, made every church, and therefore every member, directly involved in the common

ventures of the new Southern Baptist Convention. The issue of how
to structure the denominational agencies, however, did not arise
as a cause of controversy before the split of 1845 had taken place.
What had prepared the way for the rupture was intermittent grum-
bling over the allocation of funds by the Home Missionary Society.
Sometimes more seemed to be poured into the coffers of the agency
from the South than was spent on missionary work in Southern territory. In reality, however, between 1832 and 1841, Baptists in the
South contributed $29,093, while expenditures there amounted to
the greater sum of $30,842. The South was not actually the victim
of discrimination, but nevertheless a feeling that it was being sold
short persisted. There was even a call in 1835 for a separate organization to serve the West and South. The sense of grievance, however,
reflected deeper-seated resentments against the North.

The chief chafing issue over the years was the question of slavery,
a subject that will be discussed more fully in chapter 9. The Southern
states were the home of the cotton plantations where slaves worked
the fields and served in the households. There had been some anti-
slavery sentiment in the South in the years around 1800, but by the
1820s it had become accepted opinion among Baptists there that
slavery was economically necessary and biblically defensible. In the
North, by contrast, opinion swung against the institution of slavery, and, from the 1820s, immediate emancipation was urged as a
Christian obligation with increasing vehemence by the anti-slavery
movement. In 1836 the Maine Baptist Association branded slavery
"the most abominable" of all systems of iniquity that had cursed
the world.[12] The South responded by rallying behind its ramparts.
Abolitionism, according to the Baptist Convention of North Carolina
in 1835, was "uncalled for, intrusive, and pernicious."[13] Lines were
already being drawn between the two sides. A series of controversies surrounding the issue of the legitimacy of the Home Missionary
Society's employing slaveholders as its agents culminated in the
1845 decision to create a separate Southern convention. The central
question was certainly whether or not slavery was compatible with
Christian civilization, but, as in the prelude to the political rupture
in 1861, when the states that became the Confederacy seceded from

the Union, more was at stake. For the South, its distinctive values were under assault; for the North, there was a threat to the unity of Americans. The division between Northern and Southern Baptists, rather like the schism between Eastern and Western Christianity in 1054, was a matter of a clash of cultures with divergent values.

THE CAMPBELLITE CONTROVERSY

Baptists were also troubled by a more directly theological controversy that led to schism. Alexander Campbell, originally a Seceder Presbyterian from northern Ireland, was impressed by Scottish efforts to discover New Testament simplicity in church order and, on moving to America, joined the Baptists of Pennsylvania in 1812. Campbell increasingly felt that Baptists needed to change their ways in order to conform to the pattern of the earliest church. More deeply swayed by the spirit of the Enlightenment than his contemporaries who followed Andrew Fuller, Campbell was extremely rational in his approach to religion. He decided that priestcraft was responsible for importing obscurities into the faith. "Instead of the apostles' doctrine," he wrote in 1823, "simply and plainly exhibited in the New Testament . . . we have countless creeds, composed of terms and phrases, dogmas and speculations, invented by whimsical Metaphysicians, Christian Philosophers, Rabbinical Doctors, and Enthusiastic Preachers."[14] This farrago of nonsense, he argued in his *Christian Baptist* newspaper, must be swept away so that the original simplicity could be restored. Confessions of faith must be dropped and the New Testament treated as an authoritative law book. Then, he claimed, it would become apparent that faith is purely assent to the proposition that Jesus is the Son of God; that baptism is designed for the remission of sins and so is a requirement for salvation; and that the Lord's supper should be observed weekly. Other Baptists found none of these positions acceptable. Faith, they held, was a matter of trust in a person, not merely assent to a proposition; baptism was a question of obedience rather than a mediator of saving grace; and there was no duty to hold communion so frequently. Campbell's "Reform" movement met stout resistance.

The struggle between Campbell's followers and his opponents was fought out in many churches. At Nashville, Tennessee, for instance, the Baptist church, which had been established there in 1820, called Phillip S. Fall as pastor six years later. Fall had been sought as a potential pastor only a year after the church's foundation, but in the intervening period had been persuaded by Campbell's views. On his first Sunday he started the weekly observance of the Lord's supper, a month later he stopped the examination of the experience of baptismal candidates on the ground that a bare statement of belief in Jesus as Son of God was the only requirement, and in 1828 the church adopted the New Testament as its sole rule of faith and practice. Eventually, in 1830, five members withdrew to form the nucleus of a fresh church since the original congregation had altered its character so drastically. In Britain congregations adopting Campbellite views, though far less numerous than those in the United States, were often constituted from former Scotch Baptist churches. These bodies, holding to the theology of Archibald McLean, had existed since the first was founded in Edinburgh in 1765. Inspired largely by a small Scottish sect, the Glasites or Sandemanians, they believed in closely imitating the apparent practice of the New Testament by holding communion weekly and having more than one elder. The Scotch Baptists also adopted the Sandemanian doctrine of faith, which held that it was a matter of the head rather than the heart. They were therefore natural recruits to Campbell's cause. Only slowly in either America or Britain did it become apparent that the Reformers were emerging as an entirely distinct body, which eventually became known as the Disciples of Christ or (on its conservative wing) as the Churches of Christ. Eventually, however, it was clear that the new body was a rival to the Baptists rather than a movement within their ranks.

The Landmark Movement

At mid-century another powerful faction among Baptists arose. The Landmark movement can best be seen as a response to circumstances created by the strength of the Methodists and the appeal of the Campbellite reformers in many parts of the American South.

Baptists faced fierce competition in their quest for souls. The leading exponent of Landmarkism, James R. Graves, was a self-educated man of immoderate Baptist zeal. Ordained in 1842, he wanted to demonstrate through the pages of the *Tennessee Baptist* that his own denomination was exclusively right. Wanting to combat the Campbellites, he adopted much of their attitude toward the New Testament. "Every positive law, ordinance or practice, in the church," he held, "not expressly commanded or exampled, is positively forbidden." Only those ordained among the Baptists were true ministers of the gospel, and so no others should be allowed to preach. Authentic baptism required not just the mode (immersion) and subject (believers) to be correct, but also the administrator to be the commissioned official of a true Baptist church. Hence baptism by others was "alien immersion" and so invalid. Other congregations that failed to follow New Testament ecclesiastical instructions were not proper churches but mere societies. "There is no church," Graves contended, "but a body of immersed believers, who have been immersed by one who has himself been immersed, after conversion and a hope of salvation."[15] The logic of that position required a remarkable historical claim. If an administrator of baptism himself needed to have been properly baptized, there must have been a succession of valid baptismal practice down through the centuries—meaning that contemporary Baptist immersion must go back in an unbroken chain to Jesus himself. Graves did not flinch from this view. Just as contemporary Anglo-Catholics adopted the doctrine of apostolic succession, whereby the true church had been preserved over the ages through the consecration of bishops by those validly consecrated, so Graves propagated the idea of baptismal succession. Here was a High Church appeal to tradition.

A distinctive Landmark position was first publicly avowed by a meeting at Cotton Grove, Tennessee, in 1851, when it was declared that preachers of other denominations could not be recognized as gospel ministers. Thereafter, the progress of similar views steadily gathered pace. In 1854 James M. Pendleton, Baptist minister at Bowling Green, Kentucky, gave the movement its name by publishing a tract called *An Old Landmark Re-set*, in which he treated the exclusive mission of Baptist ministers as the landmark to be restored. Graves began efforts to make his own publications the standard staple of Sunday school literature among Southern Baptists, and created sharp disputes in the process. The strength of Landmark views by the end of the century was apparent in the Whitsitt controversy. William T. Whitsitt, a church historian who, in 1895, was appointed president of the flagship Southern Baptist Theological Seminary at Louisville, Kentucky, made the point in an encyclopedia article that Baptists adopted immersion around 1641. This true statement ran athwart the a priori assumption of the Landmarkists that there must have been a succession of immersionist practice since the time of Jesus. Baptist associations, stirred up by elements in the denominational press, passed resolutions of protest, and Benjah H. Carroll, the redoubtable minister of First Baptist Church, Waco, Texas, headed a campaign for Whitsitt's dismissal. Eventually, in 1898, Whitsitt resigned. In 1931 Carroll's brother, James M. Carroll, was to publish *The Trail of Blood*, a popular classic that set out the supposed line of authentic Baptist witness over the years. By then two small Landmark Baptist denominations were in existence. Landmarkism stirred up intense debate and left an enduring legacy. There was a temporary exclusion of Landmarkers from Dallas First Baptist Church in 1879, but, in general, before 1900 the movement did not generate actual schism.

Language, Race, and Grace

There were more peaceful groups in Baptist life, however, that did pursue separate paths during the nineteenth century. Baptist convictions spread over the continent of Europe from shortly before the middle of the century, especially through the superbly organized work of Johann Gerhard Oncken that will be discussed in chapter 15. Many members of the new communities of faith joined the tide of emigration to North America, so that ethnic groups of Baptists established their own churches in the United States and Canada. There was a German Baptist denomination from 1851 and a Swedish equivalent from 1879. Welsh-speaking Baptists led a substantially separate existence in Pennsylvania throughout the century. Language, in fact, operated as a significant dividing factor. Only race was a stronger barrier. At first, as we shall see in chapter 9, black and white Baptists usually worshiped in the same buildings, but, in the immediate aftermath of the Civil War, distinct African American churches were formed in the South. State agencies gradually emerged, and the burgeoning black Baptist press also took its place in binding the churches together. The most effective tie between the churches on a large scale, however, was their common concern for overseas missions. From 1880 many of the previous disparate efforts were unified under the American Baptist Foreign Mission Convention, and another body, the American National Baptist Convention, founded in 1886, initially planned to maintain close cooperation with white Baptists in overseas work but increasingly turned to other tasks. Together with a National Baptist Educational Convention, set up in 1893 to advance black ministerial training, these bodies came together in 1895 to form a truly united organization, the National Baptist Convention. The new convention, under E. C. Morris as president right down to 1922, at last fulfilled the hopes of African American Baptists for a national expression of their identity. Language and race were probably the most salient forces separating nineteenth-century Baptists from each other.

The oldest division of all was that over the doctrines of grace between the General, or Free Will, Baptists and the Particular, or Calvinist, Baptists. In America Free Will Baptists had been almost extinguished by Particular Baptist proselytism in the eighteenth century, but a small group survived in North Carolina and engaged in energetic expansion in the early nineteenth century. Benjamin Randall's body of Free Willers, introduced in the previous chapter, flourished in northern New England, while more General Baptists were found in Kentucky and Indiana. All were Arminian in doctrine and all continued into the twentieth century, when, in 1911, the bulk of the New England group was absorbed by the Northern Baptists who sprang from Particular roots. In a similar way, Baptists of Arminian and Calvinist background in the Maritime provinces of Canada merged in 1906. In England, most of the older General

Baptists moved steadily into rationalist views and eventually became indistinguishable from Unitarians. The New Connexion, however, as the fruit of the Evangelical Revival, remained orthodox and enterprising, and grew into a sizeable community during the nineteenth century. Some of its members gave support to the Baptist Missionary Society before they created their own equivalent, and from the beginning of the Baptist Union there were affiliated New Connexion churches. As Calvinist theology mellowed during the century, there was less hostility in Particular ranks to Arminian views and members began to be transferred between churches of the two traditions without qualms. In 1891 the New Connexion was wholly absorbed into the Baptist Union, only a few years before the equivalent events in Canada and the United States. The blending of the General and Particular bodies in all three countries was possible because they shared a common ethos that was generically Evangelical rather than specifically Calvinist or Arminian. The nineteenth century was marked by convergence as well as by disruption.

The most marked feature of the great majority of Baptists during the nineteenth century was their shared allegiance to Evangelical priorities. Like the Methodists, they were relentlessly evangelistic, often (especially in America) enjoying revivals that spurred growth. They formed a plethora of organizations to advance the cause of the gospel, throwing themselves into Bible, tract, and Sunday school work, and much else. Denominational agencies were among the new structures, but these bodies, whether associated with the Baptist Union in England or the Triennial Convention in America, aroused deep suspicions. Churches of higher Calvinist views saw the novel institutions as tainted with a false theology and withdrew to their own Primitive or Strict and Particular associations, maintaining the style as well as the thought of the past. The rest of the English Baptists debated whether to open the Lord's table to those not baptized as believers, concluding in the main, by contrast with their American cousins, that they should. Meanwhile, Baptists in America divided permanently over the sectional difference symbolized by slavery.

They were also troubled by Alexander Campbell's Reform movement, which led to a parting of the ways with the Disciples, and by the Landmarkers, who agitated in the South for an uncompromising theory of Baptist tradition. Differences of language and race kept many Baptists apart from each other, but the inherited antagonism between Calvinist and Arminian faded. The confluence of these two streams is an indication of the extent to which most nineteenth-century Baptists were remolded by a common Evangelicalism.

FURTHER READING

Baker, Robert A. *The Southern Baptist Convention and Its People, 1607–1972*. Nashville: Broadman, 1974.

Bebbington, David W. "The Democratization of British Christianity: The Baptist Case, 1770–1870." In *Ecumenism and History: Studies in Honour of John H. Y. Briggs*, edited by Anthony R. Cross, 265–80. Carlisle: Paternoster, 2002.

Briggs, John H. Y. *The English Baptists of the Nineteenth Century*. Didcot, Oxfordshire: Baptist Historical Society, 1994.

Crowley, John G. *Primitive Baptists of the Wiregrass South: 1815 to the Present*. Gainesville: University of Florida Press, 1998.

Dix, Kenneth. *Strict and Particular: English Strict and Particular Baptists in the Nineteenth Century*. Didcot, Oxfordshire: Baptist Historical Society, 2001.

Fitts, Leroy. *A History of Black Baptists*. Nashville: Broadman, 1985.

Hughes, Richard T. *Reviving the Ancient Faith: The Story of Churches of Christ in America*. Grand Rapids: Eerdmans, 1996.

Wamble, Hugh. "Landmarkism: Doctrinaire Ecclesiology among Baptists." *Church History* 33 (1964): 429–47.

Chapter 7

THEOLOGICAL POLARIZATION
AMONG BAPTISTS

The disturbances of the nineteenth century culminated in a tendency for Baptists to divide into two camps. The divergence was not unique to Baptist life, but part of a larger process in the Protestant world. The theology of Evangelicals in almost all denominations, which had been a bond that withstood the various tensions over other issues during most of the nineteenth century, began to unravel. Between the 1870s and the 1930s, those who had previously been conscious of a unity based on a shared message increasingly looked askance at others within the Evangelical movement as either too narrow or too broad. The trend peaked, especially in North America, in controversies during the 1920s between Modernists wanting to bring theology up to date and Fundamentalists determined to resist the loss of cherished truths. Not all denominations suffered from these fierce struggles, for in some bodies, such as Congregationalism on both sides of the Atlantic, liberal theology was too powerful to be expelled, and in others, such as the so-called Plymouth Brethren, there was no question of accepting liberal fancies. In other bodies, however, there were strongly placed adherents of both sides and so there were outbreaks of doctrinal dispute. Among the Presbyterians of America, though not those of Scotland, the struggles were intense and led to institutional schism. The Baptists also suffered from internecine debates and permanent divisions. It is true that, alongside those who arraigned their fellow Baptists for either intellectual backwardness or doctrinal faithlessness, there were others who maintained a more tolerant attitude toward other points of view than their own. Yet the tendency for some to adopt more liberal theological positions and for others to protest against these developments was a salient feature of the period leading up to and just after the First World War. There was an overall tendency toward polarization.

In the middle years of the nineteenth century the inherited body of Evangelical theology seemed firmly in place. It followed, in its predominant Calvinist form, the outline of the thought of Jonathan Edwards, who had expressed the core of Puritan theology in a style more acceptable to the rising Enlightenment of his day. Among the Baptists the chief exponent of theology within the Edwardsian paradigm was Andrew Fuller. Although he had died in 1815, Fuller remained the touchstone of orthodoxy over half a century later. Edward Steane, secretary of the Baptist Union of Great Britain and Ireland, remarked in 1872 that Fuller had done the most to shape the characteristics of modern Calvinism. The New Hampshire Confession, approved by the state Baptist Convention in 1833 and widely adopted elsewhere in America, followed Fuller's moderate version of Reformed theology. Fuller had expounded the classic doctrines of the faith, but had made them palatable to an enlightened epoch. He interpreted the atonement, for example, as a demonstration of the public justice of the Almighty, a vindication of his orderly government of the world. For an era schooled by Newtonian science into valuing the principle of order, this was a way of viewing the cross that carried conviction. Furthermore, Fuller abandoned the old Calvinist insistence that Christ died for only the elect. The atonement, according to the theologian, was sufficient for all, a teaching that appealed to the belief of the age in universal benevolence. Fuller was one of those who thoroughly integrated Evangelical theology into the legacy of the Enlightenment, which continued to shape thinking in most spheres of life for much of the nineteenth century. The Baptist message fit the mindset of the day.

Calvinism, however, became less fashionable as the nineteenth century wore on. Although many Baptists still adhered to Reformed doctrines, and the greatest Victorian preacher, Charles Haddon Spurgeon, resolutely championed them, they steadily fell into decay. One reason was the allegiance to the Bible that marked the Baptists. Increasingly it was felt that the scriptures alone formed a sufficient guide to doctrine. James Acworth, president of Rawdon College in Yorkshire, urged his students to study the Bible for themselves, unfettered by existing human systems. "Make your own system" was his standard advice.[1] Another reason was the prestige of Arminianism. Because Methodism advanced more rapidly than any other denominational group during the nineteenth century, its message of a salvation that was available for all seemed to be the right one for the hour. Baptists often cooperated with Methodists, especially on the American frontier, and from the 1870s they frequently supported joint evangelistic efforts under the interdenominational preacher D. L. Moody and his imitators. Moody did not simply teach Arminian doctrines, for he upheld the eternal security of the believer, but he did try to be as acceptable to Methodists as to Presbyterians and so toned down the Calvinist content of his addresses. In England, as the last chapter indicated, General Baptist churches were admitted to the Baptist Union from its foundation in 1832 so that there was close fellowship between churches with Calvinist and Arminian origins. "The two great sections, Particular and General," declared the *General Baptist Magazine* in 1859, "are so blended as scarcely to maintain the old line of demarcation."[2] By the final decade of the century their convergence was so complete that the General Baptists abolished their separate denominational agencies altogether. Shortly afterwards, as we have seen, there were similar mergers between Baptists of Arminian and Calvinist backgrounds in Canada and the United States. So Calvinism was in many places ceasing to be even the formal doctrinal position of Baptist churches.

ROMANTIC CULTURAL INFLUENCES

The Enlightenment component of Baptist theological attitudes also began to be called into question. The nineteenth century witnessed a revolution in cultural attitudes as the legacy of the age of reason was challenged by new views associated with Romanticism. The older stress on reason as the supreme human faculty was gradually replaced by emphases on will, spirit, and emotion. Human imagination seemed more admirable than the cold temper of scientific investigation. The universe was treated less as a static machine and more as a theater of natural growth. Values no longer appeared uniform over time and space but varied as the historical process evolved and according to the community that professed them. This cultural relativism, closely bound up with an awareness of history and a sense of national distinctiveness, became a hallmark of the new way of thinking. The Germany of the age of Goethe was the source of many of these notions, and the most influential channel for their transmission to the English-speaking world was the poet Samuel Taylor Coleridge. His philosophical theology ensured that these ideas impinged not just on literature but on religion from the early years of the nineteenth century onwards. Edward Irving, a Scottish Presbyterian minister serving in London who formed a friendship with Coleridge, injected them into the bloodstream of British Evangelicalism during the 1820s; and William G. T. Shedd, an Old School Presbyterian in the United States, published an edition of the works of Coleridge in New York in 1853. Baptists were, in general, slow to be touched by such fresh ways of thinking. By and large, they were unaffected until the second half of the century, and even then the Romantic revolution impinged more on taste than on theology. Where they could afford it, Baptists began to follow the general trend toward Gothic architecture, building in the medieval style of the age of faith, and some of their most respectable urban congregations began to imitate the more formal and elaborate patterns of worship pioneered by the Anglicans. The reciting of the Lord's Prayer, for example, was introduced for the first time into Baptist services. But beyond the ranks of Baptists the theological environment was beginning to change.

The first of the Evangelical denominations to show signs of adaptation in its theology to the new cultural mood was Congregationalism. In America Horace Bushnell, acknowledging his debt to Coleridge, urged that there was no gulf between the natural and the supernatural, so that, for example, the child was likely to be brought to faith by the ordinary processes of family life rather than by dramatic conversion. In England the comparable views of James Baldwin Brown, another Congregational minister, were condemned by the Baptist John Howard Hinton as "deficient in the truth and power of the gospel."[3] Hinton was defending the older synthesis of Evangelical teaching with Enlightenment thought against subversion by a drastically new way of expressing Christian teaching. Over the years, however, the new style gained further ground. The general tendency was to make the Christian message milder. Instead of picturing God chiefly as an impartial governor of the world, as Fuller had done, those touched by Romantic sensibility saw him primarily as a kindly Father caring for his wayward family. The atonement became not a demonstration of divine justice but an exhibition of the eternal generosity of the Father toward his children. Doubts began to arise about whether a God of that character would consign his creatures to hell and the idea was canvassed that there might be a second chance of salvation beyond the grave. In 1877, Samuel Cox, minister of Mansfield Road Baptist Church, Nottingham, published a book, *Salvator Mundi*, which ventured to hope that in the end all human beings would be saved. The opinion was recognized as so radical that Cox was dismissed from his position as editor of the interdenominational *Expositor*, but he continued to serve his congregation. The more liberal theology introduced by Romantic taste was beginning to impinge on the Baptists.

At the same time, theologians were beginning to take a fresh view of the Bible. The milestone publication was *Essays and Reviews* (1860), a collection of articles by Anglicans from outside the Evangelical fold that called into question received opinions about the nature and effects of inspiration. The underlying assumption, drawn largely from the critical scholarship of Germany, the heartland of Romanticism, was again that there is no contrast between the natural and the supernatural, so that the Bible should be read like any other book. Baptists joined the chorus of Evangelical disapproval. Soon, however, similar critical views appeared among Baptists. Crawford H. Toy, who had spent two years studying Semitic languages in Berlin, was in 1869 appointed professor of Old Testament at Southern Baptist Theological Seminary, then situated in Greenville, South Carolina. He wrestled with the application of German philosophical theology to the understanding of the Bible, and was eventually persuaded by the Dutch biblical scholar Abraham Kuenen that the Old Testament should be seen as the natural evolution of the religious spirit of mankind. The interpretation of the Old Testament by Jesus was not decisive, but "the science of hermeneutics must be the final authority."[4] Such startling sentiments attracted criticism, which in turn led to Toy's resignation in 1879. There is no doubt that Toy's views were highly unusual among Baptists at the time, but similar opinions made long strides among the more scholarly in the denomination before the end of the century. In 1892 the progressive English Baptist leader John Clifford published *The Inspiration and Authority of the Bible*, circumspectly commending the new critical views arriving from the continent. Its appearance provoked a circle of theological conservatives to launch a Bible League designed to resist attacks on the Bible. Although the organization remained small, it was a sign of sharper conflict to come.

A further novelty of the age that caused great debate was the idea of evolution. Charles Darwin's book *The Origin of Species* (1859) had startled the religious world by proposing that plants and animals evolve from one species into another through the mechanism of natural selection. The main Christian objections were not that Darwin contradicted the Bible but that his account undermined the apologetic case, extremely popular during the era of the Enlightenment and afterwards, that, since each species shows evidence of design, it follows that there must be a divine Designer. If, as Darwin taught, each species develops naturally into another, then a divine hand in the process is superfluous. In the early years after Darwin's publication, however, many theologians took his arguments in their stride. They contended that Darwin merely revealed the methods used by the Creator. Broader-minded theologians went on to argue that evolution revealed the extent to which God was involved in the ordinary processes of his universe, so highlighting the doctrine of divine immanence. There was a marriage between evolution and the Romantic theme of growth in nature, helping to make the idea of development toward a better future a common theme around the year 1900. John Clifford was one of those who was happy to accept evolution as a triumph of modern discovery, and he even included Darwin in a book called *Typical Christian Leaders* (1898). Other Baptists, on the other hand, saw evolution as a threat to Christian beliefs. In 1882 a tutor at Spurgeon's College protested in his lectures "against being considered a blood relation of the ape or the oyster."[5] Human beings, on this understanding, must be seen as a separate creation, distinct from the animal kingdom. Although scientific theories of evolution were becoming more widely accepted, some Baptists remained resolutely skeptical.

CONSERVATISM AND LIBERALISM

Worries about the theological drift, though not about evolutionary thought, surfaced most strikingly in the Downgrade Controversy of 1887–1888. Charles Haddon Spurgeon, who enjoyed enormous prestige across the world because of his powerful preaching ministry at the Metropolitan Tabernacle in London, had been concerned for many years about the direction of Evangelical thought. "From our inmost souls," he wrote in 1867, "we loathe all mystic and rationalistic obscurations of the plain and full-orbed doctrines of grace."[6] Although Spurgeon was more than a little touched by Romantic inclinations, he remained a stalwart exponent of Calvinist doctrine in its moderate Fullerite form. Those who were allowing their message to be modified by the newer intellectual currents of the age, he came to believe, were betraying the gospel. He objected, for instance, to the statement of the younger Baptist minister J. G. Greenhough that "our preaching of hell wins none but the base and cowardly. . . . Hopes are much larger than creeds."[7] In 1887 one of the students whom Spurgeon had trained in his college described the theological decay—or "Down Grade"—among Nonconformists in the eighteenth century. Spurgeon added his endorsement, drawing attention to the similar risks in his own day. The great preacher called for action by the Baptist Union to halt the tide of unfaithful teaching, but, when nothing was done, he resigned from the denominational body. The shock of his departure led to frantic but fruitless efforts to bring him back. Spurgeon wanted the Baptist Union to adopt a statement of faith such as that of the Evangelical Alliance, but most of his contemporaries were averse to being fettered by a creed. In the spring of 1888 the Baptist Union assembly went no further than issuing a short declaration of doctrines commonly believed in its churches. That did not satisfy Spurgeon, who remained outside the union for the rest of his career. Only a few Baptists followed him into isolation, but the effect of his public protest was to make the great bulk of Baptists who remained in the union more cautious about avowing broad-minded ideas. Although a number of ministers continued to canvass novel lines of thinking, Spurgeon's action helped rein in theological liberalism among Baptists in Britain.

In the Northern United States, by contrast, there were Baptists who gave fuller expression to the impulse to adapt traditional theology to modern culture. William Newton Clarke of Hamilton Theological Seminary, New York, published in 1898 *An Outline of Christian Theology* that presented a systematic statement of doctrine. The work followed the traditional order of theological compendia and there was no repudiation of orthodoxy, but the starting point, in the manner of the early nineteenth-century German theologian Friedrich Schleiermacher, was "the religious sentiment."[8] Clarke's book was to remain a standard text for much of the twentieth century. Similar tendencies were evident at the University of Chicago, founded as a Baptist institution in 1890 and largely funded by the oil magnate John D. Rockefeller, himself a devout Baptist church member. At the Chicago Divinity School was Shailer Mathews, who had studied briefly in Berlin. Mathews was willing to recast old doctrines into radically different shapes. "The sublime truth that stands out in the resurrection of Jesus," he wrote in 1910, "is the emancipation of the spiritual life from the physical order as culminating in death, not information as to physiological details."[9] In subsequent years Mathews became the standard-bearer of the Modernist cause. Nor was the South, though barely touched by such developments, entirely immune to them. Also in 1910 William O. Carver, a professor at Southern Baptist Theological Seminary published *Missions and Modern Thought*, in which he unequivocally argued that the missionary enterprise must be adapted to modern assumptions. Carver's view that religion consists in a sense of dependence on God betrays again the influence of Schleiermacher. Advanced opinions were making steady progress in the seminaries.

There were other Baptist theologians who, while keeping abreast of the intellectual developments of the day, wanted to keep them within tighter bounds. Augustus H. Strong, president of Rochester Theological Seminary, New York, from 1872 to 1912, was for much of that time the most influential figure among the Baptists of the North. His *Systematic Theology* (1876) was the textbook that reigned before Clarke's *Outline* and continued afterwards to vie with it for sway over pastors in training. It provided an accessible statement of Evangelical teaching without any significant remolding of doctrine along modern lines. Later, however, Strong published a work entitled *Christ and Ethical Monism* (1899) that adopted many of the premises of German thought. Truth, he now held, was not propositional, but to be found in the person of Christ. Strong did not wholly resolve the tension between the older and the newer positions in theology, wanting to be up-to-date without sacrificing central doctrines. Similarly in the South, Edgar Y. Mullins, president of Southern Seminary from 1899 to 1928 and author of *The Axioms of Religion* (1908), the most persuasive apologia for Baptist convictions issued in the early twentieth century, tried to reconcile the two intellectual worlds of objective propositions and subjective feelings. "Calvin and Schleiermacher," he wrote, "are the two great names which stand forth in the doctrinal history as most significant for these two standpoints."[10] The solution lay in a synthesis of the two positions. Mullins can properly be called a mediating theologian, attempting to bring together the inherited faith springing from Reformed roots and the thought of the modern world associated with developmental philosophy. Most Baptists, like Strong and Mullins, did not wish to reject modern scholarship but did want to retain a grasp on the Evangelical verities.

A rising tide of opinion, however, was more inclined to take a hostile stance toward modern views. The primary intellectual allegiance of these more assertive voices was usually to distinctive views of prophecy. The normal conviction among Evangelicals in the early nineteenth century had been the postmillennial view that the second coming of Christ would take place only after ("post-") the arrival on earth of the millennium, an age when the preaching of the gospel worldwide would have ushered in an age of peace and plenty that they found predicted in Old Testament prophecy. From the 1820s, however, premillennial teaching slowly gathered force, contending that, on the contrary, the return of Christ would come before ("pre-") the millennium. Premillennialism was perceptibly connected with the emergence of Romantic influences in the religious world, foretelling dramatic happenings soon to come. Some premillennialists supposed that episodes prophesied in the Bible could be correlated with world events, and so ventured to predict the date of the end of the age. Thus William Miller, a Baptist preacher in Vermont, announced that Christ would return in 1843/44, and, even after disappointment in those years, many of those who shared his expectations continued to believe that the end could not be long delayed, inaugurating the Adventist movement. From the 1830s, however, there developed a futurist strain of premillennialism that held that all the events of the book of Revelation lay in the future. The most influential version of this belief, first propounded by the Irish leader among the Brethren, John Nelson Darby, was known as dispensationalism. Holding that history was divided into epochs, or "dispensations," in each of which divine dealings with humanity operated on different principles, Darby taught that the present age would imminently end with the rapture of the true saints to heaven. Meanwhile, the professing church would degenerate and so fall under judgment. Such views spread during the later nineteenth century and were codified in the notes of the Scofield Bible of 1909. Dispensationalist ideas made little headway in seminaries (in 1919 only 7 out of 236 North American seminaries surveyed accepted them), but they did gain the ear of a broader Christian public. Baptists who embraced a dispensationalist world-view were inclined to look for signs of theological declension around them and give them apocalyptic significance.

Another trend of thought reinforced the eagerness to identify failings in the modern church. The teaching of John Wesley that the Christian may attain a state of perfect love, or entire sanctification, spilled over from Methodism into the broader Evangelical community in the later nineteenth century. A Baptist minister named W. E. Boardman published *The Higher Christian Life* (1859), urging believers to seek a state of more advanced spirituality. From 1875 there was at Keswick in the English Lake District an annual convention of those who believed that the way to holiness lay through an act of full surrender. The tone of Keswick teaching was once more tinged with Romantic feeling: it cultivated poetry, loved nature, and took "the rest of faith" as its goal. Although most of the early adherents of Keswick were Anglicans, one of its prominent leaders by the turn of the twentieth century was F. B. Meyer, an English Baptist minister and widely published author. Meyer was a main speaker in 1903 at the first convention on Keswick lines in Wales, an event that did much to inspire the Welsh Revival of 1904–1905. This stirring of the whole principality led to mass conversions and, through the publicity it gained across the world, a fresh global appreciation of a more intense style of devotional life that would have no truck with compromise. The novel Pentecostal movement, which spread rapidly from Los Angeles in 1906, seconded the sense of quickened spirituality with its teaching that speaking in tongues was a sign that an immense revival was afoot. Although Baptists generally repudiated "the tongues movement," it contributed to the heightened expectations of the period. Very often, as in the Keswick movement, the new styles of devotional teaching mingled with premillennial doctrine to create a powerful ideological blend. The many Baptists affected by these new currents of thought were not satisfied with the worldly tone of denominational bureaucracies and the liberal nostrums of college instructors. They formed an audience prepared to listen to calls to arms.

FUNDAMENTALIST CONTROVERSIES

The summons came from a series of pamphlets issued between 1910 and 1915 called *The Fundamentals*. Dispatched to every minister in America and Britain, they catalogued the weaknesses in the liberal teaching that was spreading. The virgin birth, future judgment, and the objectivity of the atonement were some of the fundamental doctrines of the faith that were under attack. Even the divinity of Christ was being called into question. Most space in the booklets, however, was devoted to condemning biblical criticism. Once the scriptures were subject to human whim, the authority for all the other doctrines was undermined. In the fevered atmosphere of the First World War, which the United States entered in 1917, tensions among Baptists snapped. Some of the premillennialists, looking to supernatural remedies for the ills of the times, objected to American involvement in worldly struggle. Shailer Mathews and others from Chicago Divinity School denounced them for their unintelligent and unpatriotic views, charging them with receiving German gold. Their opponents retorted that the liberalism of Chicago was made in Germany. William Bell Riley, pastor of First Baptist Church, Minneapolis, and a champion of dispensationalism, published *The Menace of Modernism* (1917), in which he identified the source of the crisis as the colleges where students were taught to "sneer at Scripture."[11] In the following year Augustus Strong added to the furor by reporting that American Baptist missionaries abroad were abandoning many of the central doctrines. At the close of the war, Riley determined to act. In 1919 he summoned a World Conference on the Fundamentals of the Faith to launch an interdenominational crusade against false teaching. The struggle between Fundamentalism and Modernism had begun.

One of the central contests was within the Northern Baptist Convention. Since this institution, which drew together American churches from coast to coast outside the South, had existed for less than fifteen years, its trajectory was not yet fixed. Its destiny seemed worth fighting over. In 1919 its annual convention meeting ratified support for the Interchurch World Movement, an organization designed to coordinate the home and foreign missions of all the

Evangelical denominations. Convinced that this creedless body was a sign of the last days, Riley mounted a successful campaign against Baptist participation that helped cause its collapse. The theological conservatives, fired by their triumph in the campaign, met in 1920 to plan how next, according to a celebrated article in the denominational newspaper that coined the term "Fundamentalists," to "do battle royal for the Fundamentals."[12] At the Fundamentalist gathering, Riley indulged in some of the unsparing rhetoric that was his hallmark. "The Samson of Modernism," he declared, "blinded by the theological fumes from Germany, feels for the pillars of the Christian temple and would fain tear this last one away and leave Christianity itself in utter collapse."[13] The demand of the Fundamentalists for an inquiry into the denominational schools, colleges, and seminaries was accepted, but they were dismayed

William Bell Riley (1861–1947)
Baptist Fundamentalist Leader

when, at the 1921 convention, the inquiry's report vindicated most instructors and refused to consider removing any unfaithful teacher. The remedy seemed to lie in adopting a statement of faith. Accordingly, at the 1922 convention, Riley proposed the adoption of the New Hampshire Confession, with its firm declaration of moderate Calvinism. But he was outmaneuvered. A liberal counter-proposal rallied the moderates at the heart of the denomination to affirm that "the New Testament is an all-sufficient ground for Baptist faith and practise."[14] Thereafter, Riley turned, with like-minded men, to organizing a Baptist Bible Union that would cover the whole of North America. Although sniping at Modernism within the Northern convention long continued, the creation of a fresh organization was a confession that the Fundamentalist assault on denominational policy had failed.

Although the Southern Baptist Convention, steered by Mullins and his circle, remained free of similar broils during the interwar period, there was a parallel controversy in the Baptist Union of Great Britain and Ireland. A call, in the wake of the First World War, to establish a federation of the Free Churches that embraced liberal-minded Congregationalists as well as Baptists aroused the fears of theological conservatives that it would lapse into unorthodoxy. A Baptist Bible Union, the source of the title subsequently adopted in America, was formed by dispensationalists, Keswick supporters, Bible Leaguers, heirs of the Welsh Revival, and admirers of Spurgeon's stand against the Downgrade. It targeted individuals whom it supposed to be unsound in the faith, especially T. R. Glover, a Cambridge classical scholar who was proposed as vice president of the Baptist Union in 1923. Glover was accused of writing with "flippant humour and half-contemptuous comment" about the scriptures.[15] Glover, however, was resoundingly elected to his post and the leaders of the Baptist Bible Union soon realized that they would make little impact. Accordingly, the organization turned, in 1925, into a nondenominational agency that rapidly lost its way. There was no equivalent of W. B. Riley to provide energetic leadership in Britain, and there moderate conservative voices restrained the ardor of the Fundamentalists far more effectively. Although a few churches did leave the Baptist Union over Glover's election, the controversy did not gain the headlines of its American counterpart. Fundamentalism proved much weaker in Great Britain than in the United States.

The questions at issue were largely the same on the two sides of the Atlantic, but their balance and treatment were different. The Bible was the chief bone of contention, with Fundamentalists in Britain as well as America believing that disloyalty to its plain teaching was the source of the other follies of the age. In America, however, the conviction that the Bible is wholly free from error was widely canvassed, whereas in Britain few spokesmen advocated inerrancy, being happier with terms such as "infallibility" or "trustworthiness," and not entirely repudiating the venture of biblical criticism. That moderation tended to make the Fundamentalist movement in Britain less self-assured. Again, belief in the premillennial second advent united most of the militant opponents of Modernism. Dispensationalism was the received eschatology spread by a range of agencies such as the Moody Bible Institute in the Northern United States. It is striking, too, that when the Southern Baptist Convention adopted its first *Baptist Faith and Message* in 1925, it modeled the document on the New Hampshire Confession but added a clause on the second coming. It was necessary in the United States to display adventist credentials in order to appease Fundamentalist sympathizers. In Britain, however, the Christian hope was less widely formulated in dispensationalist terms, even among conservative Evangelicals. Consequently, the British challenge to liberalism was normally presented in less apocalyptic language. Opposition to evolution, furthermore, was voiced on both sides of the Atlantic, but it was far stronger in the United States. Darwin was often criticized and, in 1926 the Southern Baptist Convention explicitly resolved against the view that humanity had an ancestry among the lower animals. In Britain, by contrast, the main thrust of Darwinian evolution was generally accepted among Evangelicals as scientific truth, their objections being reserved for attempts to remodel doctrine in evolutionary terms. So in the key areas of controversy—scripture, eschatology, and evolution—the prevailing British attitudes of conservative Evangelicals were much milder.

Polarization was therefore most acute in North America. The Baptist Bible Union soon precipitated schism in Canada as well as in the United States. Two of its prominent leaders, T. T. Shields from Toronto and J. Frank Norris from Texas, could not remain in denominations that tolerated liberalism. Shields' departure from the Baptist Convention of Ontario and Quebec was the signal for the creation of three new Canadian denominations between 1927 and 1933. Likewise, the Baptist Bible Union gave birth in the United States to the General Association of Regular Baptist Churches (1932). W. B. Riley resisted the separatist impulse longer, and remained in his convention until 1947, the year of his death. Those who thought like him created the Conservative Baptist Association of America in that year. Like many other pastors in the North, Riley had effectively functioned outside his denominational agencies for many years, forging an empire around his Bible and Missionary Training School. The Bible schools, operating apart from the taint of denominational seminaries, provided an institutional backbone for separatist Fundamentalism. During the 1930s and 1940s they were to flourish, sending out trained Christian workers to serve churches that had left their denominations or else to found entirely new causes. Media and parachurch agencies also bound together the Fundamentalist network. "The Old-Fashioned Revival Hour" radio program, aired on Sunday evenings from 1937 by Charles E. Fuller, himself a Baptist pastor, was profoundly influential. So was Youth for Christ, begun by Torrey Johnson at the end of the Second World War as a vigorous evangelistic agency with Billy Graham as its best-known staff member. Both were ordained Baptists. Much of the dynamism in Baptist life had been transferred to interdenominational channels.

The Evangelical synthesis of the mid-nineteenth century broke down during the years between the 1870s and the 1930s. Calvinism fell into decay and new attitudes stemming from the Romantic revolution against the Enlightenment impinged drastically on religion. A milder theology and biblical criticism came into vogue, sometimes associated with Darwinian evolution. Spurgeon protested against the new theological developments in the Downgrade Controversy, but some Baptists, especially in America, began to advocate distinctly liberal doctrinal positions. Although many of the leaders of opinion in the Baptist denominations remained moderate Evangelicals, those who adopted dispensationalism and a heightened spirituality began to pull apart from their contemporaries with broader views. The First World War precipitated hostilities between the Fundamentalists and the Modernists. A struggle ensued for control of the Northern Baptist Convention, with the Fundamentalists being beaten off. In Britain, though there was controversy at the same time, the issues were less sharply drawn and the outcome less serious. In the United States and Canada, by contrast, a separatist Fundamentalism that included many Baptists but eschewed denominational agencies became a powerful force. That does not mean that the mainstream Baptist bodies, the Northern and Southern conventions, ceased to be predominantly Evangelical. Although the Northern Baptists continued to include in their ranks those professing liberal views, their congregations were overwhelmingly likely to support Billy Graham from the middle of the twentieth century; and Graham was himself a Southern Baptist minister, entirely at home in the denomination even though he normally worked outside its agencies. The middle group among Baptists, averse to repudiating sound scholarship but loyal to the core of the gospel, was numerous and influential even in the 1920s. The theological polarization of the interwar years was far from total.

FURTHER READING

Bebbington, David W. "Baptists and Fundamentalism in Inter-war Britain." In *Protestant Evangelicalism: Britain, Ireland, Germany and America, c. 1750–c. 1950: Essays in Honour of W. R. Ward,* edited by Keith Robbins, 297–326. Studies in Church History Subsidia 7. Oxford: Blackwell, 1990.

Hopkins, Mark. *Nonconformity's Romantic Generation: Evangelical and Liberal Theologies in Victorian England.* Carlisle: Paternoster, 2004.

Hutchison, William R. *The Modernist Impulse in American Protestantism.* Cambridge, Mass.: Harvard University Press, 1976.

Marsden, George M. *Fundamentalism and American Culture: The Shaping of Twentieth-Century Evangelicalism, 1870–1925.* New York: Oxford University Press, 1980.

Trollinger, William V. *God's Empire: William Bell Riley and Midwestern Fundamentalism.* Madison: University of Wisconsin Press, 1990.

Wacker, Grant. *Augustus H. Strong and the Dilemma of Historical Consciousness.* Macon, Ga.: Mercer University Press, 1985.

Chapter 8

BAPTISTS AND THE SOCIAL GOSPEL

The period between the 1870s and the 1930s was marked not only by a tendency to theological polarization but also by a desire to engage with the ills of society. In this era there emerged a social gospel. Some of its staunchest advocates disliked the label because they claimed that what was called the "social gospel" was, in reality, the true gospel, the message of Christ for society at large and not just for particular people. Individuals might need to be saved from their sins, but so, they claimed, did the whole community. Christian standards must be proclaimed and, if possible, enforced—at home, in business, and in public life. The existing social order must be turned into an approximation to the kingdom of God. "It is not a matter of getting individuals into heaven," declared the leading Baptist social gospeler, Walter Rauschenbusch, "but of transforming the life of earth into the harmony of heaven."[1] Christians must engage far more with the problems of contemporary society. The initiative in this new phase of social awareness came not from Evangelicals but from Anglicans of broader views. In England in the years around 1850 a group of so-called Christian socialists—J. M. Ludlow, F. D. Maurice, and Charles Kingsley—had urged greater public concern for

Walter Rauschenbusch (1861–1918)
Baptist Advocate of the Social Gospel

the welfare of the working people, themselves undertaking evening classes for their education. By later in the century, partly inspired by their predecessors, other Anglicans took up the cause on both sides of the Atlantic. The Church Association for the Advancement of the Interests of Labor was established in New York City in 1887, and subsequently spread over much of the United States; two years later, the Christian Social Union was formed within the Church of England and became an influential grouping of those seeking to apply Christian principles to socio-economic practice. Evangelicals rarely associated with either body, but from around the same time some of them began to take up similar causes. Amongst them were a number of Baptists.

The explanation for this development is partly that it was a response to contemporary circumstances. The economies of Britain and America had forged ahead during the nineteenth century. Britain, the first industrial society, had generated wealth for the families of the early factory owners, but it was ill distributed and many employees suffered low wages and poor working conditions. Although the average real income of working families was growing in the later nineteenth century, there were still many working-class people whose lives were precarious. The dock laborers of the East End of London were employed on only a daily basis; the miners of the coal mining districts lived in terror of disasters underground. It was symptomatic that, in 1894, a prosperous Baptist textile manufacturer in the northern town of Bradford, Alfred Illingworth, provoked his mill girls into a strike by demanding extra work for no additional pay. The state of the cities, though improved since the middle years of the century, was often insanitary and the housing overcrowded, with several families living together in cramped rooms. Industrialization and urbanization exerted an even more drastic effect on parts of the United States because the processes happened later and so over a shorter period of time. In 1865, 80 percent of Americans still lived in rural areas with fewer than 2,500 inhabitants; by 1920, more than half lived in towns and cities. The rapid growth of the economy in the years after the Civil War generated huge fortunes for the super-rich, but many of their employees were exploited. A series of major strikes against wage cuts in 1877, 1886, and 1894 revealed the acute industrial tensions underlying the rising prosperity. The problems were accentuated in the United States by floods of immigrants who wanted a share in the American dream but discovered employment to be a nightmare. Some of the most outspoken in the churches started to denounce the existing state of affairs as a blight on Christian civilization. In 1894 W. T. Stead, an English Congregational journalist, wrote the sensational *If Christ Came to Chicago!*, which laid bare the exploitation and corruption of the city and called for action by members of the churches. The urban/industrial challenge of the age stirred some to take up social Christianity.

The response of the churches, however, was conditioned by their earlier attitudes. The public mind—like the theology—of the English-speaking world around the middle of the nineteenth century was shaped by a blend of Evangelical religion and the legacy of the Enlightenment. The political economy that had been devised by Adam Smith and his contemporaries was given a Christian sanction. Francis Wayland, president of Brown University and the leading Baptist intellectual of the age, published *Elements of Political Economy* (1837), a widely used textbook that embodied the blend of commercial wisdom and religious truth. The principles of supply and demand were seen as part of the divinely ordered structure of the world. Wages could not be maintained at high levels when there was a fall-off in demand for products. Conversely, hard work would be rewarded by the Almighty with success. Such convictions were persistent. Russell H. Conwell, pastor of the Baptist Temple, Philadelphia, from 1882, delivered an enormously popular lecture over 6,000 times called *Acres of Diamonds*, which retold the tale of a man who pursued a fruitless quest for diamonds when all the while a jewel mine lay undiscovered in his own back yard. Opportunities were there if they were seized. "I say," he declared, "that you ought to get rich, and it is your duty to get rich."[2] The address was uncompromising in its recommendation of self-help as the remedy for all ills. This prevailing set of attitudes discouraged any effort to propose remedies for the deficiencies of the industrial economy. Such views helped reinforce the prevailing philosophy of laissez-faire, the belief that the state should do as little as possible in order to allow the people to engage in vigorous entrepreneurial activity. The new British Baptist newspaper *The Freeman*, it was announced at the end of 1854, would be "the strenuous advocate of progressional measures, though it will look for social remedies, not so much to any external interference, as to the gradual development of the intellectual, the moral and the industrial capabilities of the people."[3] This ideological stance meant that the churches were wary of taking up any measures to improve the lot of the victims of economic change.

ANTECEDENTS OF THE SOCIAL GOSPEL

At the same time, another feature of the melding of Evangelicalism with Enlightenment thought encouraged hopes that the future would be better for all. Most Evangelicals of the nineteenth century professed postmillennialism, the belief that conditions would improve as a result of the preaching of the gospel so that the second coming would not take place until the world was fit to receive its king. The earth, on this understanding, was moving steadily toward the millennium, the thousand years predicted in the book of Revelation when Satan would be bound so that truth and righteousness could flourish. The idea blended readily into the Victorian idea of progress, a major fruit of the Enlightenment. The eighteenth-century hope that humanity would exercise greater control over the environment seemed to be finding fulfillment. With railroads, steamships, and the electric telegraph abolishing distance, progress seemed a reality. These innovations were regarded as harbingers of the millennial glory. In 1854 the English *General Baptist Magazine* was sanguine about the prospects of the world as the millennium approached. The gospel would triumph, war would cease, and famine would be no more. Crime, drunkenness, "lewdness," slavery, oppression, scandal, loose talk, false teaching, idols, popery, and paganism would all be swept away. There would also be an end to "the oppressive weight of taxes that grind nations to the dust."[4] The author of the article expected that this formidable set of changes could be accomplished by 2016. The millennium might take place only in God's good time, but Christians should try to bring about this happy state of affairs. The success of the gospel, according to the American *Baptist Watchman* in 1857, "contemplates the organization and supremacy of goodness in human society—the doing of God's will on earth—the coming of His Kingdom hither, as well as our going hence to it. . . . It is ours, not only to fit ourselves and others for a better world, but to labor to make this world better."[5] This confidence in the earthly future, together with the associated summons to prepare for it, was a precursor of what the leading social gospelers were to say in later generations. Postmillennial teaching led Baptists and their fellow Evangelicals toward greater social commitment.

There was, in any case, a deep-seated tradition of philanthropy among the churches. Even when political economy inhibited Evangelicals from urging social changes, they believed in combining charitable work with spreading the gospel. Baptist churches customarily made collections at the Lord's table for relieving the needy of their congregations. The rich within their ranks were often generous with their resources. Thus Sir John Barran, a Leeds manufacturer of ready-made clothing, provided a battery of services for his employees and their families. A large number of interdenominational voluntary societies sprang up in the earlier years of the nineteenth century to cater to the needs of the poor, the weak, and the sick. Free blankets, soup kitchens, and ragged schools for the deprived children of the cities were among the benefits provided. There was particular interest in the welfare of the young. In London, for example, the Baptist minister George M'Cree established the National Refuges for Homeless and Destitute Children. In the same city, Charles Haddon Spurgeon founded an orphanage in connection with his Metropolitan Tabernacle. It would be entirely mistaken to suppose that, because there was a prevailing belief in self-help, there was no concern for those who found it hard to help themselves. The American evangelist D. L. Moody, whose gospel campaigns were often supported by Baptists, was also an advocate of compassionate efforts on behalf of the less fortunate. In England, F. B. Meyer, a prominent Baptist minister and an early supporter of Moody on his first evangelistic tour of the country, published a book called *The Bells of Is: Or Voices of Human Need and Sorrow* (1894) to publicize his efforts in Leicester to assist released prisoners. They were met at the prison gate, given help with food and shelter, and provided with a career in selling wood or cleaning windows. Meyer, while remaining resolutely conservative in his theology, was soon to become an English advocate of the social gospel. It was an easy transition, as Meyer illustrates, from supporting practical measures of relief to endorsing a wider program of social Christianity.

The long-standing Evangelical practice of calling for moral reforms had a similar effect. The summons to repentance was associated with campaigns for "the reformation of manners" in society at large. Changed lives required changed behavior. In particular, the temperance movement pushed Baptists toward urging a specific remedy for the ills of the day. Drunkenness was widespread, leading to violence, sexual license, and incapacity to work, and so giving up strong drink seemed a solution to many problems. In the 1820s a campaign was launched in America to urge the disuse of distilled spirits, the most serious cause of intoxication. The movement spread to other parts of the English-speaking world and broadened to encompass voluntary abstinence from all alcoholic beverages. Some Baptists were initially cautious, thinking the temperance message might prove to be an alternative to the gospel. Other Baptists, however, joined in enthusiastically. Jabez Tunnicliff, for example, an English General Baptist minister, was a founder of the Band of Hope movement that aimed to educate children in the risks incurred by drinking alcohol. The churches gradually became more closely identified with temperance in the later years of the nineteenth century. Although the London Baptist Association retained wine at its meetings as late as 1880, a Baptist Total Abstinence Association had already been founded in England in 1874. It was increasingly rare to find a pastor who drank at all. The churches, especially those of the Methodist and Baptist denominations, became hotbeds of demands for the entire legislative prohibition of the sale or manufacture of alcohol. Prohibition was adopted in the state of Maine as early as 1851 and was imitated in states and counties elsewhere in America. This development was crucial for Baptist attitudes to social policy. The older philosophy of laissez-faire had entailed minimizing action by public authorities, but the call for a ban on alcohol opened the door to seeing a wider role for law in promoting righteousness. Thus Samuel Z. Batten, perhaps the leading activist of the social gospel among Northern Baptists, came by his conviction that the state could play a major role in Christianizing the nation through participation in the temperance movement. The struggle against alcohol was a major factor in the rise of social Christianity.

Another moral preoccupation that fed into the social gospel was the question of sexual ethics. Evangelicals in the middle years of the century spent time trying to rescue prostitutes. In London, for example, George M'Cree joined in organizing midnight meetings for women who were willing to come in from the streets to hear the gospel. When, in the 1860s, the government introduced legislation to enforce inspection of the health of prostitutes working within reach of naval or military bases, an Evangelical campaign to repeal these Anti-Contagious Diseases Acts was launched. The legislation appeared to endorse the sexual exploitation of women. The leading figure in the pressure for repeal, Josephine Butler, was the wife of an Anglican clergyman, and it was a cousin of hers, C. M. Birrell, a Liverpool Baptist minister, who was responsible in 1871 for carrying a resolution at the Baptist Union condemning the acts. A sustained effort over the next fourteen years led eventually to the abolition of the Anti-Contagious Diseases Acts and also to the rousing of feeling in all the Evangelical churches on questions of sexual morality. Thus when, in 1885, the journalist W. T. Stead showed how easy it was to procure a young girl for immoral purposes, there was an outcry that led to the raising of the age of consent to sexual relations from thirteen to sixteen. The same cause was taken up in America by the Woman's Christian Temperance Union that, under the leadership of the redoubtable Methodist Frances Willard, extended its remit into the sphere of sexual ethics. Willard's campaigns led to the raising of the age of consent in successive states to sixteen or even eighteen. Baptists became sensitized to taking action on questions of what was euphemistically called "social purity." F. B. Meyer, for instance, was active in promoting efforts by local government agencies to restrict prostitution in the areas around the successive churches where he served. The effect, once more, was to make many Baptists more willing to see action by public authorities as a potential tool for improving the moral standards of the community. That conviction was near the heart of the social gospel stance.

A broader shift in the intellectual climate was pointing in the same direction. The principles of political economy, the discipline that provided the justification for limiting state power to the minimum, were coming under question in the later nineteenth century. It was increasingly felt that its axioms were not timeless, but had to be adapted to the circumstances of each successive age. In England the eminent Congregationalist R. W. Dale reached the conclusion that Evangelical Nonconformists had unduly restricted the responsibilities of public bodies. The state, he held, had a specific place in the divine purposes. Leaders among the Baptists, who highly respected Dale, began to ponder whether there was a wider role for government. By the 1870s in the city of Birmingham, where Dale proclaimed a "civic gospel," the authorities were improving urban life by taking utilities such as the gas supply into the hands of the community. This "municipal socialism" seemed a sign of what could be done to remedy the problems of the Victorian city. In America another approach to socialism was canvassed by Henry George in his *Progress and Poverty* (1880). George argued that economic problems were the result of the private ownership of land. His panacea was to make land public property. George's views first turned the mind of the leading Baptist social gospeler Walter Rauschenbusch to the problems of society, and George also created a stir when he undertook speaking tours of Britain in 1884–1885 and Australia in 1890. In addition, the views of the most famous socialist of all, Karl Marx, were being publicized by the 1880s. He had used the phrase "social gospel" in the *Communist Manifesto* (1848) and offered a more profound economic analysis than Henry George. Marxism was unappealing to Christians because of its frank rejection of religion, and yet seemed to provide perceptive insights into questions of labor and capital. Thus Rauschenbusch, who absorbed Marx, was capable of praising the German even though he dismissed the Marxist belief in economic determinism. For all but the most radical of the social gospelers, the Christian social message was a means of counteracting the potential influence of Marxism over the working classes. Nevertheless, socialism was in the air from the 1880s, and as a result many of the advocates of the new approach to the problems of the age, including Rauschenbusch, were willing to call themselves socialists.

A further influence on the emergence of the social gospel was German theology. Just as Germany generated the developments in biblical criticism that challenged received interpretations of the scriptures in the later nineteenth century, so it produced the ideas that were most central to the social gospel. Albrecht Ritschl of Göttingen, who died in 1889, had taught that the earliest message of Christianity was the kingdom of God. Jesus had preached it and the early church had upheld it. Ritschl's disciple Adolf Harnack, a church historian of Berlin, contended that the simplicity of this message had been corrupted by the Hellenization of Christian teaching and the consequent rise of complicated dogma. What was needed was a radical return to the proclamation of the principles of the kingdom, the Fatherhood of God, and the brotherhood of man. These ideas were particularly influential over Rauschenbusch, himself the pastor of a German-speaking Baptist church in New York. In 1891 he spent nine months on a trip to Germany, absorbing Ritschl and hearing Harnack. The kernel notion that the gospel had originally been focused on creating a just earthly community became the hallmark of Rauschenbusch's thought. The community was the kingdom of God. "This doctrine," he wrote, "is itself the social gospel."[6] In 1892 Rauschenbusch was one of a circle of Baptist ministers who formed the Brotherhood of the Kingdom to discuss issues surrounding the application of religion to contemporary social issues. The original teaching of Jesus, they supposed, was the remedy for the strained relations in industry and the abject deprivation of the poor in the growing cities. "The Spirit of God," according to the brotherhood's aims, "is moving men in our generation toward a better understanding of the idea of the Kingdom of God on earth."[7] The same teaching about the kingdom, rather than the church, being Jesus' overriding concern became current in Britain around the same time. Here was a German theological innovation that provided an intellectual stimulus for social Christianity.

THE CONTENT OF THE SOCIAL GOSPEL

The social gospel movement that resulted from these various factors has often been seen as an expression of liberal theology. The belief that the kingdom of God, something much broader than the church, was to be built up on earth was itself a breach with older orthodoxies. The expectation that the kingdom would steadily advance was often associated with the idea of evolutionary progress common among the liberals of the age. And many of the social gospel advocates were influenced by the personalism of Rudolf Herman Lotze, a colleague of Ritschl's at Göttingen who held that personal ethical development is the goal of religion, so that each individual is enlarged or diminished by the actions of others. Shailer Mathews of Chicago Divinity School, one of the most prominent Baptist liberal theologians, was swayed by this body of thought, and argued in his book *The Social Gospel* (1910) that the church will "emphasize personality" and so teach fraternity between employers and workmen and promote the personal well-being of the laborers.[8] There was certainly a correlation between theological liberalism and the social gospel. Two-thirds of the leaders of theological liberalism of all denominations between 1875 and 1915 played some part in the social gospel movement. The most advanced English Baptist social gospeler, Charles Aked, minister of Pembroke Chapel, Liverpool, was also a theological radical, judging that Calvinism was no better than "the poison of the rattlesnake and the blood-lust of the tiger."[9] Aked, however, was exceptional among Baptist upholders of social Christianity in severing his ties with the Evangelical ethos of the denomination. Even Mathews, whose preponderant liberal theological allegiance is undoubted, showed signs of his Evangelical roots. If society was to be reconstructed on a Christian basis, he argued, its inhabitants must be authentic Christians. "It takes sound timber to make a sound ship,"[10] he wrote, "and it takes regenerate souls to make a regenerated society." Again, the task of the church was not just to bring in the kingdom: "the first duty of the church is to turn men from sin to God."[11] Mathews, as a Baptist, did not wholly shed his Evangelical clothing.

The same is more markedly true of Walter Rauschenbusch, who was not only the most eminent Baptist exponent of the social gospel but also, in the estimation of most commentators, the leading spokesman of the movement in any denomination. His classic work, *Christianity and the Social Crisis* (1907), sold as many as 50,000 copies between its publication and 1910. It is true that Rauschenbusch was drawn to a broader theology than was normal among Baptists. While he was still a student at Rochester Theological Seminary, New York, long before he encountered Ritschl, Rauschenbusch incurred the censure of the president, Augustus H. Strong, for adopting, under the influence of Horace Bushnell, a moral influence theory of the atonement rather than upholding the standard Evangelical substitutionary view. At the end of Rauschenbusch's career, Strong was still protesting that the younger man was weak on the doctrine of the cross. "Your theology," Strong told him, "is one of love, but not of righteousness like that of Paul."[12] Yet, in between, Strong had employed Rauschenbusch as a faculty member at Rochester Seminary and had defended him against his critics. The younger theologian was sufficiently in tune with the Evangelical temper of the denomination to retain widespread confidence. He praised the conference held at Northfield by the evangelist D. L. Moody; he translated the sacred songs of Moody's partner, Ira D. Sankey, into German; he arranged for visiting speakers to give testimonies to his seminary classes; and he published *Prayers of the Social Awakening* (1910), hoping to ensure that engagement with contemporary issues did not drift apart from spirituality. In an article on the "New Evangelism" in 1904, Rauschenbusch contended that fresh methods of spreading the gospel must not break with the old. Instead, the new evangelism "will have to retain all that was true and good in the old synthesis."[13] Rauschenbusch saw his teaching as expanding the tradition rather than as undermining it. His version of the social gospel, though molded by German liberalism, still retained many hallmarks of Evangelical religion.

APPLICATION AND OPPOSITION

There was a great variety of views within the social gospel movement about the degree of change required in the present order. Rauschenbusch believed in "practical socialism," but he declined to join the Socialist Party that aimed to transfer control of industry to the people. His socialism was a form of idealism, a celebration of the value of community. Many, however, wanted to avoid socialism altogether. Mathews dismissed Rauschenbusch's *Christianity*

and the Social Crisis as "favorable to socialism," preferring the existing capitalist pattern. The church, Mathews, held, "will favor neither workmen nor employer as such."[14] Businessmen who identified
with social Christianity naturally concurred in this type of moderate teaching. The Baptist oil magnate John D. Rockefeller, who
had amassed a fortune of around $900 million by 1913, saw his
Christian responsibility as primarily the careful disbursement of
charity. The deployment of his munificent gifts contributed largely,
for example, to the elimination of the hookworm in the American
South. Likewise, the English paper manufacturer Edward Robinson,
Lord Mayor of Bristol in 1908, started a generous pension fund for
his employees and eventually instituted a profit sharing scheme. The
efforts of such men were affected by the social gospel impulse, but
they had no desire to tamper with the existing structure of society.
In the American South, where the movement made more impact
than was once supposed, this conservative brand of teaching prevailed. Thus J. M. Dawson, pastor of First Baptist Church, Waco,
Texas, from 1915, had preached in the previous year on social questions, but had taken pains not to endorse labor unions or criticize
capital. The message of those who identified themselves with social
Christianity could be far removed from socialism.

There were some, however, who went much further than
Rauschenbusch into advocacy of drastic change. Richard Heath, an
English Baptist, wrote a radical critique of the churches, *The Captive
City of God* (1904), urging that, in the spirit of the Anabaptists,
they should be active in the cause of democratic socialism. Charles
Aked, the Liverpool minister, joined the Fabians, a group of social-
ists committed to persuading politicians to adopt collectivist measures for the welfare of the weak. So eloquent were his exhortations
that, in 1906, he was invited to the pulpit of Fifth Avenue Baptist
Church, New York—ironically the congregation where Rockefeller
was a member—before moving on to a Congregational church in
San Francisco. Another Fabian was John Clifford, the most distinguished Baptist minister of his generation in England. In 1889
Clifford urged the Baptist Union to pursue the "social gospel,"
long before the phrase was in regular use. In the 1890s he acted as

president of the Christian Socialist League, a body that called for drastic social reconstruction. "This country," according to Clifford in 1893, "cannot accurately be called Christian so long as the people in their collective arrangements practically deny the fatherhood of God and the brotherhood of men."[15] By 1898 he was advocating a full-blooded version of socialism. "Only," he wrote, "when the people own or control the necessary instruments of production in the large industries will formal be translated into substantial freedom."[16] Clifford rose to prominence in national politics, leading the denunciations of the Boer War as an imperialistic venture between 1899 and 1902, and heading the protests against the 1902 Education Act that gave public money to Anglican and Roman Catholic schools. Although Clifford remained loyal to the Liberal Party until after the First World War, he did much to make socialism a practical option for Nonconformists and so to help the rise of the Labour Party. The radical form of the social gospel among Baptists had major repercussions in Britain.

Likewise, in North America the social gospel made a political impact. It was part and parcel of the Progressive movement that, in the earliest years of the twentieth century, set the pace in American politics. Although there were many secular influences on Progressivism, such as the application of principles of business efficiency to government, the churches played a major role in mobilizing demands for greater concern for the victims of economic change. The social gospel theologians in America were rarely so active in public life as was Clifford in Britain. The achievements of the Brotherhood of the Kingdom, for example, were restricted to such minor matters as the introduction of sandpiles for children's play into New York parks. Yet the ideals of social Christianity generated much of the steam for the civic reforms of the time, such as concern to regulate working conditions, child labor, and standards of purity for food and water. Demands for constitutional change—measures such as the referendum, the direct primary, and woman suffrage—stemmed from a desire to ensure popular control over politicians for the sake of securing integrity in public life. Baptists could be the objects as well as the agents of Progressive critiques: one of the most salient campaigns of the times, opposition to the huge trusts that dominated certain sectors of the economy, was for a long time focused primarily against Rockefeller's Standard Oil. Yet Baptists were likely to be in the van of Progressive causes. They were at the heart of the crusade for prohibition that culminated in the passing of the Eighteenth Amendment to the Constitution of the United States in 1919. Samuel Z. Batten, for example, sustained his primary commitment to the temperance cause when he became secretary of social education for the American Baptist Publication Society in 1912, zealously advocating prohibition. In Canada, likewise, Baptists rallied behind the Progressive impulse. A. L. McCrimmon, Chancellor of McMaster University, a Baptist institution then in Toronto, was one of the Christian leaders who, in the wake of the First World War, promoted social reform by forging a link between the Social Service Council, which represented the churches, and the federal government. There were substantial political consequences of the social gospel.

It is not surprising that a development with potentially drastic implications for theology, society, and politics should encounter stiff opposition. Before the opening of the twentieth century, while social Christianity was still diffuse and relatively marginal, expressions of disquiet were muted. Conservative Evangelicals, drawing on their long tradition of social engagement, agreed with efforts to improve the lot of the poor. In 1900, however, in England, William Cuff, one of Spurgeon's trainees, declared that he had no faith in the social gospel because salvation was the message of the church. Others began to express similar fears that newer concerns were squeezing out older ones. Victor Masters, secretary of the Southern Baptist Home Mission Board, was by 1915 voicing the worries of many in the South that social service must not be equated with redemption. Businessmen who were alarmed by the alignment of social gospelers with workers against employers added their voices to the rising chorus of disapproval. The chairman of the board of Rochester Seminary, a businessman from Cincinnati, called without success for the dismissal of Rauschenbusch after the appearance of his *Christianity and the Social Crisis*. The strongest criticisms came from the dispensationalists, who recognized a sharp theological division between the social gospelers and themselves. The kingdom of God, according to the social gospel, with its roots in postmillennialism, would gradually emerge on earth; but, according to the dispensationalists, it would not arrive until after the dramatic return of the Savior. Rauschenbusch referred to "the vagaries about the second coming" professed by his critics;[17] they, in turn, began to denounce unsparingly the optimistic eschatology of the social gospelers. In 1911 Isaac Haldeman, pastor of First Baptist Church, New York City, called *Christianity and the Social Crisis* "a dangerous bit of reading" because it rejected the New Testament's "plain apocalyptic statements and catastrophic promises concerning the kingdom."[18] From the 1920s onwards it became normal in Fundamentalist circles to condemn the whole enterprise of the social gospel, theory and practice, as a repudiation of the message of the scriptures. Similarly, in the 1930s the neo-orthodox theologians who looked to Reinhold Niebuhr for inspiration saw the enterprise of Rauschenbusch and his contemporaries as having neglected the God-centered themes of the Bible for the sake of man-centered ideals of philanthropy. To both schools of thought the social gospel seemed a departure from the true gospel.

Yet, for many Baptists, the impetus to social Christianity was no diversion from the Evangelical faith. A large number of those who took up social work from around the turn of the twentieth century did so without any theological reconstruction. The needs of the age simply required more elaborate measures to fulfill the mandate to love one's neighbor as oneself. F. B. Meyer managed to combine a conservative and premillennial Evangelical theology with continuing insistence on the obligation of the churches to engage in social work. There sprang up throughout the English-speaking world a series of institutional churches, congregations that took pains to provide facilities to help the working people around them with such services as reading rooms, indoor and outdoor games, evening entertainments, and even employment exchanges. By 1906 there were over a hundred such institutional churches in New York City alone. Many of them, there and elsewhere, were Baptist. Thus John

Milton Waldron, a black Baptist pastor, started Bethel Institutional Church in Jacksonville, Florida, in 1901, complete with a kindergarten, cooking school, and night school. In the postwar period, economic conditions worsened in many parts of the world. By the Great Depression of the 1930s, it was hard for churches to stand aside from the pressing demands of the times. In England, H. Ingli James, minister of Queen's Road Baptist Church, Coventry, for example, preaching to a large number of Welsh families who had migrated to the city because of the decline of coal mining in their native land, proclaimed that social justice was inherent in the gospel. Back in Wales, some of the Baptist chapels in the afflicted industrial areas opened soup kitchens for the unemployed. In that decade, the social gospel may have gone out of fashion in many theological circles, but on the ground the imperative of Christian charity still moved Baptists to speak and act in its spirit.

The development of social Christianity in the late nineteenth and early twentieth centuries was partly a response to altered circumstances. The large cities and burgeoning industries of the age created a range of social problems that seemed to call for church involvement. Although at first Baptists were inhibited by the assumptions of political economy, they were subsequently roused to more systematic engagement with social issues by a number of facets of their corporate life. Their postmillennial theology anticipated the transformation of earthly conditions into something better, their philanthropic traditions required them to help the needy, and their growing commitment to temperance and social purity made them more willing to contemplate public interference in the socio-economic order. Some in their ranks were swayed by external stirrings of socialist theory, German theological influence, and the broader liberal theological currents of the times. The Baptists who participated in the social impulse, however, were by no means shaped solely by liberal theology, and many were resolute Evangelicals. Although the resulting social gospel affected Baptists less than some other bodies, the denomination nevertheless produced two towering figures of the movement, Walter Rauschenbusch and John Clifford. Rauschenbusch wrote several of its most influential texts. Although many Baptists were far more cautious than Rauschenbusch, Clifford went further in advocating specific socialist measures. There was, therefore, no common front on social issues among Baptists in this period, but they did tend to support Progressive political measures. The social gospel encountered shrill resistance from those who saw it as a surrender of the old gospel, and by the 1930s it was becoming unfashionable. A willingness to meet the needs of the people around their doors, however, persisted in Baptist churches even after the rationale in terms of kingdom theology faded away. The social gospel may have passed, but charity never failed.

Further Reading

Evans, Christopher H. *The Kingdom is Always but Coming: A Life of Walter Rauschenbusch*. Grand Rapids: Eerdmans, 2004.

Flynt, Wayne. "Dissent in Zion: Alabama Baptists and Social Issues, 1900–1914." *Journal of Southern History* 35 (1969): 523–42.

Harper, Keith. *The Quality of Mercy: Southern Baptists and Social Christianity, 1890–1920*. Tuscaloosa: University of Alabama Press, 1996.

Hopkins, Charles H. *The Rise of the Social Gospel in American Protestantism, 1865–1915*. New Haven, Conn.: Yale University Press, 1940.

Jones, Peter d'A. *The Christian Socialist Revival, 1877–1914: Religion, Class and Social Conscience in Late Victorian England*. Princeton, N.J.: Princeton University Press, 1968.

Minus, Paul M. *Walter Rauschenbusch: American Reformer*. New York: Macmillan, 1988.

Chapter 9

GOSPEL AND RACE AMONG BAPTISTS

The Baptists carried the gospel to people of many backgrounds. Confident that the message of salvation was for sinners of whatever hue, they drew in people of color from an early stage. A black slave named Jack was baptized into First Baptist Church of Newport, Rhode Island, as early as 1652, and a free black woman called Peggy Arnold joined the Seventh Day Baptist Church at Newport in 1719. The Great Awakening exerted a significant influence over African Americans. By 1790 in Virginia, nearly a third of Baptists were black. Native Americans in the United States and indigenous people elsewhere were attracted into church fellowship. Often racial differences were forgotten as members of distinct origins supported the common aim of mission. Yet race was a profoundly divisive issue. For much of the history of the Baptists, many of the white members of their churches saw themselves as inherently superior, while members of other racial groups were victims of neglect, disdain, or far worse. In particular, slavery was enforced by white Baptists on black people who were often their coreligionists. Human beings were bought, sold, and treated as pieces of property like sheep or cattle. Even after the abolition of slavery, Baptists in the United States deliberately denied full civil rights to their fellow citizens on the basis of race. There is, however, another side to the story. Baptists participated in the struggles against the slave trade and the institution of slavery. Subsequently they played a foremost part in the campaign against the denial of civil rights. So, at times, some members of the denomination were perpetrators of racial discrimination, but equally others became champions of its demise. The Baptists' engagement with racial questions forms a remarkably checkered history.

RACIAL OPPRESSION

Because the institution of slavery was unknown in England, its operation was confined to the New World. Black slaves brought from Africa were owned in the English colonies of the Caribbean during the seventeenth century and a few were found on the American continent on the Chesapeake and in the Carolinas. Since their numbers were so small, they posed little potential threat to their owners and sometimes seem to have mingled freely with the white workforce. From the early years of the eighteenth century, however, slaves were imported in much larger numbers. They began to be seen as a source of danger to the white community should they ever decide to throw off their bonds. The slaves were subjected to a draconian code of discipline and fierce punishment for infringing it. Generally, owners were reluctant to encourage the spread of Christianity among them, fearing that the new religion might foster aspirations to freedom. The traditional forms of ancestor worship and witchcraft therefore persisted long after Africa had been left behind. From around 1725, however, the slave community began to take on a more settled existence. Instead of individual males leading separate lives, whole families subsisted in servitude. More children were born each year into slavery than were imported from across the seas. It seems likely that parents were attracted by the rites of passage associated with the Christian faith to help mark major events in family life such as birth and death. At the same time there were elements in traditional West African belief that prepared the way for Christian teaching. Although most forms of sub-Saharan spirituality accepted the existence of a variety of deities, there was a received conviction that behind and above them was a single Creator not so different from the God worshiped by Christians. There was also an acute supernatural awareness, an expectation of divine intervention in the events of daily life, which bore a distinct affinity with the beliefs of the early Evangelicals. So, when vigorous Baptist evangelism began to spring up from the Great Awakening, slaves as well as blacks who had already been freed by their masters were drawn into the growing churches.

White Baptists often looked askance at the institution of slavery in the later eighteenth and early nineteenth centuries. In 1788, for instance, Isaac Backus expressed the desire that his nation could move gradually toward the abolition of slavery. In 1808, even in the deep South of America, where slaveholding was common, the Mississippi Baptist Association resolved that its member churches should take disciplinary action against members "whose treatment of their slaves is unscriptural."[1] There was little sense anywhere, however, and least of all in Mississippi, that slavery itself should soon come to an end. The transport of slaves across the Atlantic was another matter. From the late 1780s, Evangelicals in Britain, recognizing the inhumanity of the slave trade, led a campaign for its abolition that drew in a large number of Baptists. Many gave up tea because it was grown with slave labor. The parliamentary efforts against the trade coordinated by William Wilberforce culminated in its abolition in 1807, and in the following year the United States also prohibited the Atlantic trade. Dislike for slavery itself grew over subsequent years. By the 1820s, opinion among Evangelicals in Britain and the American North was beginning to veer in favor of the total extinction of the institution. Many of them began to classify slaveholding as a sin and therefore to call for its immediate termination. Although the Baptist Missionary Society carefully instructed its missionaries to the Caribbean to avoid discussing the subject as too political, planters considered missionary teaching a potential cause of slave rebellion. When, in 1831, a slave revolt actually took place in Jamaica, the slave owners decided to eject the missionaries from the island. William Knibb, a Baptist missionary at home in Britain, traveled around the land, urging that the question was now whether slavery or the gospel survived in the nation's overseas territories. His inflamed oratory stirred the country on the eve of the 1832 general election, leading in the following year to parliament's voting to abolish slavery throughout British dominions. The Baptists in Jamaica celebrated when, in 1838, the institution was swept away.

In the American South, however, slavery persisted. Another slave revolt took place in 1831 in Virginia, led by a black Baptist lay preacher, Nat Turner, who saw himself as called by God to lead his people to freedom by the sword. There were black casualties and Turner was executed, but over fifty whites were killed and the episode led to even tighter discipline of slaves. The institution of slavery had become a way of life and the badge of an entire culture. Baptists in the South resented and resisted calls from some of their Northern brethren and from Britain to bring bondage to an end. Already, in 1822, Richard Furman, pastor of First Baptist Church, Charleston, had composed an eloquent defense of slavery. "Had the holding of slaves been a moral evil," he wrote, "it cannot be supposed, that the inspired Apostles, who feared not the faces of men, and were ready to lay down their lives in the cause of their God, would have tolerated it."[2] Furman and his white fellow Baptists in the South believed that, since slavery was assumed to be an acceptable part of life in the world of the Bible, it remained so in the nineteenth century. They neglected the consideration that slavery in the ancient world was not restricted to people of one color, so that the situations were not strictly comparable. Yet Christian slave owners did increasingly see it as their responsibility to advance the gospel on their plantations. Converted slaves usually worshiped with their masters, though they were frequently accommodated in a separate part of the meeting house, perhaps at the back or in a gallery. Addresses to the slaves often dwelt on the scriptural injunctions to obey their masters, and black members did not even necessarily possess a vote in church decisions. Yet church was the one place where a semblance of egalitarianism could be found. African Americans, like their white fellow members, were generally called "Brother" and "Sister," they could serve as deacons and Sunday school teachers, and they could even give evidence in disciplinary cases against white members, a practice banned in the secular courts. The antebellum ethos of the Baptist churches of the South did something to counterbalance the degradation of the prevailing social system.

Native Americans were not usually enslaved, but they were frequently treated as enemies by white immigrants into North America. Outright warfare punctuated the seventeenth and eighteenth centuries and, subsequently, frontiersmen were often in hostile contact with the people who were being displaced from their ancestral lands. Between 1830 and 1860 it was the policy of the United States government to remove the tribes from the settled eastern states to territories west of the Mississippi. Baptists concurred in this project: Isaac McCoy, a missionary appointed in 1817 by the Triennial Convention to the indigenous peoples of Indiana and Michigan, acted as an agent for removal programs. Yet McCoy championed the right of Native Americans to be treated fairly and, with a growing band of fellow missionaries, founded schools as well as churches among some of the tribes. It was often an uphill struggle. "The White people," complained another missionary, "are constantly opposing every effort to instruct the poor benighted Indians. The great objection urged by most people in these parts is the enmity of the old wars in which some of their friends have been killed by them."[3] Even when the object of dealings with Native Americans was to benefit them, the attitude of the missionaries could be condescending. This was equally true throughout the British Empire—in Canada, Australia, and southern Africa—when Baptist settler communities tried to bring the gospel to their indigenous neighbors. It was their assumption that the original inhabitants were at a lower level of civilization, and so needed to be brought out of savagery as well as out of paganism. There was an insensitivity to indigenous culture that few were able to transcend. Nevertheless, for long into the nineteenth century it was believed that there was no inherent barrier to prevent native peoples from rising to civilized status. Their handicap was not their birth but their lack of facilities for advancing. Consequently, Baptists provided a range of educational institutions designed to teach the skills of settled life. The college founded for the coeducation of Native Americans and Anglophone whites by Almon C.

Bacone, a missionary to the Oklahoma Territory from 1878 and himself a Native American, was a notable instance. Wherever the idea prevailed that indigenous peoples could make progress through agencies of this kind, white Baptists did not suppose that the intellectual capacities of other groups were limited. However circumscribed their views, they were not the victims of racial prejudice.

THE LEGACY OF SLAVERY

The most acute tensions over race developed in the American South. The victory of the North at the end of the Civil War in 1865 brought emancipation to the enslaved population. The freedmen naturally looked for a comparable emancipation in their church life. Thus the black Baptists of Richmond, Virginia, the former Confederate capital, took over several of the churches of the city by June of that year, appointing their own pastors for the first time. In most places African Americans started their own wholly autonomous congregations, worshiping in whatever place they could. Initially their white coreligionists deplored the exodus, but the persistent white refusal to recognize the ex-slaves as equals ensured that the separation of the races went ahead. In the North, by contrast, except in the largest cities, the far smaller number of African Americans normally continued biracial worship. In the South, however, white Baptists soon bowed to the inevitable, and most of the divisions were harmonious. Academy Baptist Church, Mississippi, for instance, called a conference in 1869 "for the purpose of organizing the colored people of Academy into a separate church by a unanimous request from them."[4] By the early 1870s the departure of African Americans from Southern churches was virtually complete. Even the Primitive Baptists, with their strong tendency to retain the customs of the past, divided between blacks and whites. This juncture marked the beginning of an enduring polarization of Baptists along racial lines.

White attitudes toward blacks in the South were a compound of genuine compassion and blatant bigotry. On the one hand, there was a real eagerness to ensure that the black population heard the authentic gospel. There was a deep-seated fear, as the Tishomingo Baptist Association of Tennessee put it in 1869, of "the colored people, if left alone, retrograding into superstition."[5] Beliefs brought from Africa had not been entirely banished from black Baptist religion, and there was a widespread concern that inadequate instruction from untrained ministers would allow them to flourish. On the other hand, there was a nostalgic attachment to slavery, powerfully reinforced by novel racial theories associated with social Darwinism. The white race, it was supposed, was destined to dominate the world because, in the competition for resources, it was better adapted to its environment. Whites would survive because they were fittest. There was much talk of "pure Anglo-Saxon blood." The combination of ideas could issue in outright rejection of the principle enshrined in the American Declaration of Independence that "all men are created equal." "We think," announced an editorial in the Georgia Baptist newspaper in 1883, "that our own race is incomparably superior to any other."[6] An official report of the Home Mission Board of the Southern Baptist Convention in 1891, though less brash, echoed similar assumptions. "Nothing is plainer," it declared of the "Colored People," "to any one who knows this race than its perfect willingness to accept a subordinate place, provided there be confidence that in that position of subordination it will receive justice and kindness."[7] It was such views that generated the Jim Crow laws, depriving African Americans of the vote and establishing racial segregation from the last years of the nineteenth century onwards. White Baptists were often their most enthusiastic supporters.

The new dispensation in the South was often enforced by systematic vigilantism. The Ku Klux Klan was the best-known organization that imposed racist terror on African Americans. "Belonged to the Ku Klux Klan," ran the epitaph of a Confederate veteran, "a deacon in the Baptist Church and a Master Mason for forty years."[8] During the 1890s, incidents of lynching, the mob murder of defenseless blacks by hanging, took place at a rate of over a hundred each year. In the face of such developments, voices of protest from white sources were all too few. Northern Baptists, though active in supporting schools for training black people, often turned a blind eye to institutional racism and the methods used to buttress it. The desire for national reconciliation after the Civil War inhibited them from criticizing the policies of Southern states. Even social gospel writers in the North neglected Southern problems. Walter Rauschenbusch did not take up the treatment of African Americans until the last few years of his life; Shailer Mathews never mentioned the subject in his social gospel handbook of 1910. When the message of the social gospel was taken up in the South, its advocates did sometimes speak about the issue. John E. White, an Atlanta Baptist pastor who was a vice president of the Southern Sociological Congress that aimed to relate the faith to contemporary problems, urged better race relations. Yet those who were especially concerned with "the negro question" remained paternalist in their attitudes, supposing that white assistance was needed to raise the level of black attainment. Thus Benjamin Riley, the Baptist author of *The White Man's Burden* (1910), argued for the older view that black people were held back not by the handicap of racial inferiority but by the accident of circumstances, yet believed that they required "the most rudimentary training in morals."[9] There was a gulf of understanding that remained unbridged.

The black response to oppression and incomprehension varied. Some Baptists believed in accommodating themselves to the situation as far as possible. Booker T. Washington, a black Baptist of broad theological views who served as president of Tuskegee Institute, Alabama, from 1881 onwards, urged that African Americans should avoid militancy, believing that black progress would come gradually through industrial training for the mass of his people. Washington set out his views in a celebrated speech at Atlanta in 1895, in which he rejected any struggle for justice and urged cooperation between the races. For some years, his approach was seen by many, white as well as black, as the way forward for racial relations. In particular, his fellow African American Baptists tended to agree with him. By means of hard work, they supposed, they would earn the esteem of their fellow citizens and eventually eliminate discrimination. Elias Camp Morris, the initial president of the National Baptist Convention that, for the first time, linked black Baptist congregations nationwide from 1895, declared that there must be "no cessation of our efforts to become taxpayers, owners of homes and constructive builders of our own fortunes."[10] Others, however, believed in greater activism. They were typified in the early career of Sutton E. Griggs, a Texas-born black Baptist pastor, who wrote a novel, *Imperium in Imperio* (1899), about the struggles of a black protagonist against racism. His hero was "a new Negro, self-respecting, fearless, and determined in the assertion of his rights."[11] When serving in Nashville, Tennessee, Griggs helped organize a boycott of the city's streetcars in protest against their segregation in 1905–1906, joined in the Niagara Movement that was designed to defend African American interests, and supported the foundation of its successor, the National Association for the Advancement of Colored People (1909). The inspirer of these bodies, the black intellectual W. E. B. Du Bois, wanted blacks to maximize their education, enter the professions, and agitate for their rights. He shared with Washington the aim of racial uplift, but insisted that protest against injustice must accompany hard work. Du Bois, like Washington, spoke from National Baptist Convention platforms. There was no single strategy among black Baptists for improving their lot.

The black churches, as the chief corporate vehicle for African American aspirations, achieved a great deal for their members. At a time when black people were excluded from the public space of parks, libraries, restaurants, and meeting halls, churches provided a place where they could assemble for virtually any purpose. The Baptists, who enjoyed the support of far more African Americans than any other denomination, therefore provided the chief institutional agency for black advancement. In 1916 the National Baptist Convention reported more church members than either the Northern or the Southern Baptist Convention. By that time the distribution of the black population was beginning to change. In 1890, 90 percent still lived in the South but, subsequently, job opportunities in the manufacturing industry drew them to Chicago, Detroit, Pittsburgh, and other Northern centers of population. By 1936, more black church members lived in cities than in the countryside. In both North and South, black ministers were the natural leaders of their communities. Most continued to recommend caution and self-help to their flocks, but some played a full part in interwar campaigns against lynching and in favor of the removal of barriers to full voting rights for African Americans. Thus, from 1931 onwards, Adam Clayton Powell Jr., who was to succeed his father as minister of the Abyssinian Baptist Church, Harlem, headed protest marches against discrimination in New York. He sat in Congress from 1944, and, though he eventually departed from doctrinal orthodoxy and financial probity, was an eloquent champion of his people. Because of the strength of the churches in African American life, Baptist pastors were spokesmen for the whole community.

In these years there emerged for the first time a substantial intellectual elite among black Baptists. At Howard University in Washington, D.C., Mordecai W. Johnson, its first black president, Benjamin E. Mays, the dean of the School of Religion, and Howard Thurman, the dean of the Divinity School, constituted a formidable trio of Baptist ministers. It was their achievement to forge a new strategy for addressing the racial injustice of American society. In 1936 both Thurman and Mays traveled to India and met Mahatma Gandhi, the leader of the national struggle for independence from Britain. Gandhi had developed a technique of non-violent protest that was capable of mobilizing the masses. Although he expounded his approach in terms of Hindu philosophy, he had learned his methods long before from newspaper reports of the Passive Resistance movement against the 1902 Education Act in England. There, Nonconformists, led by the Baptist John Clifford, had allowed their goods to be seized rather than submitting to unjust legislation. The part of Gandhi's thinking that swayed the Baptist visitors was therefore itself of Baptist origin. Subsequently, Thurman wrote *Jesus and the Disinherited* (1949) to argue that Jesus, as a Jew on the margins of the Roman Empire, was on the side of the oppressed in all ages. The book endorsed Gandhi's method of non-violent protest. It was this technique, a morally acceptable form of action against oppression, that was to be the mainspring of the civil rights movement of later decades. Martin Luther King Jr. always carried a copy of Thurman's *Jesus and the Disinherited* in his briefcase.

THE CAMPAIGN FOR CIVIL RIGHTS

The crisis of the Second World War did much to undermine the foundations of racial injustice. The conflict against Nazism was in part a struggle against a regime that upheld an ideology of Aryan domination of other races. "Nazism," according to George D. Kelsey, a Baptist professor at Morehouse College, "exposed racism in all its cruel nakedness and extreme idolatry."[12] During the war, segregation was abolished in the armed forces and the Fair Employment Practices Commission began the same process in civilian life. In the flurry of rhetoric about freedom and self-determination, the National Association for the Advancement of Colored People revived. Just after the war, the Baptist State Convention of North Carolina resolved that "segregation of believers holding the same tenets of faith because of color or social status into racial or class churches" is a "denial of the New Testament affirmation of the equality of all believers."[13] It was, however, a decision of the Supreme Court that heralded revolutionary change. In 1954 it was authoritatively settled in the case of *Brown v. Board of Education* that the doctrine of "separate but equal" could not be used as an excuse for keeping schools segregated. African Americans rejoiced that at last they had the law unequivocally on their side and took courage. On December 1, 1955, when asked to give up her seat on a bus in Montgomery, Alabama, to a white man, Rosa Parks refused. The black people of the city began a bus boycott that launched the civil rights movement. Martin Luther King Jr., then a young black Baptist minister in Montgomery, was propelled to prominence and became the executive head of the Southern Christian Leadership Conference that coordinated the ongoing campaign. Deeply molded by his pastor father's conservative Evangelical theology, King had absorbed much broader thinking during his education, though he was always wary of liberal optimism about the human condition. He determined to put into practice the philosophy of non-violent action he had learned from Benjamin E. Mays and George D. Kelsey, his professors at Morehouse College. King emerged as the leader of the demand for full civil rights for all Americans.

There was stout resistance by white Baptists in the South. There can be no doubt that a majority of Southern Baptists believed in segregation. Although a conviction that the church should be solely concerned with spiritual affairs often masked the extent of aversion to mixing with their black fellow citizens, the general assumption was that the races were happier when living apart. When a report sponsored by the Christian Life Commission of the Southern Baptist Convention endorsed the decision in *Brown v. Board of Education*, there was a howl of protest. W. A. Criswell, the prestigious pastor of First Baptist Church, Dallas, Texas, denounced the Brown ruling as showing that its framers must be "dying from the neck up."[14] Carey Daniel, pastor of First Baptist Church, West Dallas, in the same state, issued a pamphlet called *God the Original Segregationist*, arguing that Genesis 10:32 and Acts 17:26 showed that the Almighty had assigned distinct living areas to each race. Although many would have hesitated to appeal explicitly to the Bible to endorse their case, prejudice ran deep. "Since the church was organized by Christ," declared an Arkansas minister in 1963, "it has always stood for segregation."[15] The legacy of the pseudo-scientific racial theories of earlier years fused with defense of the culture of the South against outside interference. The blend was powerfully reinforced in these years by the atmosphere of the Cold War. Many Southerners considered Martin Luther King's venture a Communist plot against inherited freedoms. The consequence was a profound distaste for desegregation. As late as 1968, only 11 percent of Southern Baptist churches admitted African Americans to membership. Most white Baptists in the South wanted nothing to do with civil rights.

There were, however, more progressive voices among white Baptists. Between 1950 and 1966, the American Baptist Convention of the North passed annual resolutions favoring moves toward closer relations between the races, and from 1956 urged churches to become fully integrated. Even if rhetoric was rarely translated into action, a public stance was taken. Martin England, who represented the convention's ministers' retirement scheme in the South, went further during the 1960s, taking part in protest marches and managing, in the process, to sign Martin Luther King up for insurance benefits. In 1968 a caucus of African American ministers in the American Baptist Convention demanded greater participation, and in the very next year the denomination elected its first black president. The National Baptist Convention, representing the largest black Christian constituency, was hardly more advanced in its position. Its powerful president, Joseph H. Jackson, believed that the existing treatment of minorities in the United States was sinful, but rejected the method of civil disobedience and so disapproved of King's flamboyant efforts. Gardner C. Taylor, minister of Concord Baptist Church, Brooklyn, opposed this cautious policy, called for alignment with the developing civil rights movement, and challenged Jackson's leadership, apparently winning the denominational presidency in 1960. Jackson, however, refused to leave office, and, after a violent confrontation at the 1961 annual meeting, the Taylorites, including King himself, left the denomination to form the Progressive National Baptist Convention. Although the most prominent spokesmen for the civil rights cause were forced out of the National Baptist Convention, it is clear that the movement enjoyed a great deal of support in its ranks.

Even the Southern Baptists included many who were more sympathetic to the elimination of discrimination against African Americans. The evangelist Billy Graham, a member of Criswell's church in Dallas, ended segregation at his crusades from 1953, and so set a weighty example. T. B. Maston, professor of social ethics since 1922 at Southwestern Theological Seminary, Fort Worth, Texas, advocated desegregation on theological grounds. Segregation, he roundly concluded in a book of 1959, is "contrary to the spirit and teachings of Christ."[16] The head of the Southern Baptists' Christian Life Commission from 1960, Foy D. Valentine, though necessarily careful not to provoke a reaction within his constituency, personally endorsed policies of integration. In the year of his appointment, the Christian Life Commission report (which was accepted as information rather than adopted by the convention) urged Southern Baptists "to make use of every opportunity to help Negro citizens to secure . . . [equal] rights through peaceful and legal means and to thoughtfully oppose any customs which may tend to humiliate them in

Martin Luther King Jr. (1929–1968)
Baptist Civil Rights Leader, with Leaders of Southern Baptist Theological Seminary

any way."[17] In 1961 the Southern Baptist Theological Seminary at Louisville took the bold step of inviting Martin Luther King to address its students in chapel, and lost some of its financial support in consequence. By 1969, a survey established that more than half the delegates to the Southern Baptist Convention, admittedly a sample tending to be more open-minded than some others in the denomination, believed that race should not be a factor in determining church membership, and only 6 percent believed that it should. By that date, the progressives in the Southern Baptist Convention dominated its policies. They had taken a significant part in the downfall of segregation in the South by persuading their fellow Baptists that change was inevitable or even desirable.

The civil rights campaign, however, was primarily a black achievement. Its rank-and-file members were mobilized on the basis of their Christian affiliation. Thus Fannie Lou Hamer, a member of Williams Chapel Missionary Baptist Church in Ruleville, Mississippi, volunteered in 1962 to register to vote, knowing that she would earn a punishment. She was duly beaten in the county jail, but went on to be a civil rights orator. "I believe," she declared, "that God gave me the strength to be able to speak in this cause."[18] Martin Luther King continued to take the lead in the process. By carefully calculated publicity measures, he ensured that the campaign for equality between the races was kept before the American public. His letter from Birmingham Jail, written in April and May 1963, was a masterly call for white Christians not to rest content with well-meant sympathy but to align themselves publicly with the civil rights movement. The march on Washington in August of that year was another media coup. "I have a dream," King proclaimed in the heart of the capital, "that my four little children will one day live in a nation where they will not be judged by the color of their skin but by the content of their character."[19] Already the government had announced its intention to proceed with legislation to achieve King's central goal. The Civil Rights Act of 1964 and the Voting Rights Act of the following year put an end to the most blatant forms of institutional discrimination. Thereafter, King's own standing tended to decline as other more radical voices competed for the public ear. In particular, Malcolm X, the son of a Baptist preacher but now an orthodox Muslim, called for greater militancy in the campaign for full black rights. King, however, did not flinch from danger and eventually fell to an assassin's bullet on April 4, 1968. The naming of many American roads in his honor and the eventual designation of a public holiday in his memory bear testimony to the impact of Martin Luther King on the life of his nation.

Elsewhere the racial issue continued to trouble Baptist life. In South Africa in particular, the years after the Second World War brought not greater interracial harmony but stronger separation between the races. The government policy of apartheid was reflected among Baptists in the contrast between the predominantly white Baptist Union and the largely black Baptist Convention. Although the assembly of the Baptist Union resolved in 1976 that it was open to all churches without regard to race or color, the institutional division from the convention lasted into the twenty-first century. Britain was becoming the setting for another black community in the postwar years. Although there had been people of African and Caribbean descent in the country over the centuries, mass immigration, initially from Jamaica, began only in 1947. In the midst of local prejudices, Baptists usually tried to welcome the newcomers. Wednesbury Baptist Church in the West Midlands, for example, declared that it was "not in favour of any Colour Bar that may exist in the town and surrounding area."[20] When tensions in community life culminated in riots in Notting Hill, London, in 1958, two Baptist ministers of the area announced their determination to work for reconciliation. A number of black-led congregations subsequently became affiliated with the Baptist Union, and, by the end of the century, the largest church in membership of the union was a black congregation in the East End of London. The Baptist World Alliance, well aware of the simmering unrest over racial relations, periodically recorded its abhorrence of discrimination on the basis of color. The United States, though it was the land that attracted by far the most worldwide attention, was not the only one where differences of race had to be overcome by the spirit of the gospel in the later twentieth century.

In 1995 the Southern Baptist Convention formally apologized to African Americans for involvement in slavery in an earlier age and "for condoning and/or perpetuating individual and systematic racism in our lifetime."[21] There was cause for the resolution. Slavery flourished down to the Civil War, stripping black people of their dignity, terrorizing them with cruelty, and often preventing them from pursuing Christian family life. At the same period, Native Americans and indigenous peoples in lands occupied by British settlers were treated as needing to be civilized as well as to believe the gospel. Although Baptists in Britain and the North took up the cause of anti-slavery, in the South white Baptists defended it until they went down to military defeat. Slaves themselves, however, had adopted the Christian faith in growing numbers and overwhelmingly in its Baptist form. In the wake of the Confederate debacle, freedmen seized their religious autonomy but then faced the entrenchment of racial oppression in the South. Shifting in large numbers to Northern cities in the early twentieth century, black people continued to find their churches places for the fulfillment that was denied them elsewhere and their ministers the champions they required to defend their interests. It was only after the Second World War, however, that there was a concerted effort to end the subordination by race that was the legacy of slavery to the Southern states. Baptists played a prominent part in the struggle, albeit on the side of defending segregation as well as in the cause of struggling for its extinction. The racial issue was one that sharply divided Baptists, affecting them outside America as well as within, and damaging their professed belief in a gospel that brings peace among the peoples. But Martin Luther King and his colleagues won much of what they sought in the civil rights movement. If racial inequalities survived, by the end of the twentieth century the most damaging aspects of the bequest of slavery had been overcome.

Further Reading

Boles, John B., ed. *Masters and Slaves in the House of the Lord: Race and Religion in the American South, 1740–1870*. Lexington: University Press of Kentucky, 1988.

Harvey, Paul. *Freedom's Coming: Religious Culture and the Shaping of the American South from the Civil War through the Civil Rights Era*. Chapel Hill: University of North Carolina Press, 2005.

———. *Redeeming the South: Religious Cultures and Racial Identities among Southern Baptists, 1865–1925*. Chapel Hill: University of North Carolina Press, 1997.

Manis, Andrew M. *Southern Civil Religions in Conflict: Black and White Baptists and Civil Religion, 1947–1957*. Athens: University of Georgia Press, 1987.

Martin, Dana. "The American Baptist Convention and the Civil Rights Movement: Rhetoric and Response." *Baptist History and Heritage* 34 (1999): 21–32.

McLoughlin, William G. *Cherokees and Missionaries, 1789–1839*. New Haven, Conn.: Yale University Press, 1984.

Newman, Mark. *Getting Right with God: Southern Baptists and Deseg-regation, 1945–1995.* Tuscaloosa: University of Alabama Press, 2001.

Noll, Mark A. *God and Race in American Politics: A Short History.* Princeton, N.J.: Princeton University Press, 2008.

Chapter 10

WOMEN IN BAPTIST LIFE

The role of women among Baptists has generally been neglected by historians. Pastors and theologians have normally been male, and so accounts of local church life and studies of doctrinal developments have alike tended to concentrate on the work of men. Books have sometimes been written in the past that ignore the existence of women altogether. Even in this volume, on account of the prominence of men as church leaders and theologians over the years, the lion's share of coverage is taken by men. Yet a majority of church members have normally been female. The ratio has varied over time, but for much of the time, at least in England, there were commonly two women for every man on church rolls. Women have therefore constituted a larger section of the Baptist community than men, and so their history amply deserves to be written. In recent years there has been a measure of redress. Historians have turned their attention to women's history and sometimes they have taken Baptist women into consideration. It has emerged that there were capable female leaders in Baptist denominational life as well as innumerable faithful church members who were women. The story of some of the outstanding figures has started to be written. Several, such as

Helen Barrett Montgomery, the first woman to lead a Protestant denomination in the United States, and Nannie Helen Burroughs, the corresponding secretary of the National Baptist Convention's women's organization for over sixty years, will be mentioned in this chapter. There will also, however, be an effort to consider the rank and file of women who sustained the churches, staffed their agencies, and undertook much of their outreach. The very existence of a Baptist cause often relied on women. Even when leadership was partly or wholly male, female members were at the core of church life. Their place will be discussed in the following pages.

It would be ideal if the subject of the chapter could be not one sex but the issue of gender among Baptists. Many historians have come to appreciate that the history of women is not best treated as a separate topic. Women have not lived apart from men, but the two sexes have had dealings with one another, whether as wife and husband, buyer and seller, or listener and preacher. Consequently, an analysis of the way in which the two sexes have interacted presents a fuller picture of past reality than any study of women alone. Furthermore, when gender is taken as a theme for analysis, it reveals not just the activities of women and men but also the different understandings of being female or male that were in circulation at any given time and place. Gender history is generally about the representation of femininity and masculinity. The language of people in the past can be examined so as to lay bare expectations about what womanhood or manhood entailed at particular junctures. This approach, however, has barely begun to be applied to Baptists. There are a few exceptions. We know, for example, how prominent black Baptist women in the late nineteenth century related their racial and gender identities. We also know that the great Victorian preacher Charles Haddon Spurgeon made the proper role of men a major topic of his sermons and writings. He habitually contrasted, for example, the contemporary idea of a gentleman with his own image of a man: whereas a gentleman was artificial in his manners, affected in his speech, and effeminate in his tastes, a true man was frank, outspoken, and bold. Spurgeon's army of admirers throughout the world, and especially the preachers he trained, often adopted a similar ideal of manhood and tried to act on it. Yet it would be impractical to explore Baptist understandings of the feminine and the masculine—and their interaction—until far more research has been done. We must be content for the present to examine the place of women in denominational life.

The Place of Women in Church and Society

Early Baptists wrestled with the biblical evidence for the proper role of women as they sought to reproduce the earliest pattern of the church. On the one hand, they read that women should remain silent in church, should seek guidance from their husbands at home, and should not teach or dictate to men. On the other, they knew that the Spirit would be poured out so that women would prophesy, that women were the first to testify to the resurrection, and that among those who had been baptized into Christ there were no distinctions, whether of race, rank, or gender. At the same time, the Baptist pioneers were swayed by the contemporary assumption that the subordination of women to men was part of the natural order. Men, it was generally supposed in the seventeenth century, held patriarchal authority over women and children. It is not surprising, in those circumstances, that in 1607, while moving toward a Baptist position, John Smyth asserted that the prophets in the church, the expositors of God's word, must be male only. Women, together with young people, were treated as unqualified for that office. Yet, in the setting of the time, what is remarkable is that Smyth accorded women and young people a share in the decision-making of the church. Over against the congregation led by Francis Johnson, Smyth, arguing from the kingship of all believers, believed that the church as a whole held authority over its elders. Hence, the female members as much as the male members could share in the choice of church leaders. Women and young people who had been admitted to church fellowship could speak their minds: "If any dissent, they may speak, either woman or youth, and yet the rule of the Apostle [is] not violated."[1] Women, furthermore, could act as deacons. By this provision, Smyth meant that widows over sixty could visit and relieve the needy as official representatives of the church. The founder of the first General Baptist church was prepared to give women a much higher place in church order than virtually all his contemporaries.

In a similar way, the early Particular Baptists debated how fully women could participate in church affairs. At the English West Country Association meeting in 1658 the issue of when women may speak was thoroughly aired. It was agreed that they might not teach publicly. Nor might they speak in order to act as rulers in the church, or pass sentence on doctrinal or disciplinary cases, or offer prayer as the representatives of the corporate body. It was settled, however, that they could confess their faith as candidates for baptism and church membership, that they could give testimony in disciplinary cases, and that they could express public repentance for any sins for which they had been rebuked by the church. The longest discussion surrounded the question of whether a woman could speak out against a candidate for admission to the church if she knew anything against the person's character. The decision was that she could. In practice, it is clear that women could play a prominent part in church life. In the New World in 1639, Catherine Scott, herself a preacher, encouraged Roger Williams to form the first Baptist church on American soil, at Providence, Rhode Island, though, like Williams, she soon abandoned her Baptist allegiance. In England in the following year the formidable Dorothy Hazzard took the lead in refusing to attend Anglican services in Bristol, and so began the separatist congregation that became Broadmead Baptist Church. Her church, when by the 1660s it had become openly Baptist, appointed a deaconess with the same role that Smyth envisaged for his female deacons; and, in 1679, the experiment having evidently succeeded, four women were appointed to the same office. Like Smyth's church, too, some Particular Baptist congregations allowed women to vote in church meetings. At Fleur de Lys Yard, Southwark, in London, for instance, it was agreed that they had this privilege, "being equally with the brethren members of the mystical body of Christ."[2] At the main London Seventh Day Baptist Church, women were even allowed to prophesy so long as, in accordance with apostolic instructions, they were not bare-headed. Baptists were much less forward than Quakers, among whom women could speak freely in worship and serve as recorded ministers. Yet they were much more prepared to give women a public role than the Church of England or most other Dissenters.

The revival of the eighteenth century accentuated that tendency. In stirring times, when the Holy Spirit was perceptibly poured out, the Old Testament prediction that daughters as well as sons would prophesy seemed to vindicate female participation in evangelistic efforts. In America, the Separate Baptists, the children of the Great Awakening, permitted women to offer public prayer in gatherings where men were present. To the more traditional Regular Baptists this appeared so scandalous a breach of biblical order that they refused fellowship with the Separates. Martha Stearns Marshall and Sarah Johnston Stearns were partners with their husbands, the founders of the Sandy Creek Association in the Carolinas from 1755, in setting up a host of new congregations. In Virginia in 1770 a woman undertook a preaching ministry alongside the male itinerants. The Separates sometimes went so far as to appoint not just deaconesses but "eldresses." Their sphere was the women of the churches, but they had a wide remit. They reported to the elders on the spiritual welfare of their charges, they baptized female converts, and on occasion they preached and prayed before audiences of men as well as women. When, in the 1780s, the Free Will Baptists began in northern New England a revival ministry similar to that of the Separates in the South, they gave great freedom for female involvement. The same was initially true of their English equivalents, the vigorous General Baptist evangelists who turned into the New Connexion. The strategy of the early preachers from the Barton church in Leicestershire was to hold gospel meetings in cottages, the homes where women were in charge. There a form of "domestic religion" developed in which women were the chief spiritual guides. Sometimes women shared with men the leadership of whole new churches. Mary Fowler, as much as her husband William, was responsible for establishing a fresh cause in the Nottinghamshire village of Beeston shortly after 1800. The impetus of the revival era brought women to the fore.

The Particular Baptists, though eventually swept into the stream of revival, were generally more cautious about the role of women. In 1746 the Philadelphia Association, the organization representing the main body of Calvinistic Baptists in America, received the query, "Whether women may or ought to have their votes in the church, in such matters as the church shall agree to be decided by votes?" The gathered delegates of the churches pondered the passage from 1 Corinthians that directed women to keep silent. That provision, they decided, could not exclude female participants in church meetings from possessing, "as members of the body of the church, liberty to give a mute voice, by standing or lifting up of the hands, or the contrary, to signify their assent or dissent to the thing proposed, and so augment the number on the one side or on both sides of the question." The silence commended in scripture, furthermore, could not be absolute, because otherwise women would not be able to confess their faith to the church as a condition of baptism or to speak on matters of discipline, including defending themselves when any charges were brought against them. That right, the association agreed, was "a privilege of all human creatures by the laws of nature, not abrogated by the law of God." Therefore a woman might speak on such occasions, at least by asking leave of the brothers to address them. But then she must not "open the floodgate of speech in an imperious, tumultuous, masterly manner." Yet, if she voted in an unusual way, "her reasons ought to be called for, heard, and maturely considered, without contempt."[3] In these discussions there was an evident desire to be faithful to biblical teaching at the same time as being practical. If there was a suspicion that women might prove garrulous, there was also a regard for their dignity.

As the eighteenth century gave way to the nineteenth, there was increasing talk of a "separate sphere" for women. They were expected to look after home and family, and leave the men to pursue business and public affairs. While it has come to be recognized by historians that it was no novelty for women to be allocated these priorities, there was more insistence in the advice given during this period that women should find fulfillment in domestic duties. Growing wealth allowed middle-class husbands to provide leisure for their wives in homes that were separate from the workplace, and Evangelical writers explained that child rearing was the overriding responsibility of women. Baptist authors contributed to the torrent of literature on this theme. William Landels, for example, the Scottish minister of Regent's Park Chapel in London, in his *Woman's Sphere and Work Considered in the Light of Scripture* (1859), explicitly endorsed the idea that the female sex should aim to become exemplary wives and mothers. Yet it is instructive that, whereas in this book Landels expected women's role to be tightly circumscribed, in a work of only eleven years later, *Woman: Her Position and Power*, he shifted his ground sufficiently to suggest wider possibilities for women. The existence of the office of deaconess in the early church, he mused, might indicate the legitimacy of a form of female ministry. Notions of what women should be allowed to do were more flexible than has been supposed. In any case, among the working people it was often impractical for women to be restricted to the home. In the growing cities most unmarried working-class girls went to work, often as domestic servants. Although they generally left employment on marriage, a high proportion of older women from poorer homes, both single and married, had to find a job to eke out household finances. So the ideal of separate spheres was, in practice, far from rigidly observed.

In church, the putting into practice of contemporary views on the proper role of women was variable too. The physical separation of the sexes was a common feature of Baptist meeting houses in the eighteenth century, and many of the buildings had different doors for men and women. Country churches, especially in the American South, continued this pattern long into the nineteenth century, though urban congregations increasingly abandoned it for the sake of seating members of the family together. Women were also more integrated with men in voting practices. The South and the British Isles slowly came more into line with the American North in generally allowing the two sexes to participate equally in decision-making. There were still exceptions, even in the North, where First Baptist Church, Philadelphia, denied the vote to women until as late as 1898. Nevertheless, gender egalitarianism was endorsed by a fascinating episode in 1830 when the trustees of the Mill Yard Seventh Day Baptist Church in London determined to transfer the chapel into other hands on grounds that the congregation consisted of only a handful of women. Those women, however, resisted the decision, claiming that they were still a properly constituted church. Eventually their stand was vindicated by the General Body of London Dissenting Ministers, who agreed that they did indeed remain a true church of Christ. And the work of the church undoubtedly gave an outlet for women's energies. Thus Maria Allen, a lock-keeper's daughter living in Derbyshire in the English Midlands, was "a conscientious General Baptist, and could give an enlightened reason of her hope, and faith, and practice." Wearing "a smile of cheerful urbanity," she loved the company of her friends at the local chapel. She was not deterred by flooded fields from regularly making the journey of a mile and a half to the services. Her natural and spiritual qualities "constituted her a fit agent for many departments of christian effort." And this girl, though only in her early twenties when she died in 1849, had the resolve to rebuke "three ungodly young men" who wanted to pass through her father's lock to use the boat on a Sunday, reportedly persuading them by three tracts "to keep holy the Sabbath day."[4] Clearly Christian service provided ample fulfillment for Maria. It was almost as though church was a third sphere, neither wholly private nor wholly public but sharing some of the qualities of each, where women such as Maria could flourish.

WOMEN'S ROLES

There were several aspects of church life in which women could play a particularly significant part. One was the cultivation of Christian experience. Women were often to the fore in expressing their spiritual exercises both individually and communally. Thus Abigail Harris, a member of Salem Baptist Church, New Jersey, in the early years of the nineteenth century, recorded her aspirations in a journal. "O that this day may be indeed a Sabbath day to my soul," she wrote one Sunday in 1813, "that I may not [only] . . . read & hear & pray but also . . . feel the influences of the Holy Spirit, witnessing with my spirit that I am thine."[5] Since Abigail felt this degree of commitment, it is not surprising that, on at least one occasion, her pastor's wife summoned her to offer public prayer at an evening meeting. Likewise, English Baptist women displayed a deep devotion. Around the middle of the nineteenth century, for example, a Mrs. Berry, a widow of sixty-five, was "full of love for Jesus" following her conversion.[6] The obituaries of ordinary female church members give particular attention to their regular prayer, their daily Bible reading, their use of hymns for private devotion, and their habit of keeping spiritual diaries. Women on both sides of the Atlantic would gather for special meetings of their own sex. Abigail Harris attended a society of "single sisters of the church" for Bible reading, hymn singing, prayer, and mutual support.[7] In a similar way, at Prospect Place New Connexion Chapel, Bradford, Yorkshire, between 1837 and 1852, women conducted experience meetings for the exchange of spiritual lessons and advice. Altogether, the practice of spirituality was a female forte.

Women could put their spiritual sensibilities into print. In the eighteenth century, Anne Dutton, the wife of the pastor of the Baptist meeting at Great Gransden in the English county of Huntingdonshire between 1732 and 1747, was a prolific writer. Several treatises, including *A Discourse on Walking with God* (1735), discuss Christian discipleship. Anne's autobiography contains a defense of the right of women to use the pen, notwithstanding the apostolic command to silence. She composed and published sixty-one hymns, and left her Bible to another Baptist hymn-writer, Anne Steele. This second Anne, the daughter of a pastor and timber merchant at Broughton in Hampshire, was the most popular Baptist hymn-writer of either sex in the eighteenth century. Her legacy in *Poems on Subjects Chiefly Devotional* (1760) includes "Father of mercies, in thy word, what endless glory shines," a hymn still commonly sung. These pioneers of hymn-writing had successors in the following century such as Maria Saffery and Elizabeth Trestrail, but their compositions generally made less impact. In America the best known female author of hymns in the nineteenth century was Annie S. Hawks, of Brooklyn and then Vermont, the writer of "I need Thee every hour," another enduring piece. It was common for Evangelical women to move on from composing verse to writing fiction, often initially in the religious magazines that flourished in the Victorian era. Sallie Rochester Ford, originally a Presbyterian in Kentucky but from 1855 the wife of a Baptist minister, contributed a story called "Grace Truman" to her husband's *Christian Repository*. It was published as a separate novel in 1857. Grace, the Baptist heroine, marries a Presbyterian, but cannot in conscience receive communion in her husband's denomination. After much debate, she triumphantly persuades the whole family, together with the Presbyterian minister, to join the Baptists. Probably the most productive Baptist woman writer was Marianne Hearn of Northampton in the heart of England, who adopted the pen-name Marianne Farningham. A regular contributor to the weekly *Christian World*, she published poetry, stories, and biographies, and, from 1885, served as editor of the *Sunday School Times*, molding the Christian instruction of millions. Farningham showed how influential a Baptist woman could become.

Because childcare was normally regarded as a female province, the spiritual welfare of sons and daughters in the home was seen as the responsibility of women. Mothers agonized over their children. "O keep them from the power of the devourer," wrote a Baptist servant in Bath in the 1850s about her two infant children, "from the snares and temptations of this deceitful wicked world, and from their nearest and most dangerous enemy, their own treacherous and deceitful hearts."[8] It was natural for the church's care for children to be assigned largely to women. Sunday schools in Britain, which were designed almost exclusively for the young, changed from having a majority of male teachers at the start of the nineteenth century, when they were largely concerned with teaching reading and writing, to being staffed largely by women at the end of the century, when their main task was instruction in Bible knowledge. Sunday school responsibilities extended, at least for conscientious women, beyond the classroom to preparing carefully and visiting absentees. Women also went full-time into education, and started schools of their own to provide training in a Christian atmosphere. Even higher education could seem a special responsibility of women. Thus, in 1886, the Alabama Baptist Women's Convention was founded with the single aim of raising money for the black Baptist Selma University. Whatever concerned the young usually fell to women to supervise. Hence, charities designed for children often had women in charge. Two south London orphanages were run by Baptist women. Mrs. T. H. Montague was superintendent of the Brixton Girls' Orphanage; Charlotte Sharman was the founder of another in West Square, where, though unmarried, she called her tasks "mother's duties."[9] Women carried the care for children that rested on their shoulders within the home into the wider spheres of the church and society at large.

In the broad field of philanthropy women also played a prominent role. In Britain, America, and elsewhere in the English-speaking world, the nineteenth century was an era of private enterprise for charity. Voluntary societies were created, usually under Evangelical auspices, for a vast range of activities on behalf of the poor, the sick, and the needy. Sometimes they were institutions run by women. Thus, in the United States there were such bodies as the Newark Female Charitable Society and the Female Missionary Society for the Poor of the City of New York. The societies raised funds, paid wages, and organized these agencies on business lines, but they were very much considered Christian ventures. Baptists were active alongside members of other denominations in these nonsectarian organizations. In the societies run by men, women were often the chief money raisers. Some of the largest sums raised for their objects came from bazaars, large-scale sales of goods exclusively staffed by women. In the charitable efforts of individual churches, women were also the chief workers. They often had the time during the work week to visit the distressed. District visiting, going around an area door by door, though originally undertaken by men as much as by women, became a virtual female monopoly before the end of the nineteenth century. In the course of the women's visits they would often spend as much time collecting money as dispensing charity. Altogether, women could often be constantly up and doing. Mrs. Harris, a Baptist from the English town of Leicester, was described by her obituarist as engaged in "unwearied activity in promoting the temporal and spiritual welfare of others."[10] Whether philanthropy was a matter of organized societies, money raising, or simple visiting, women took the lead.

In particular, they were a mainstay of home support for missions. Women, as chapter 13 will show, were often significant figures in the mission field. In the first generation of Baptist overseas missions at the opening of the nineteenth century, wives of missionaries were sometimes active partners of their husbands. Hannah Marshman, married to a member of the first group of British Baptists to go to India, was a full participant in the Serampore mission, and Ann Judson, the wife of the first missionary supported by American Baptists, joined in her husband's work and ultimately died in childbirth in Burma. Such devotion stirred women at home to organize support for the missionary cause. Sometimes, as might be expected, their time was spent coordinating children's efforts. Around the middle of the nineteenth century, between 15 and 20 percent of the annual income of the Baptist Missionary Society based in London came from Sunday schools and juvenile associations. Female mission societies in individual churches flourished in America. In 1847 the first women's missionary organization at denominational level, the Free Will Baptist Female Missionary Society, was established. There was a surge of larger bodies like this one about twenty years later. In 1867 in London, a Ladies' Association was formed for supporting specialist female missionary work among the women of India. The Baptist women of Boston, on behalf of the Northern United States (1871), and those of the Maritime Provinces of Canada (1884) set up their own missionary support organizations, and in 1888 there followed the Woman's Missionary Union, an auxiliary to the Southern Baptist Convention that raised money for evangelism at home as well as abroad. These agencies, though by no means feminist, were insistent on the rights of their sex. When the last of them was requested in its early years to adopt a policy proposed by men, there was a robust reply: "This is a Woman's Missionary Union, and there is no need for gentlemen to frame our resolutions."[11] Although these bodies may have made it harder for women to achieve prominence within the larger denominational home organizations, over the years they also provided a means by which women could plan their own mission strategy. They became a distinctive voice for women.

In society at large Christian women played an increasing role as reformers as the nineteenth century wore on. In its earlier years, female Baptists were to be found in the Northern pressure groups designed to abolish slavery, and they were active in the burgeoning temperance movement on both sides of the Atlantic. The Woman's Christian Temperance Union, founded in 1873 in order to achieve the prohibition of alcohol, mobilized more American women than any other organization of the century. The campaign for social purity also gathered large-scale support, aiming to rescue prostitutes from their way of life, to oppose the double standard in sexual moral-ity that tolerated male patronage of brothels, and to protect chil-dren from sexual exploitation by raising the age of consent. By the First World War it was expected that Baptist women would endorse a range of good causes. The Woman's Missionary Union of the Southern Baptists announced in 1917 its support for "those forces in our country which make for righteousness: patriotism, Sabbath observance, the sacredness of the home, the effort toward a more general re-establishment of the family altar, and the crusade against poverty, disease, illiteracy, vice, and crime."[12] These causes brought women into the political fray even though they did not have the vote. Some saw exclusion from the franchise as an injustice to be fought, and Baptists were to be found in the ranks of those demanding votes for women. In Scotland, for example, a prominent suffrage worker was Jessie Yuille, the wife of the secretary of the Baptist Union of Scotland. Baptist women, though usually dutiful toward their fathers and husbands, were by no means always silent and passive.

Helen Barrett Montgomery illustrates this principle power-fully. Montgomery played a very public part in Rochester, New York, where her father had been minister of Lake Avenue Baptist Church, and on a wider stage. She remained a lifelong member of the same church, where she took a Sunday school class for women and became a licensed preacher. Montgomery attended Wellesley College, where she imbibed ideals of active female citizenship,

Helen Barrett Montgomery (1861–1934)
Baptist Social Reformer and Leader

and, while running the home of her businessman husband, served as president of the Rochester Women's Educational and Industrial Union from 1893 to 1911, encouraging self-improvement among the poor and promoting educational reform. She was an advocate of equal suffrage for women, a believer in temperance reform (though not initially prohibition), and an opponent of brothels. Her commitment to foreign missions led to her *Western Women in Eastern Lands* (1910), an immensely popular account of the female role in global missions. It was Montgomery who conceived the idea of a Women's World Day of Prayer, which became a reality in 1919.

She acted as president of the Northern Baptist Convention, the first woman to hold that office, and served in 1921–1922, the boisterous year when the Fundamentalist controversy reached a climax; for good measure, in 1924, she also published a translation of the New Testament. "Jesus Christ," she told the Baptist World Alliance in 1923, "is the great Emancipator of woman."[13] Her own career was a vindication of that judgment.

Equally prominent in her sphere was Nannie Helen Burroughs, a descendant of slaves who joined the staff of the National Baptist Convention as a secretary. At twenty-one years old in 1900, she addressed the denomination's annual convention in Richmond, Virginia, voicing eloquently the "righteous discontent" felt by African American women in churches as a result of being, as she put it, "hindered from helping."[14] The outcome was that a women's convention was formed in her denomination, and Burroughs became its first corresponding secretary, continuing in that position, extraordinarily, until her death in 1961. Burroughs was a successful speaker on "women's work" at the first Baptist World Congress in London in 1905. In 1909 she was the founder of the National Training School for Women and Girls in Washington, D.C., designed to teach young black women a range of skills that would equip them to become professional housekeepers. It reflected her pithy philosophy of the three B's—Bible, bath, and broom—to promote clean lives, clean bodies, and clean homes. Ever a forceful personality, Burroughs, who never married, criticized the federal government during the First World War for failing to deal with lynching or segregation and was placed on a list of potentially dangerous radicals. Burroughs, like Montgomery, showed something of the ability of Baptist women to play a significant part in American society.

WOMEN IN MINISTRY

The female contribution to the churches and to society was rarely matched by any official role in the ministry. Women were not acceptable as ordained ministers, or even as preachers, in most Baptist bodies during the nineteenth century. There were exceptions. The Free Will Baptists, with their revivalist inheritance, licensed at least one woman as a preacher in the 1840s and ordained a handful in the 1870s. The small Seventh Day Baptists ordained a woman in 1885. Among the Baptists of the North, there was in 1882 an exceptional ordination of a woman, May C. Jones, by the Baptist Association of Puget Sound, occasioning a walk-out and a claim that, if a significant number had not left, the event could not have gone ahead. There were instances of female lay preachers, as at Bradford, Yorkshire, in the 1840s, and the gifted evangelist Emilia Baeyertz served in Australia from the 1870s. But in general the apparently biblical prohibition of women speaking in church still prevailed. Although there were influential champions of women becoming deacons, there were widespread reservations because holders of that office were normally expected to offer prayer at the Lord's supper. In both England and the United States there seems to have been a handful of female deacons in the later nineteenth century, but in America it was probably more common, in the manner of the seventeenth century, for women called deaconesses to serve as unordained assistants to the deacons. From 1890 there existed in England an order of deaconesses, uniformed church workers who initially undertook primarily nursing duties but who gradually assumed broader pastoral responsibilities; and four years later a similar body was organized in New York City by Rauschenbusch and his circle. Women with a calling to Christian ministry were still placed in a separate category.

It was the two waves of feminism of the twentieth century that transformed the opportunities of women to act as church leaders. The first wave, associated with the demand for female suffrage, led to much greater prominence for women. In Britain votes for women were partly conceded in 1918 and wholly granted in 1928. There, the Baptist Women's League, designed initially to raise money for home missions, became a vehicle for female participation in denominational life from 1910; in the following year women were co-opted to the Baptist Union Council for the first time; and in 1918 the first female minister was recorded as having charge of an English Baptist church. The Baptist Union Council formally decided in 1925 that there were no objections to women entering the ministry. Some women could achieve positions of real prominence. Hettie Rowntree Clifford, wife of the superintendent of the West Ham Central Mission in east London, though not herself ordained, was a dynamo of activity and preached as powerfully as her husband. In America the eminence of Helen Barrett Montgomery illustrated the very similar potential for women among Northern Baptists. By 1920 at least a hundred women had been in the formal ministry among them. The National Baptists and the Southern Baptists (like the denomination in other lands such as Australia and Canada), however, remained resistant to female ordination in the earlier twentieth century. Yet even the Southern Baptists were touched by the spirit of the age. Women had in the past been rejected as messengers to the annual convention, but in 1918, the year when American women secured the vote, they were admitted as delegates. A decade later they were allowed to speak at the convention. When, in 1941, the Fundamentalist Baptist evangelist John R. Rice published a sermon entitled "Bobbed Hair, Bossy Wives and Women Preachers," he was pointing, despite the provocative title, to a relationship between new female secular fashions and the emergence of women in ministry that actually existed. Changing attitudes toward women's role in society were affecting judgments about their place in Baptist life.

The second wave of feminism from the 1960s onwards was equally transformative. As women entered the job market in larger numbers and their champions called for equality in all spheres, nearly every denomination, including the Baptists, was affected. In Britain in 1962, there were still only two ordained Baptist women; by 2000, there were 155. Australia had its first female ordination in 1978 and other countries followed. The General Board of the American Baptist Churches of the North affirmed in 1985 that "the Gospel of Jesus Christ liberates all persons, female and male, to serve in any ministry to which they have been called by God and for which they have God-given talents."[15] By 2003 in American Baptist Churches, some 9 percent of senior pastors were female. The fact, however, that 32 percent of associate pastors were then female illustrates a phenomenon almost universal wherever women were allowed to minister: there was still a reluctance to appoint women to the most responsible positions. In the Southern Baptist Convention the issue of female ordination became a cause of acute controversy. A slowly growing number of churches permitted female deacons. In 1964 Addie Davis became the first woman ordained to the ministry, and in 1983 an organization of Women in Ministry was formed in the denomination. There was, however, a backlash. In 1973 a convention resolution noted "a great attack by the members of most women's liberation movements upon scriptural precepts of woman's place in society."[16] The broader-minded in the denomination shuddered that the biblical case for equality between women and men was being brushed aside. The issue then became entangled with the conservative/moderate controversy that wracked the Southern Baptists during the 1980s. A 1984 resolution, passed by the conservative majority against stiff moderate opposition, denounced the determining of Christian faith and practice by contemporary trends and rejected ordination for women. The conservatives adopted what was becoming known as a complementarian standpoint, believing that women should be subject to men in the home and undertake roles other than preaching in church. The egalitarian standpoint of the wider society, however, prevailed among the moderates and the Cooperative Baptist Fellowship that emerged from the denominational controversy. Disagreement over the proper role of women was one of the fissures that rent the Southern Baptists apart.

Over the centuries, women have formed a sizeable majority of Baptists, but that has not usually been reflected in histories of the denomination. Their leaders have rarely been female, and so the activities of women have been unduly minimized. Early Baptists, in trying to follow New Testament principles, scrutinized the biblical evidence for the place of women in the church and so awarded them a fuller role in decision-making than was customary in most other Christian communions. The revival of the eighteenth century had the same effect, though Baptists still normally wanted to ensure that they obeyed the limitations on women's speech that they understood as an enduring scriptural axiom. When, from around the early nineteenth century, there was an insistence in much Christian advice literature on the proper sphere of women being within the home rather than in public places, Baptists, like many other Evangelicals, in practice gave women a third sphere for fulfillment in the church. In many areas of life Baptist women found an outlet for their energies. They could express their spiritual experience in meetings as well as in private; they could put their thoughts into literature and hymns; and they could assume responsibility for children and their education. Baptist women were active in charitable work, achieving great feats of money raising; they were particularly energetic in supporting missions, creating their own organizations for the purpose; and many of them took up reform campaigns to attain goals that they conceived to be Christian. Helen Barrett Montgomery and Nannie Helen Burroughs showed what women could achieve in many of these fields. Yet, until the twentieth century, women were rarely allowed positions of leadership in the churches. Feminist developments in wider society encouraged fresh consideration of biblical guidelines so that women began to enter the ordained ministry. There was, however, a strong sense in some quarters that this interpretation did scant justice to scripture, and so conflict over the role of women ensued. All, nevertheless, agreed that churches could not exist without the varied forms of female ministry. Women were at the heart of Baptist life.

Further Reading

Briggs, John H. Y. "She-Preachers, Widows and Other Women: The Feminine Dimension in English Baptist Life since 1600." *Baptist Quarterly* 31 (1986): 337–52.

DeWeese, Charles W. *Women Deacons and Deaconesses: 400 Years of Baptist Service.* Macon, Ga.: Mercer University Press, 2005.

Higginbotham, Evelyn Brooks. *Righteous Discontent: The Women's Movement in the Black Baptist Church, 1880–1920.* Cambridge, Mass.: Harvard University Press, 1993.

Mobley, Kendal P. *Helen Barrett Montgomery: The Global Mission of Domestic Feminism.* Waco, Tex.: Baylor University Press, 2009.

Prochaska, Frank K. *Women and Philanthropy in Victorian England.* Oxford: Clarendon, 1980.

Wilson, Linda. *Constrained by Zeal: Female Spirituality among Nonconformists, 1825–75.* Carlisle: Paternoster, 2000.

Chapter 11

CHURCH, MINISTRY, AND SACRAMENTS AMONG BAPTISTS

There are certain convictions about the nature of church life that Baptists have upheld with a high degree of consistency. Prominent among them has been their belief in the principle of a gathered church. Over against those Christian communions—whether Orthodox, Roman Catholic, or Protestant—that regarded all the people of a given territory as their adherents, Baptists insisted that only those recognizing Christ as Savior should be accepted as church members. Churches, they held, were to be voluntary organizations in the sense that they were to be the result of deliberate choice by those applying to join. No applicants were deemed worthy except those who could give evidence that they possessed authentic Christian experience. As John Smyth quaintly put it in the year before he baptized himself, the "true matter" of the church was "sayntes only."[1] None, that is to say, but real believers, those described in the New Testament as "saints," were to belong to a valid church. This conviction was shared with early Independents, the later Congregationalists, who equally insisted that congregations were to consist of "visible saints." The Particular Baptists, as we have seen in chapter 4, also shared the Independent view that each church was wholly independent of every other, whereas the General Baptists followed a more connectional pattern that allowed some decisions to be taken in general assemblies of all churches and permitted some supervision of the churches by messengers. But both Baptist bodies, again like Independents, held that members of churches were to govern themselves. That view has normally been sustained down through the centuries, with ultimate responsibility for decisions resting not with pastors or deacons but with the committed church members as a whole. The churchmanship of the Baptists was not unique, for it was upheld as fully by Independents, but it was an unusual position in Christendom, arising from Baptists' belief in a regenerate church membership.

The attitude of Baptists to the ministry has contained elements of consistency and of variation. They were consistent in holding a view of ministry that was different from the normal understanding among many other Christians. The Orthodox and Roman Catholic belief was that the church should be led by priests, separated sharply from laypeople so that they could represent them before God, and the Church of England, though it included a range of opinions on the subject, retained the word "priesthood" for its ministry after the Reformation. All those who were unambiguous heirs of the Reformation, by contrast, believed in the priesthood of all believers. Hence Lutherans, Calvinists, Arminians, and Anabaptists denied the existence of any distinct priestly order within the Christian community. Nevertheless, Presbyterians ordained men to the ministry of word and sacrament, seeing the responsibility as conferring a special dignity on its holders. Baptists, again like Independents, were rather more equivocal. On the one hand, they possessed ministers; but on the other, they often denied that ministers held any particular authority or status. Some tended to maintain a higher view of the ministry not unlike that of the Presbyterians, but others upheld an altogether lower estimate, contending, for example, that there was no reason why a layperson should not preside at the Lord's table. There was also, as we have seen, a difference between early General Baptists and Particular Baptists. The General Baptists alone appointed messengers with apostolic powers to supervise congregations of which they were not themselves members. But both bodies of Baptists held that, in the local church, there were only two forms of ministry, those of elder and deacon. The bishops, or overseers, of the New Testament were identified with the elders described there, and in later years they were often called ministers or pastors. The deacons concerned themselves with the more secular affairs of the church. The nature and powers of each office were nevertheless the subject of debate. Attitudes to ordination and ministerial authority changed considerably over the centuries. Despite the unanimous rejection of a separated priesthood, there was great variation in Baptist attitudes toward ministry.

The Baptist doctrine of the sacraments, that is of baptism and the Lord's supper, was also marked by a mixture of diversity and constancy. The very word "sacrament," initially used by many Baptists, was long rejected by almost all of them. They preferred the word "ordinance" on grounds that the two events were ordained by Jesus. But on the defining practice of the denomination, believer's baptism, there was greater consistency. For the first two centuries of their existence Baptists had to contend that their own pattern of initiation was right and that the pattern observed by all the other Christians they encountered was wrong. Even when other bodies observing believer's baptism arose—the Churches of Christ and the so-called Plymouth Brethren in the nineteenth century and Pentecostals in the twentieth—the Baptists were the chief champions of the practice. They generated a barrage of literature designed to vindicate their conviction that infants should not be baptized and that the proper way to administer the rite was by immersion. "For as there is one Body," wrote Edward Barber in 1641, "one Spirit, and beleevers called in one hope of calling, one Lord, one Faith: so also one dipping which was to be administered onely on those that were made disciples."[2] The chief apologetic was concerned with the candidates for baptism, the contention being that the rite ought to be administered only to those who had come to a conscious faith. That did not mean restricting it to adults, as their opponents often supposed. Baptists upheld believer's baptism, not adult baptism, and so allowed children to be immersed so long as they showed the faith that was required. The secondary theme of their defense concerned

the mode of baptism. Although, in the earliest days of the movement, baptism was administered by pouring water from a bowl, the
Baptist requirement from the 1640s onwards was that a candidate
should be totally submerged under water. The aim was to reproduce the imagery of Romans 6, where the lowering of the body into
water reproduces Christ's descent into the grave and the lifting of
the body out of it represents his resurrection. The symbolism vividly
conveyed the message of the new start in life at regeneration. Here
was an act that all were content to call an ordinance and that some
were willing to term a sacrament.

On the second ordinance, the Lord's supper or communion service, Baptists were unanimous in rejecting two alternative views.

Charles Haddon Spurgeon (1834–1892)
Baptist Preacher

They repudiated the Roman Catholic teaching of transubstantiation, the belief that the elements of bread and wine are transformed into the body and blood of Christ. They also dismissed the Lutheran idea of consubstantiation, the conviction that, although the bread and wine remain, the body and blood of Christ are actually present as well. Baptists held that, on the contrary, the physical presence of the Lord had left the earth at the ascension and did not return in the communion service. They differed among themselves, however, on the significance of the ceremony. For many it was for remembrance only. Thus John Fawcett, an influential Yorkshire Baptist minister at the end of the eighteenth century, wrote that the Lord's table is "wisely and graciously designed to revive in our minds the remembrance of him who gave his life a ransom for our souls."[3] This position, which is usually called "Zwinglian" after the Swiss reformer Huldrych Zwingli, was for long so widespread that it was supposed to be the only Baptist doctrine of communion. There was also, however, another view, derived from the other great Swiss reformer John Calvin, which made a higher estimate of what happens in the Lord's supper. On this understanding, the bread and wine are signs that convey, by the power of the Holy Spirit, something of what they signify. The elements transmit to believers the authentic presence of the Christ who died for them. They function as a seal of salvation, ratifying human faith and divine gift alike. This Reformed view was taught by Charles Haddon Spurgeon. "As surely," he wrote, "as the Lord Jesus came really as to His flesh to Bethlehem and Calvary, so surely does He come really by His Spirit to His people in the hours of their communion with Him."[4] Those Baptists who, like Fawcett, adopted the Zwinglian view usually preferred to call the Lord's supper an ordinance. Those who, like Spurgeon, took the Calvinist view were sometimes, though by no means always, willing to call it a sacrament.

EARLY BAPTIST VIEWS

The early Baptists cherished their ecclesiology. They inherited from the Reformation the conviction that it was imperative to identify the correct patterns of church polity and worship. Ecclesiastical principles were therefore of the utmost importance. It was to "a true constituted church," according to the 1678 Orthodox Creed, "and not elsewhere, [that] all persons that seek for eternal life, should gladly join themselves."[5] Applicants for baptism and membership had to present their conversion narratives to the gathered community, and only after examination were they accepted. The aim was to ensure, as far as possible, that the church contained none but the regenerate. Those who were admitted commonly subscribed a covenant setting out the doctrines of the church and binding themselves to its life. They agreed to give and receive spiritual support for each other. Each new recruit undertook, as Morgan Edwards explains of the churches of the Philadelphia Association in 1774, to behave "henceforth as a member of a spiritual body; and accountable to it, subject to its control, and no otherwise separable therefrom than by consent first had, or unreasonably refused."[6] The control was exercised through church discipline. Members acted together as a court, bringing and hearing charges against each other when informal rebukes had failed to prompt repentance. Failure to attend the Lord's table, sabbath breaking, marrying outside the community, sexual immorality, and excessive drinking were among the common forms of behavior that were subject to disciplinary hearings. Those found guilty were reprimanded, excluded from communion for a while, or, in serious matters, dismissed from church membership. Long into the nineteenth century, Baptists, for all their championing of liberty of conscience in the wider society, normally expected conformity to tight standards within their own ranks. The upholding of discipline was one of the signs of a high Baptist regard for the visible church.

In the first two centuries of their existence, Baptists also maintained a high view of the ministry. A church without pastoral leadership, they agreed, was anomalous. Ordination was a public and formal occasion, attended by ministers from adjacent churches and solemnized by the laying of hands on the candidate. Usually, in order to avoid the ordination of the unfit, a pastor would officiate in his church for some time, often long years, before being called by the church to submit to the rite. It was generally accepted that only the ordained could administer the Lord's supper. John Gill, the chief authority on church order in the eighteenth century, stipulated not only that a private member should be prohibited from presiding at the Lord's table but also that a minister should not officiate at the ceremony in a church other than his own. In the seventeenth century it had been normal for churches to have more than one elder or minister. That was John Smyth's expectation, and it was also the practice of the open-communion church at Bedford where John Bunyan was one of the pastors. The Scotch Baptists begun in 1765, led by Archibald McLean of Edinburgh, were particularly punctilious about the pastoral office. They required more than one elder in every congregation and actually experienced schism when certain churches claimed the right to hold the Lord's supper with only one elder present. Baptists in general, however, believed that ministers were not to override the supreme authority of the local church. Their powers were always subject to those of the gathered community. The wider fellowship of Baptists also had to be kept in mind. Thus, in 1792, the Philadelphia Association disapproved of a single minister who ventured to constitute a church without involvement by his brother ministers. Church planting was not a solo exercise but an enterprise requiring endorsement by other churches. Altogether there was a sense of the high status of the Christian ministry, circumscribed only by a strong awareness of the requirements of church order.

Baptism was regarded in the early days as a ceremony of great moment. The act of baptism, the Baptists supposed, could not be separated from entry to the church, for it was understood to be the biblical mode of Christian initiation. Because baptism was valued as a way of having fellowship with the Savior who died and rose again, it was held to be a distinct means of grace. Since the Particular Baptists were Calvinists, they saw baptism as an instance of the Reformed concept of a seal. "For what baptism finds," wrote Henry Lawrence in 1659, "it seals."[7] The sacrament, a word Lawrence readily used, confirmed the blessings of salvation to the believer. Anne Dutton, in the eighteenth century, continued to expound the meaning of baptism in terms of a seal. She explained that the

Almighty often gives an experience of assurance to a person receiving baptism, but that, even if that does not happen, the very performance of the rite is a form of assurance. General Baptists were no less willing to see baptism as a sacramental act. Thomas Grantham, their most sophisticated theologian, understood immersion in this way. Their Orthodox Creed of 1678 declared that the two "sacraments" are "ordinances of positive, sovereign, and holy institution," identifying the two descriptions that later generations would see as antithetical.[8] The General Baptists were also strongly attached to the laying on of hands at baptism, regarding it as fundamental to the faith. That was because, in their view, the Holy Spirit came upon believers in a special way at baptism, empowering them for service. Particular Baptists were likewise punctilious about the ceremony. Many of them persisted in the laying on of hands long into the eighteenth century and they consistently required the act of baptism to be performed properly. Thus, for example, in 1792 the Philadelphia Association resolved in answer to a query from a member church that a baptism conducted by an unordained and unbaptized administrator was invalid. The consensus of opinion among Baptists in the seventeenth and eighteenth centuries gave believer's baptism a high place in their faith and practice.

Likewise, the Lord's supper was treated as a special spiritual occasion. It has been supposed that Baptists deliberately asserted a lower view of both baptism and communion because of the wording of the 1689 London Confession. Whereas the Westminster Confession for the Presbyterians and the Savoy Declaration for the Independents used the term "sacrament," the Particular Baptists' confession, though based on the two documents of the other denominations, employed "ordinance" instead. Surely, it is suggested, the replacement of a word with higher associations by one with lower connotations must have been designed to signal a different point of view. Yet this does not seem to have been the case. The terms were used interchangeably in the seventeenth century, so that the verbal alteration did not necessarily imply a change of meaning. Since "ordinance" had previously been employed in Baptist statements of faith to indicate the divine institution of baptism, it was natural to continue to use the word without any intention to modify the doctrine being expounded. The clause of the 1689 confession relating to the Lord's supper explains that the spiritual presence of Christ is to be found at the table, a statement of the Calvinist rather than the Zwinglian view. Hercules Collins, pastor at Wapping in London, could write in 1680 that in the Lord's supper we are made "verily Partakers of his Body and Blood, through the working of the Holy Ghost."[9] So the Particular Baptists continued to uphold a high view of communion. The General Baptists were happy to use the Reformed language of "seal" about the function of communion and were actually more inclined to include "sacrament" in their discourse than the Particulars. The belief that Christ is present at the communion service, spiritually rather than physically but in a way that he is not elsewhere, remained a part of the inheritance down into the nineteenth century. That is why Spurgeon could adopt a robust view in the Victorian years. "At this table," he contended, "Jesus feeds us with His body and His blood."[10] The doctrine of communion among Baptists was as high as was their doctrine of the church, the ministry, and baptism.

DECLINE OF HIGH CHURCHMANSHIP

Gradually, however, attitudes on all four points underwent a transformation. Instead of asserting the importance of the church, the ministry, baptism, and the Lord's supper as expressions of the will of Christ and aids on the path of salvation, Baptists started to treat them as insignificant aspects of the faith. Other Christian bodies might make much of them, but Baptists started to assert that it was their honorable achievement to have perceived how marginal they were to the spiritual life. The alteration of their views was already beginning in the eighteenth century and proceeded steadily down to the early years of the twentieth century. There were at least five reasons for this change. In the first place, it was partly a result of the circumstances of debate. Since Baptists were the only champions of believer's baptism, they concentrated on defending the practice from its numerous detractors. They often felt that they did not need to make elaborate statements about the church, the ministry, or the

Lord's supper, and willingly shared the apologias composed by their fellow Protestants, especially by the Independents, with whom they were in total agreement on these points. Steadily, their grasp of first principles in these areas tended to relax. When they took up arms on behalf of believer's baptism, furthermore, they characteristically argued on specific lines. Baptist advocates concentrated on vindicating the proper subjects and the correct mode of baptism. In all the clear instances in the New Testament, they argued, those who submitted to the rite were of sufficient years to possess personal faith; and the Greek word for baptize, which was used of the dyeing of materials in the ancient world, evidently meant immersion. The Baptist controversialists therefore saw little need to discuss the significance of the ceremony. The use of terms, such as "seal," that had previously been deployed to explain believer's baptism was probably deliberately avoided because of their association with infant baptism in the Reformed tradition. So Baptists felt the need to expound the meaning of their own distinguishing rite less and less.

A second reason for the alteration was a change in the intellectual climate. The rise of the Enlightenment, as we saw in chapter 5, impinged powerfully on religion during the eighteenth century, and its legacy molded the thought of theologians, however orthodox, during the ensuing century. There was, for example, a focus on usefulness that inhibited thinking about other aspects of any given phenomenon. Thus, for Andrew Fuller, the ablest Baptist theologian at the opening of the nineteenth century, the importance of baptism lay in its utility. In his widely circulated *The Practical Uses of Christian Baptism* (1802), Fuller suggested that baptism was principally "a solemn and practical profession of the Christian religion."[11] His was a much lower estimate of its significance than that professed by earlier Baptist exponents of the rite. Francis Wayland, who served as president of Brown University, the Baptist institution in Providence, Rhode Island, from 1827 to 1855, took the same principle of expediency even further. "I see nothing in the New Testament," he wrote, "which would prevent any community of Christians from adopting any form of church government which they may esteem most for their edification."[12] That concession, remarkable from a denominational leader, undercut any defense of the unique authority of Baptist polity. Traditional attitudes to Christian ministry were equally affected. For Wayland, there was no distinction between a minister and any other servant of Christ, so that other disciples could perform any of the responsibilities of church life. And the Enlightenment cast of mind also downgraded the Lord's supper. John Clifford, the English Baptist leader of the later nineteenth century who lived on until after the First World War, argued that sacraments were "not in themselves vehicles of grace."[13] This claim, which denied much in early Baptist thinking, was a result of an exaltation of reason and a denigration of mystery. The pervasive influence of an Enlightenment style of thought led to a major shift in the Baptist stance on ecclesiastical issues.

The Evangelical Awakening, in the third place, had a similar effect. For those who had experienced the power of revival to spread the gospel, other matters, such as church order, commonly faded into insignificance. Indeed, the Evangelical and the Enlightenment approaches often intertwined and reinforced each other. John Leland, an ardent champion of religious liberty in the early American republic, served as a Baptist minister in Massachusetts. Combining the ardor of an itinerant evangelist with the empiricism of a *philosophe*, he developed an aversion to communion, writing in 1811, "for more than thirty years experiment, I have had no evidence that the bread and wine ever assisted my faith to discern the Lord's body . . . I have known no instance that God evidently blessed the ordinance for the conversion of sinners, which often attends preaching, praying, singing and baptizing."[14] The absolute priority of saving souls had other consequences. Wayland, though presiding over a university, urged that the best way of preparing preachers was on the job, through training by more senior men. A liberal education was simply not required for the task of preaching the gospel. What was needed was cooperation with others engaged in the same task. So Wayland believed in acting in unison with members of other denominations to the maximum allowable extent. Consequently, he questioned whether the restriction of communion to those who had been baptized as believers was wise. That same issue, as we have seen in chapter 6, was pursued more rigorously in England by Robert Hall. The consequence was a minimizing of the importance of baptism as a precondition for communion. Wherever there were interdenominational evangelistic efforts, the same tendency to downplay distinctive ecclesiastical points came into play. The effect was visible in the field of hymnody. Down to the early years of the nineteenth century, hymn books used by Baptists in America arranged their contents with earlier sections covering the church, baptism, and the Lord's supper, and later sections dealing with salvation and Christian experience. But from the publication of *Baptist Psalmody* for Southern Baptists in the middle of the nineteenth century onwards, the order of the sections was reversed: matters surrounding conversion took precedence over the church and its ordinances. The Evangelical upsurge led to a downgrading of church order.

A fourth reason for the lowering of Baptist convictions in the area of ecclesiology was the enduring power of anti-Catholicism. Baptists were haunted by the specter of Rome—its outward display, its addition of tradition to scripture, and its grand claims for the authority of priest, bishop, and pope—and they joined in the vigorous Protestant polemic on points in dispute. Thus, in his *Notes on the Principles and Practices of Baptist Churches* (1857), Wayland asserted, against the Roman Catholic position, "the absolute right of private judgment in all matters of religion."[15] There was particular insistence on the sacrifice of the mass being a distortion of the original simplicity of the Lord's supper. It was a fundamental error, Protestants contended, to suppose that the sacrament had an automatic effect, *ex opere operato*, in transmitting saving grace to the worshiper. From the late 1830s their fears were accentuated by the rise of Tractarianism, otherwise called the Oxford Movement, a section of opinion within the Church of England that tried to foster Catholic faith and doctrine. The national church in England, and soon its sister churches throughout the world, were apparently moving in a Romeward direction. When the most prominent leader of the Oxford Movement, John Henry Newman, went over to the Roman Catholic Church in 1845, the worst apprehensions of sound Protestants were confirmed. There were marked effects on Baptist discussions of ecclesiastical affairs. Charles Stovel, a leading English Baptist minister, argued in 1843 that the Tractarian belief that infant baptism turned babies into Christians was nonsense. The strength of his repudiation moved him to deny any transmission of divine blessing at all: "The idea of a spiritual gift in baptism, together with the whole doctrine of sacramental grace, was derived from heathen philosophy by heretics."[16] Baptists in general became so concerned to rebut Tractarian claims about the church, the ministry, and the sacraments that they retreated to much lower estimates of their importance. They downgraded the corporate dimension of religion in favor of stressing the individual, dismissed any suggestion that clergy enjoyed distinctive powers, and refused to call baptism and communion anything but ordinances. Because the Anglo-Catholic heirs of the Oxford Movement continued to set the terms of discussion on these matters, Baptists had a powerful reason for minimizing the outward and institutional expressions of the faith long into the twentieth century.

A final explanation for the transformation in Baptist ecclesiological thinking, though a more ambiguous one, resulted from a major change in wider society between the late eighteenth and the early twentieth centuries: the steady advance of respectability. As wealth increased, so did expectations, especially in large urban congregations. Men of affairs required their churches to be organized on businesslike principles, with careful management, annual reports, and audited accounts. At one Scottish Baptist church, Hillhead in Glasgow, the deacons were actually called "managers." Church meetings, where decisions were taken on policy matters, turned into business conferences, often run, especially in America, according to formal rules of debate. The aim was no longer to reproduce the pattern of the earliest church but to imitate the methods of a modern corporation. Church discipline gradually faded. Those summoned to answer charges might decline to appear, as when, in 1887, a member of Springfield Baptist Church, Augusta, Georgia, refused to respond to a summons for attending the circus. Discipline often ceased to be a matter for the whole church from around the middle of the nineteenth century, and moral problems that once would have called for formal censure were now referred to a standing committee or else to the pastor and deacons. A Baptist mark of the church was disappearing. At the same time, the ministry was increasingly treated as a profession. From around the middle of the nineteenth century, Baptist ministers began to use the title "Reverend." Prosperous congregations required and could afford well-educated ministers. Training for the ministry therefore became more academic, with new colleges and seminaries being formed. Between 1870 and 1900 the number of English Baptist ministers with college training increased by a fifth. By the 1930s over a third of Northern Baptist ministers in the United States had received a seminary education. There were still, especially in the American South, many rural congregations, both black and white, led by men without any formal qualifications, but the trend was toward professionalization. The effect was often to raise the level of respect for the minister and, in that sense, to resist the tendency to a lower churchmanship. The imitation of secular professions, however, generally meant that the new breed of minister was disinclined to adopt high views of church or sacraments. He liked efficiency rather than display. Respectability tended to reinforce the decay of earlier Baptist ecclesiastical convictions.

Low Views and the Sacramental Revival

The result of these various developments was that, by the early twentieth century, Baptists held almost uniformly low views on church issues. The individual's personal experience of Christ was what mattered to conservatives, liberals, and centrists alike. The champion of the center among Southern Baptists, Edgar Y. Mullins, formulated the core of Baptist witness as the "competency of the soul in religion."[17] Each person, he meant, enjoys the possibility of access to God through Christ. Although Mullins refused to identify this principle with individualism on the grounds that human beings interact with each other in church, industry, and state, the effect of his principle, which was extremely influential in North America, was to confirm the existing low estimate of the significance of the church. In 1935 William R. McNutt, professor of practical theology at Crozer Theological Seminary, in adopting Mullins' formula, deduced that a man "has no inescapable need of church to bring him salvation or mediate to him divine grace."[18] The individual's experience did not require artificial aid, and so baptism and communion were not seen as means of grace. Baptism was nothing but "an act of obedience symbolizing the believer's faith."[19] The Lord's supper, according to Augustus H. Strong in 1907, was a symbol of a previous state of grace. "It has itself no regenerating and sanctifying power."[20] The negative tone of these comments was typical and could be replicated from members of the denomination in virtually every land. Baptists were much surer of what the ordinances were not than of what they were.

Low churchmanship meant a lack of uniformity on questions of church membership, authority, and ministry. Pragmatic considerations rather than theological convictions prevailed in the ordering of the church. In England, where the practice of open communion discussed in chapter 6 had triumphed in most quarters by the twentieth century, a high proportion of Baptists too the further step of adopting open membership. Encouraged by increasing links with other Free Churches in the earlier part of the century and also with Anglicans in its later part, many Baptist churches allowed any professing Christians to join, whatever their mode of baptism or, even, in some cases, without any form of the rite. A few churches in America also took this path by the early years of the twenty-first century. Again, the relation between church leaders and ordinary members was rarely fixed by theological criteria. The heritage of church meetings where members discussed and determined policies was often cherished in Britain, but in America congregations usually became increasingly willing to hand almost all responsibilities to the pastoral staff, the deacons, the elders (where they existed), or some combination of the three. In the huge congregations of several thousands, or even tens of thousands, that emerged during the second half of the century, collective decision-making would have been a virtual impossibility. Senior pastors had to learn management techniques drawn from business, and sometimes became ecclesiastical entrepreneurs. The understanding of the ministry underwent significant evolution too. In 1944 Arthur Dakin, principal of Bristol

Baptist College, contended that, among Baptists, the only true ministers were those in pastoral charge of a congregation, but he was answered by Ernest Payne, soon to be general secretary of the Baptist Union, who argued that ordination was for life. Whether or not an individual was in pastoral charge, Payne held, did not alter a calling to the ministry. The rising standards of professional training, which required ministers to possess a body of specialist theological knowledge, helped ensure that Payne's view prevailed. Similar professionalization continued apace in the United States, though attitudes to the meaning of ordination remained fluid there. Alongside the prosperous megachurches there were many small congregations that could not afford a full-time pastor and so were served by ordained ministers who also held a secular job. Without firm principles to serve as a guide, the theory and practice of ministry varied enormously.

The prevailing low churchmanship was challenged in Britain by a sacramental revival. The pioneer was Henry Wheeler Robinson, principal of Regent's Park College in England. As a biblical scholar, he became dissatisfied with the conventional understanding of baptism as merely an act of obedience. In the New Testament, he wrote in 1922, "water-baptism is the outward and visible sign of an inward and spiritual baptism of the Holy Spirit."[21] Consequently, he developed the case that believer's baptism ought to be considered a sacramental means of grace. After the Second World War, a generation of younger ministers adopted similar views and published, in 1959, a collection of essays entitled *Christian Baptism*. The most thorough defender of the position, George Beasley-Murray, principal of Spurgeon's College, elaborated the argument on the basis of detailed biblical exposition in his *Baptism in the New Testament* (1962). Several of his contemporaries developed a similar sacramental approach to the Lord's supper, and usually added a high understanding of the church and the ministry. It was not just biblical scholarship that lay behind this movement, for interdenominational influence was also at work. The Genevan movement, a Congregational resurgence from the late 1930s, emphasized the doctrines of church, ministry, and sacraments in a way that acted as a stimulus. The liturgical movement, which spread from the Church of England, pointed Baptists toward worship practices associated with a higher churchmanship. And ecumenical contacts multiplied in the years after the Second World War. A number of Baptists now engaged with the champions of the Anglo-Catholic tradition not as foes but as friends, absorbing their sacramental viewpoint. As denominational loyalties slackened in the postwar world, so many Baptist churches found members molded by other traditions in their ranks. From the 1960s the charismatic movement brought a new willingness to experiment in worship and to develop visual vehicles for the gospel. The outcome of all these developments was a set of attitudes much more sympathetic to higher ecclesiastical views than in the recent past.

Similar convictions rarely appeared outside Britain until much later. There were, it is true, occasional writers who expounded a more sacramental point of view. There was a German parallel to the new British statements on the significance of baptism in Johannes Schneider's *Baptism and the Church in the New Testament* (1957). Even in America, where the belief that the ordinances were nothing but acts of obedience prevailed most strongly, there were occasional dissenting voices. Thus Fred D. Howard, a Southern Baptist theologian, argued in a book of 1966 that the Lord's supper was more than a symbol, since Christ was present there in a unique way. In the United States, however, important stirrings were deferred until the end of the twentieth century. In 1997 a Baptist manifesto called "Re-Envisioning Baptist Identity" (which will call for further examination in chapter 15) was issued. Acknowledging "the church catholic," a revised version of the manifesto affirmed baptism, preaching, and the Lord's table "as powerful signs that seal God's faithfulness in Christ and express our response of awed gratitude rather than as mechanical rituals or mere symbols."[22] The inclusion of preaching alongside baptism and the Lord's table marked the document out as original thinking, and yet the use of the word "seal" pointed to an affiliation with earlier doctrines of the sacraments. A cascade of titles from the early twenty-first century provides historical evidence that backs up the claim of those associated with the manifesto that they were reviving traditional Baptist ways of thinking rather than diverging into new paths. Two of these works, published in 2003 and 2008, were provocatively called *Baptist Sacramentalism*. They were not, however, part of the mainstream of North American Baptist opinion about ecclesiastical affairs. A sermon at an Oklahoma City Baptist church in 2009 was far more representative. It set out the various views on the Lord's supper, entirely rejecting not only transubstantiation and consubstantiation, but also the Reformed belief in the spiritual presence of Christ. The Baptist view, the preacher urged, was that communion was purely symbolical. That stance, however, was under greater assault than at any point over two centuries.

The attitude of the Baptists to ecclesiology, therefore, altered greatly over the years of their existence. There were, it is true, certain constants: they upheld gathered churches of believers, rejected priestly conceptions of ministry, argued for believer's baptism by immersion, and denied the physical presence of Christ at the Lord's supper. In the early years, inheriting the conviction of the Reformation that church order must be exact, Baptists required members to be subject to church discipline, gave a respected place to their ministers, and held that the sacraments were distinct means of grace. There was, however, a gradual lowering of their normal estimate of the significance of each during the eighteenth and nineteenth centuries. The terms of debate with their opponents and the intellectual atmosphere of the Enlightenment sapped the high doctrines of their earlier years. So did the revivalism stemming from the Evangelical Awakening, the hostility of Baptists to Roman Catholic and Anglo-Catholic claims, and the rising respectability of their churches. By the twentieth century, the Baptists tended to lay so much stress on personal experience that they had little time for questions of ecclesiology, allowing great variations in church administration and patterns of ministry. In Britain, however, there emerged a sacramental revival, albeit more scholarly than popular, and, by the opening of the twenty-first century, a similar phenomenon was emerging in North America. So there was a definite trajectory in Baptist views on the church, ministry, and sacraments. The members of the first Baptist bodies favored high views of church order, but later generations came to adopt the simpler convictions that still prevail. Only in recent years did some members of the denomination turn again to a more sacramental point of view. It is therefore not the case, as is often supposed, that Baptists have adopted a uniformly low stance on these matters. It is true that, for many years, they were predominantly concerned to rebut the lofty ecclesiastical claims of others. At their origins and again in the recent past, however, they produced champions of a distinctly high churchmanship.

FURTHER READING

Cross, Anthony R. *Baptism and the Baptists: Theology and Practice in Twentieth-Century Britain*. Carlisle: Paternoster, 2000.

Cross, Anthony R., and Philip E. Thompson, eds. *Baptist Sacramentalism*. Carlisle: Paternoster, 2003.

Fowler, Stanley K. *More than a Symbol: The British Baptist Recovery of Baptismal Sacramentalism*. Carlisle: Paternoster, 2002.

Hudson, Winthrop S., ed. *Baptist Concepts of the Church*. Philadelphia: Judson Press, 1959.

Payne, Ernest A. *The Fellowship of Believers: Baptist Thought and Practice Yesterday and Today*. Enlarged ed. London: Carey Kingsgate, 1952.

Walker, Michael. *Baptists at the Table: The Theology of the Lord's Supper amongst English Baptists in the Nineteenth Century*. Didcot, Oxfordshire: Baptist Historical Society, 1992.

Chapter 12

BAPTISTS AND RELIGIOUS LIBERTY

"Baptists," declared George Truett in 1920, "have one consistent record concerning liberty throughout all their long and eventful history." Truett, the pastor of First Baptist Church, Dallas, had been chosen by the Southern Baptist Convention to deliver a speech on the east steps of the Capitol building during its meetings in Washington, D.C., on the theme of "Baptists and religious liberty." It was a grand occasion, there was an audience of many thousands, and the address was magnificently delivered. Truett eloquently voiced the conviction of his fellow Baptists that they had always been in the vanguard of calls for freedom, civil as well as religious. They had been the supreme exemplars of dedication to the separation of church and state. Baptists, Truett asserted, were the traditional champions of "absolute liberty."[1] Truett's claim, however, requires careful evaluation. The notion that Baptists had been rigorous in their demands for freedom of conscience from the start of their existence calls for scrutiny. It is true that their stance represented a major break with the long tradition, dominant since the time of the emperor Constantine in the fourth century, that any Christian ruler should try to promote true religion within his realms, by the sword

197

if necessary. Baptists did not relish the state enforcement of a particular pattern of belief and practice. Yet how scrupulous they were in their early years in upholding the rightness of religious neutrality by the authorities needs investigation. Again, the issue arises of how careful Baptists were in subsequent periods to take a firm stance on the avoidance of state interference with private convictions. They may have been inclined to favor conscientious dissent, but were they as wholly consistent as Truett believed? The attitude of Baptists to questions of religious liberty may turn out to have been rather more varied than he supposed.

RELIGIOUS LIBERTY FOR ALL

At the time in the early seventeenth century when Baptists emerged, the consensus, even among Puritans, was that right-minded rulers held a responsibility to ensure that their subjects worshiped correctly. When John Smyth reached separatist convictions, he did not immediately abandon this belief in the powers of "godly magistrates." In Smyth's *Paterne of True Prayer* (1605), he asserted that "the Magistrates should cause all men to worship the true God, or else punish them with imprisonment, confiscation of goods, or death as the qualitie of the cause requireth." Religious toleration was unthinkable, since it was "next unto Anarchie."[2] Even when, in 1609, Smyth moved on to Baptist beliefs, he did not repudiate these views, but expressed himself equivocally on the role of the magistrate. It was only later, when he was applying for membership in the Mennonite church, that he altered his opinions. By that time he shared the view of the Mennonites that the magistrate was disqualified by his office from membership in the church of Christ. There should be no coercion in the state, and the civil authorities who practiced it were showing their repudiation of Christian allegiance. It was left to Smyth's colleague, Thomas Helwys, the leader of the rump of Baptists who declined to approach the Mennonites for membership and returned to England, to expound a robust view of freedom of conscience. Helwys recognized the need for the civil authorities to wield the sword of punishment and was willing to accept magistrates as church members. But, as he explained in his

Short Declaration of the Mistery of Iniquity (1612), he believed that religion should be free from any interference by the agents of the king. It was not just that his own company of Baptists should be allowed to worship in peace. Rather, since the king was responsible only for earthly affairs, all were to enjoy liberty of conscience: "Let them be heretiks, Turcks, Jewes or whatsoever, it appertynes not to the earthly power to punish them in the least measure."[3] Here was a resounding declaration of universal toleration, probably the first to be written in England.

Helwys was not alone in expounding a principled view of acceptance for all religions. His fellow General Baptists Leonard Busher and Thomas Murton wrote in a similar vein over the next few years. The premises for the theory of toleration in all three writers were resolutely theological. There was, they argued, a spiritual realm alongside the secular kingdom, so that the authority of the civil power had its limits. The sole lord in the spiritual realm was Christ, so that the state must not intrude on his sphere by trying to enforce any form of religion. The soul was directly responsible to the Almighty: human beings, according to Helwys, "must stand themselves before the iudgment of God to answere for themselves."[4] True faith was, in any case, something that could not be generated by coercion. If the state tried to ensure religious conformity, it would only, as John Murton put it, "compel men to be hypocrites."[5] As General Baptists, these writers believed that all might accept the gospel. By persecuting those of different beliefs, the authorities were alienating those who might attain the truth. Members of other faiths must be allowed to live unharassed so that evangelism could turn their hearts to God. On these grounds, Busher was one of the first to call for Jews, who had been excluded from England since the thirteenth century, to be readmitted to the country. If there were freedom to pursue truth, this group of men argued, believers would explore the Bible more and so gain a fuller understanding. That would enable Christians to grow together and attain greater unity. The General Baptist authors also contended for toleration on the ground that it would bring the benefits of social peace and commercial success, but their main case was based on their fundamental convictions about the nature of religion. The kingship of Christ over conscience allowed no rival authority.

The stance of these earliest Baptists was reproduced in the next generation. Edward Barber, a leading General Baptist, wrote straightforwardly in 1641 that "no man ought to be forced in matters of religion."[6] Richard Overton, a coreligionist of Barber's, expressed the view in 1645 that Turks, Jews, pagans, and infidels should all be permitted to lead unmolested lives. Overton was one of the ideologues of the Leveller movement who, in the tumult of military rule at the end of the 1640s, urged an extensive program of civil liberties, including a wide franchise, the right to silence, and legal representation. Overton was carrying his defense of freedom from the religious into a wider political sphere. Nor was the case confined to the General Baptists. Samuel Richardson, who had been a signatory of the 1644 Particular Baptist confession, published *The Necessity of Toleration in Matters of Religion* (1647). The Presbyterians, now dominant in the place of the Anglicans, were strongly attached to the principle of enforced uniformity in religion. Richardson challenged their approach as cruel and destructive. "Is there no better cure of the pain of the head," he asked, "than beating out one's brains?"[7] The weapons of Christians, he argued, should be spiritual, not carnal. They might legitimately excommunicate for religious errors, but not impose civil penalties. Truth did not need the sword to make it prevail. Another Particular Baptist, Thomas Collier, took a step further than any General Baptists in formulating the breadth of toleration. Others had urged the acceptance of heretics and adherents of other religions, but in 1648 Collier called for outright atheists to be exempted from punishment for their opinions. At a time when it was supposed that belief in a deity was essential to ensure moral behavior, his appeal was an extremely radical stance. So, many Baptists of both main sections in England were staunch advocates of religious liberty.

The greatest champion of the application of the principle in the American colonies was Roger Williams, the founder of the first Baptist church in the New World. His book *The Bloudy Tenent of Persecution*, though published in London in 1644, arose from circumstances in Massachusetts during the previous decade. Williams had been critical of the magistrates for enforcing religious conformity there, and, having been banished from the colony, fled to create new settlements outside its bounds in what later became, under his leadership, Rhode Island. Williams' book responded to the case made out by John Cotton, a prominent Massachusetts Puritan minister, for the right of the magistrate to intervene in the affairs of the church for its welfare. Williams contended that, on the contrary, truth and peace could be maintained only by the severance of the magistracy from church issues. The church had suffered ever since the time of Constantine from its alliance with the state. By contrast with Israel in Old Testament times, the New Testament church was only spiritual. "And as the church," he wrote, "hath no temporal power over the magistrate . . . so the magistrate hath no spiritual power over the church."[8] The parable of the tares that were allowed to grow until the end of time showed that there must be no attempt to root out false religion in the present age. The work was a powerful plea for full liberty of conscience through separation of church and state. It cannot, however, be claimed as a Baptist book. Williams, as we have seen, regretted his adoption of believer's baptism in 1639 within four months of the event and severed his relations with the church he had founded. *The Bloudy Tenent* was based on his new views as a seeker. Religious liberty, he believed, would help usher in the millennial age, when fresh apostles would be raised up to create true churches. It is true that Williams' book widely influenced Baptists in his own and later days, but the text cannot legitimately be used to illustrate authentic Baptist views on its themes.

It also has to be said that other claims made about early Baptist views on religious liberty have often been exaggerated. For one thing, Baptists had been anticipated by others in many of their standpoints. Most Anabaptists, including Menno Simons himself, had rejected all use of force in religion. In the sixteenth century, humanists such as Erasmus and political theorists in the French Wars of Religion had argued for a measure of religious toleration; the Netherlands had even put the principle into practice, which was why English separatists emigrated to that country. Again, when Baptists were expounding their ideas, they were not alone. During the 1640s certain Independents such as John Goodwin, together with other radical groups, took the same line as many Baptists about the desirability of complete toleration. The ground of the Baptists' case had nothing to do with what made them distinctive—their adoption of believer's baptism. Rather, their case was erected on what they shared with other radicals, the wider contention that there must be an imitation of the early church. Some of the Baptists, furthermore, were not in favor of universal toleration. John Tombes, the chief Particular Baptist debater during the 1650s, for instance, did not want to extend toleration to Roman Catholics, worshipers of false gods, revilers of Christ, or deniers of the scriptures. Even Thomas Collier retreated from his previous endorsement of the acceptance of atheists, in order to argue, in 1659, that magistrates could punish blasphemy. There was, in fact, a general tendency in the later seventeenth century for the theme of religious liberty for others to fade from Baptist discourse. The Particular Baptist confession of 1677 recommended granting liberty only to opinions not contrary to scripture, and the General Baptist Orthodox Creed of a year later also objected solely to the imposition of religious obligations not found in the Bible. Baptists under persecution in these years demanded rights for themselves and their fellow Dissenters, but little for others. There was no enduring insistence on the universality of freedom of conscience.

The Toleration Act of 1689 introduced a fresh era for all Dissenters from the Church of England. The period of active persecution ended and a time of relative peace ensued. This did not mean that Baptists, along with their fellow Dissenters, could enjoy their right to worship in total security. During the reign of Queen Anne at the opening of the eighteenth century, it seemed likely that they might be subject to fresh restrictions by act of parliament, but, from the accession of George I in 1714, the greater tolerance of the Hanoverian dynasty made their position more assured. Nevertheless, legislation from the previous century was still in force and could be activated by hostile magistrates. The Test and Corporation Acts that limited membership of town councils to those willing to show their allegiance to the Church of England by taking the sacrament in the parish church were still sometimes put into operation. In the countryside Dissenters were liable to pay tithe, a proportion of their agricultural income, for the support of the local clergyman. In 1732 the congregations of the capital therefore formed the Protestant Dissenting Deputies, a board of representatives designed to keep watch over the rights of Dissenters. It maintained an active vigilance on behalf of Presbyterians, Independents, and Baptists throughout the country, protesting when privileges were invaded and taking cases to law when necessary. In these circumstances, Baptists, like the other denominations, were normally content so long as they remained free to worship without interference. They did not assert broad claims about liberty for all, nor did they agitate for the separation of church and state. Their watchword was "civil and religious liberty," by which they meant merely that they desired the preservation of toleration and a reduction, rather than an increase, in the powers of the crown. By the 1780s they felt strong enough to call for the repeal of the Test and Corporation Acts, but they did not achieve their objective until 1828. In England during the long eighteenth century, the largest dreams of Baptists were for a wider degree of toleration. A more comprehensive version of religious liberty was not on the agenda.

SEPARATION OF CHURCH AND STATE

In the colonies there was great diversity. In Rhode Island, a group of settlements created by the efforts of Roger Williams, there was complete freedom of religious practice; the Quaker colony of Pennsylvania approximated to the same policy. In New England generally, however, there was official support for Congregationalism, and in Virginia the Church of England held similar privileges to those it enjoyed in the Old World. Massachusetts gave limited toleration in 1691, but Baptists were still compelled to pay taxes for the support of the Congregational churches or else face seizure of their goods or imprisonment. In 1729 they were granted exemption from the taxes, but they were still required to obtain certificates to show that they were bona fide members of their own churches. The Great

Awakening broke the mold of the system. The Separates emerging from the revival, both Congregational and Baptist, had no right to the certificates and so were liable to be harassed into payment; at the same time, they resented having to pay for the maintenance of Old Light churches that did not preach the gospel. Tensions rose until, in 1767, the Warren Association that united Regular and Separate Baptists appointed a Grievance Committee to help those who were unfairly taxed, harassed, or jailed. It was this committee led by Isaac Backus that in 1773 took the decisive step of calling on the members of association churches to refuse either to pay the taxes or to complete certificates and then to suffer the consequences. Their Congregational fellow subjects were protesting against royal autocracy in the events leading up to the American Revolution, but seemed unaware that they were trampling on the rights of the Baptists. In the excitement of the times, the Baptist campaign of civil disobedience led to a withering of the certificate system. Backus had already in 1768 voiced the conviction that man-made laws about ecclesiastical affairs are contrary to the divine law. Now, in a memorial to the first Continental Congress in 1774, he elaborated the same principle: "As the kingdom of Christ is not of this world, and religion is a concern between God and the soul with which no human authority can intermeddle . . . we claim and expect the liberty of worshiping God according to our consciences."[9] Although he quoted Roger Williams, Backus did not go so far as the earlier writer. Backus still approved of compulsory public worship, state-sponsored days of fasting and thanksgiving, and the exclusion of Roman Catholics from public offices. Nevertheless, he was once more asserting the separation of church and state as a matter of theological principle. Backus had once been content with toleration, but here was a call for freedom of religion as a right.

In Virginia, Baptists played an equally prominent part in the quest for religious liberty. To the alarm of the Anglican gentry, the Separate Baptists grew spectacularly in the colony. From 1768 the response was a campaign of arrests, imprisonments, and assaults, especially against those who failed to obtain a license to preach. The first General Association of Separate Baptists in 1771 asserted that they needed no license because they possessed a "general license given them by King Jesus."[10] A measure of toleration was granted in 1772 and, four years later, the Virginia Declaration of Rights guaranteed the free exercise of religion, but Baptists demanded unrestricted liberty to preach the gospel. In the wake of the War for Independence, when the Virginia legislature considered a bill for paying teachers of all denominations by a general assessment, the Baptists were roused into mass petitioning. The outcome was that, in 1786, the Virginia Statute for Religious Freedom, framed by Thomas Jefferson, passed into law, establishing full liberty of worship as a natural right. In the Baptist agitation, John Leland, who united the zeal of the denomination with much of the rationalism of Jefferson, came to the fore. In Leland's *The Rights of Conscience Inalienable* (1791), he argued

John Leland (1754–1841)
Baptist Pastor and Advocate of Religious Liberty

for a strict separation between church and state. "Government," he wrote, "has no more to do with the religious opinions of men, than it has with the principles of mathematics."[11] Unusually for his day, and going much further than Backus, Leland pursued the principle to secular conclusions: there should be no publicly declared days of fasting or thanksgiving; there should be no exemption for ministers from taxation; conversely, there should be no public tax to pay chaplains; mail could be handled by the post office on Sunday; and Christians should not petition against dueling, lotteries, or alcohol. Leland was a rigorous proponent of the view that organized religion and public life must stay entirely separate.

Establishment of religion, the union of church and state, nevertheless endured into the nineteenth century on both sides of the Atlantic. The First Amendment to the Constitution of the United States, in 1791, prohibited legislation respecting the establishment of religion, but only by the federal Congress. State governments remained free to involve themselves in religion. In that year, twelve out of the fourteen states imposed religious tests for public office, Rhode Island and Virginia being the only exceptions. Five states gave financial support to Christian ministers, an arrangement that continued in Vermont until 1807, in Connecticut until 1818, in New Hampshire until 1819, in Maine until 1820, and in Massachusetts until 1833. In each case, Baptists, with Leland sometimes prominent among them, took part in the final stages of pressure for disestablishment. So, by 1833 there was no established religion in the United States. Thereafter, members of the denomination normally treated the separation of church and state as a fundamental Baptist conviction. Although English Baptists watched transatlantic developments with envy, their concern in the early years of the nineteenth century was with their practical grievances rather than with disestablishment. They had no form of legal registration for their children, since infant baptism in the established church fulfilled that function for others, and the parish clergy could refuse burial to their babies since infants were unbaptized. In addition, like other Dissenters, Baptists had to marry in a parish church; they could not use their own style of worship at burials in parish graveyards; they could not enter the

University of Oxford or graduate from the University of Cambridge; and they were subject to compulsory church rates for the upkeep of Anglican buildings. Gradually, as the century wore on, most of these disabilities were redressed. In the wake of parliamentary reform in 1832, frustration over their grievances induced some Dissenters to demand that the Church of England should be severed from the state. In 1838 the Baptist Union resolved that church establishments were "a violation of the law of Christ and the rights of conscience."[12] When, in 1844, there was created a pressure group to demand disestablishment, the union sent official delegates, and thereafter, as in America and elsewhere in the English-speaking world, disestablishment became for a time a normal feature of a Baptist's political beliefs. Partly through the pressure of Baptists and other Nonconformists, the Anglican Church was disestablished in Ireland (1870) and in Wales (1920) but never in England. The principle of the separation of church and state had not always been part of the Baptist credo, but it had turned into one of their chief convictions.

CHRISTIAN NATIONS AND RELIGIOUS MINORITIES

At the same time, the ambition of nineteenth-century Baptists was to turn their lands into Christian nations. There was, as we have seen, pressure on local and national authorities to adopt measures that would make the people less cruel, profligate, violent, and drunken. Some of the policies raised serious questions about the relations of church and state. It was widely assumed in Britain, America, and other lands of British emigration that a Christian nation must be Protestant, and so Baptists were found as earnest advocates of measures to contain Roman Catholicism. In Britain, for example, they participated enthusiastically in the outcry of 1850–1851 against the restoration of the Catholic hierarchy in England and Wales, and supported a bill that prohibited Catholic bishops from taking the titles of existing Anglican sees, an action that might be regarded as infringing on Catholic freedom. Again in the 1880s, when an atheist, Charles Bradlaugh, was repeatedly returned to parliament, Baptists were divided. Many, including even the redoubtable champion of the faith Charles Haddon Spurgeon, held that it was a matter of civic principle that Bradlaugh should be allowed to take his seat; others, however, believed that an unbeliever had no place in the nation's counsels. The issue of how far the state should be asked to uphold distinctively Christian principles was also raised by the sabbath question. Baptists were strong believers in the sacredness of the first day of the week, but they had qualms about how far they should ask the public authorities to enforce the Christian day of rest. The tension is evident in a resolution of the Philadelphia Baptist Association in 1815. The Presbyterians had asked the Baptists to join them in securing legislation against the profanation of the Lord's day, but the Baptists declined because they saw "every exercise of civil power to enforce the institutions of religion, as the assumption of an illegitimate prerogative." Nevertheless they recommended that, since sabbath desecration was "detrimental to the best interests of civil society," members of their churches should "seek the redress of this grievance by every means arising to them from the social compact which may not infringe on religious liberty."[13] This imprecise advice betrays something of the embarrassment at the clash of two principles to which Baptists were deeply attached—sabbatarianism and religious liberty.

An issue that perennially raised similar difficulties was education. Training the young was a traditional responsibility of the church, but it was also increasingly becoming a concern of the state as the nineteenth century wore on. Baptist parents wanted their children to receive Christian training, but how far could schools funded by the public legitimately provide it? When the state first provided schools in England in 1870, the question of the religious content of the curriculum was deeply divisive. The Church of England, as the established church, wanted its own doctrines taught, but Baptists did not. Some of them who were most committed to the religious neutrality of the state argued that, since it was now entering the educational field, religion must be removed from schools altogether. The curriculum must become wholly secular, leaving Christian training to church and home. By 1873 it was supposed that a large majority of English Baptists accepted that solution. In the Australian colony of Victoria, by contrast, the predominant Baptist position was that the Bible must at all costs be reintroduced into schools. There it was banished by an act of 1872 that established secular education. Catholics, who did not want Bible teaching for fear of a Protestant bias, joined with secularists to keep the schools Bible-free. Baptists, however, were among the most vocal in demanding a place for the Bible in the classroom. In both lands a minority in the denomination took the opposite point of view, and subsequently English opinion swung more in favor of Bible teaching, but for a while Baptists in England and Victoria adopted diametrically contrasting policies on how school, state, and religion should intertwine. In America it was generally assumed that the scriptures would have a place in public schools and that the instruction would be congruent. Thus when, in 1910, a history book containing "unscriptural and anti-scriptural statements" was used in Texas schools, there was a formal protest resolution by the state's Baptists on the ground that disbelief in the Bible should not be paid for by the taxes of Christian citizens.[14] For all the belief in separation of church and state in America, there was often the least anxiety there about the potential infringement of the principle in the schools.

It was easier to recognize and deplore infringements of religious liberty abroad. As Baptists gradually became rooted in lands beyond the English-speaking world, instances of persecution and harassment began to arise. In the middle years of the nineteenth century, Edward Steane, secretary in Britain of the Baptist Union and the Evangelical Alliance simultaneously, gave regular publicity to cases in continental Europe where churches were closed or the Bible prohibited. In the twentieth century, problems of this kind multiplied. During the interwar period, James Henry Rushbrooke, acting from 1928 as first general secretary of the Baptist World Alliance, was an indefatigable defender of the Baptists of eastern Europe. The resistance of the Romanian authorities in church and state to the rise of the Baptists in their land occupied much of his time, but in the 1930s the persecution of the Russian Baptists under Stalin also loomed large. In 1933, for example, when the United States first gave diplomatic recognition to Soviet Russia, the Baptist World Alliance executive committee fruitlessly urged President Roosevelt to use his influence to mitigate the sufferings of believers in that land. Nor were Baptists solely concerned for the welfare of their coreligionists. In 1905, for example, Texas Baptists resolved their horror at the persecution of the Jews in Russia, then still under the Czarist regime: the Jews should be "left to the quiet exercise of their heaven born right to worship God according to their own consciences."[15] In later decades the Baptist World Alliance acted as the chief sounding board for resolutions on questions in this field. At Stockholm in 1975, for instance, it committed Baptists to refrain from seeking privileges that might infringe on full religious liberty for others. The defense of freedom of conscience as a universal value was often more understood in international affairs than at home.

A great difficulty for the Baptists of America was to disentangle Christianity from patriotism. The two were closely intertwined in the civil religion that marked the United States. An aura of religiosity surrounded the officers and institutions of state, making it hard to see when they were biased toward causes that Baptists approved but others deplored. There was, for example, a great deal of resentment, especially among Jews, about the enforcement of Sunday legislation, and yet in 1921 the Baptists of New York, the center of Jewish settlement, recommended measures to preserve "the American Sabbath."[16] This request was hardly intended to endorse freedom of conscience. Truett's speech of the previous year on the Capitol steps showed traces of civil religion when it praised religious liberty simultaneously as "the chiefest contribution that America has thus far made to civilization" and as "pre-eminently a Baptist contribution."[17] The interwar period was a time when it seemed easy to assume a harmony between American and Baptist values. The secretary of state to Warren G. Harding, himself the first Baptist president (though usually regarded as a poor president), was Charles E. Hughes, a leading Baptist layman who went on, in 1930, to become Chief Justice of the Supreme Court. In 1921 the demand was so great for seats in Calvary Baptist Church, Washington, D.C., where both men worshiped, that tickets had to be issued. As chief justice, Hughes was particularly tender toward personal freedoms generally and religious consciences in particular. The culmination of the convergence of American and Baptist principles was the adoption, in 1939, of an American Baptist Bill of Rights, endorsed by the American, National, and Southern conventions. Its mastermind, Rufus W. Weaver, went on to establish a committee that represented all three conventions to act as a lobby for Baptist concerns. It moved to Washington in 1946 and, four years later, became the Baptist Joint Committee on Public Affairs. Its task, as its first secretary, Joseph M. Dawson, conceived it, was to act as a voice for religious liberty. The Joint Committee was designed to stand at once for Baptist convictions and the ideals of the nation.

During the 1930s and 1940s the great threat to the liberty that America and Baptists prized so much appeared to come from Rome. Catholics were seeking public financial aid for parochial schools and there were rumors of an intention to open diplomatic relations with the Vatican. These were the twin targets of Baptist protest in these years. In 1948, however, there was a legal case that pointed to a new phase of church-state relations in the United States. The Supreme Court ruled in *McCollum v. Board of Education* that religious instruction in public schools when children were released from classes was unconstitutional. The Baptist Joint Committee had backed the plaintiff, allegedly an atheist, whose complaint was vindicated, but many Baptists objected. To them the provision of good Christian teaching outside ordinary classes but in school time seemed a wise policy, not an infringement on liberties. The danger in this instance and in an increasing flow of similar cases was thought to be from rising secular forces. Dawson regretted the emergence of the new attitude among Baptists. Protestants, he argued in 1953, who were clamoring for their own type of religious instruction through the public schools were no better than Catholics. They were "assailing the American system under the charge that it is promoting secularism, a new kind of devil."[18] The perceived dangers of secularism were to grow. Meanwhile, however, the Joint Committee continued to stand for the divorce of religion from public support. It opposed continuing Catholic pressure to gain public money for parochial schools, deplored the increasing efforts of educational administrators to secure funding for institutions that remained denominational, and in 1962–1963 endorsed Supreme Court rulings that organized classroom prayer and Bible reading must cease in public schools. During the 1960s the Joint Committee resisted demands for a constitutional amendment to allow prayer and Bible reading to return to the classroom. Like Baptist bodies generally, it maintained the position of strict separation between church and state.

A large volume of rank-and-file discontent with this stance came to the surface from the late 1970s in the New Christian Right. The election of Jimmy Carter, another Baptist president, in 1976 raised hopes of more distinctively Christian policies in the White House. Some expected, in particular, that, after the *Roe v. Wade* decision of the Supreme Court in 1973 that struck down laws against abortion, there would be an effort to protect the life of the unborn fetus. When Carter's inaction on this and other fronts proved disappointing, a mood arose in conservative circles that organized political efforts were required. Jerry Falwell, an Independent Baptist, became the leader of Moral Majority, a pressure group designed to reinstate family values in public affairs. Falwell was prepared to change the First Amendment so that the federal government could promote religious causes. W. A. Criswell of First Baptist Church, Dallas, announced in 1984 that the separation of church and state was "the figment of some infidel's imagination."[19] The Southern Baptist Convention, which in 1982 endorsed President Reagan's proposal to reinstate school prayer, was shifting its position on religious liberty. Its spokesman on ethics and religious liberty in the 1990s, Richard Land, distanced himself from the New Christian Right, insisting that he still believed in the separation of church and state. Equally, however, he stood apart from the strict separationist viewpoint still backed by the Baptist Joint Committee in Washington, and argued instead for what became known as accommodationism. It was legitimate, according to accommodationists, for the state to respond to claims by religious groups for exceptional treatment beyond what was required by the First Amendment in order to ensure the "free exercise" of religion. The new position of the Southern Baptists was so divergent from that maintained by other Baptist groups that, in

1992, it left the Joint Committee. Critics accused the convention of abandoning the Baptist heritage of religious liberty altogether; its defenders contended that they were adjusting to the new circumstances in which the threat to the welfare of true religion came from secular humanism.

Clearly the path of the Baptist profession of religious liberty has been more tortuous than has often been portrayed. The earliest General Baptists did compose eloquent pleas for freedom from state interference in religion, making a remarkable break with the overwhelming tradition of Christian teaching since Constantine. Particular Baptists shared the conviction that toleration was essential in public policy. Roger Williams, however, was not a Baptist when he eloquently championed religious liberty, Baptists were neither first nor alone in their stance, and many of them qualified their defense of freedom in spiritual affairs. They ceased in the later seventeenth century to advocate claims on behalf of others, instead concentrating, after 1689, on ensuring the preservation of the toleration they had been granted. The Great Awakening stirred a fresh phase of Baptist advocacy of the separation of church and state, and contributed to the embodiment of the principle in the law of Virginia and the Constitution of the United States, but Isaac Backus professed a more qualified version of this creed than John Leland. Baptists helped achieve disestablishment in all American states by 1833, but their efforts on the other side of the Atlantic produced the same result only in Ireland and Wales. The desire of members of the denomination to Christianize their nations often inhibited their commitment to religious liberty, but they still defended the principle on the international stage. In America the Baptist position seemed a close fit with national values, but when the perceived threat to religious liberty changed from being primarily Catholic to being chiefly secular, the enthusiasm of many Baptists for a strict form of the principle waned. Some were willing to drop the libertarian heritage; others wished to modify it. Consequently, it has to be said that George Truett's claim that Baptists were consistent defenders of liberty turns out to misrepresent the historical record.

Baptists were certainly disposed to favor freedom of religion, but their versions of the principle varied greatly over time. The divisions of recent times over the interpretation of religious liberty are a faithful reflection of the variations of the past.

FURTHER READING

Coffey, John. "From Helwys to Leland: Baptists and Religious Toleration in England and America, 1612–1791." In *The Gospel in the World: International Baptist Studies*, edited by David W. Bebbington, 13–37. Carlisle: Paternoster, 2002.

George, Timothy. "Between Pacifism and Coercion: The English Baptist Doctrine of Religious Toleration." *Mennonite Quarterly Review* 58 (1984): 30–49.

Goen, C. C. "Baptists and Church-State Issues in the Twentieth Century." *American Baptist Quarterly* 6 (1987): 226–53.

Hankins, Barry. "The Evangelical Accommodationism of the Southern Baptist Convention Conservatives." *Baptist History and Heritage* 33 (1998): 54–65.

McBeth, H. Leon. *English Baptist Literature on Religious Liberty to 1689.* New York: Arno, 1980.

McLoughlin, William G. "Isaac Backus and the Separation of Church and State." *American Historical Review* 73 (1968): 1392–1413.

Chapter 13

BAPTISTS AND FOREIGN MISSION

The most important development in which Baptists participated during their four centuries of existence was the foreign missionary movement. In the course of the nineteenth and twentieth centuries Christianity was implanted in a range of lands where previously it had been all but unknown. Baptists joined in spreading the gospel beyond the bounds of Christendom to Asia, Africa, and other parts of the globe. Some of the achievement, as we shall see in the next chapter, was the result of migration and individual initiative, but more of it was a result of organized missionary work in foreign countries. The historian Kenneth Scott Latourette, himself at one time president of the American Baptist Foreign Mission Society, wrote a seven-volume *History of the Expansion of Christianity* (1937–1945). The first eighteen centuries were covered in only three volumes; the period of less than a century and a half since 1800 required four volumes. There would have been more on the later years if the books had not appeared before the middle of the twentieth century. The dynamic missionary impulse of the nineteenth and twentieth centuries required so many pages because of its extraordinary geographical reach and increasing degree of success. Christianity was freed from its confinement in Europe and North America and, by the opening of the twenty-first century, had become the predominant faith in many parts of Africa and the Pacific and had established a strong minority presence in several parts of Asia. Anglicans, Congregationalists, Lutherans, Methodists, Presbyterians, Roman Catholics, and other smaller denominations all took a full share in the movement, but the worldwide spread of the gospel was a phenomenon that had a major Baptist component.

In the first two centuries after the Reformation, the advance of Christianity had been far more a Roman Catholic than a Protestant endeavor. Catholic states saw it as their duty to promote the faith in the vast territories under their control. The Spanish, Portuguese, and French empires officially sponsored missions by religious orders that planted the Christian religion in the Far East and in Central and South America. Although seventeenth-century Puritans made sporadic efforts to convert the neighboring Native Americans, Protestants rarely planned missions to go to regions where they had not settled. The earliest Protestant missionaries were men who acted as chaplains to communities and garrisons scattered around the globe. The Society for the Propagation of the Gospel, an Anglican organization founded in 1701, was designed primarily for the benefit of North American colonists, but during the eighteenth century it did undertake preaching among the Native Americans. A more single-minded missionary venture was begun in 1706 by Frederick IV, King of Denmark, who dispatched a party of Lutheran Pietists from Halle in Prussia to spread the gospel in India. Settling at Tranquebar on the southeastern coast, they translated the Bible and other books into Tamil and established a small but enduring indigenous Lutheran community. But the chief eighteenth-century missionary project was undertaken by the Moravians. Originally followers of the Czech reformer Jan Hus from Moravia, they were reorganized in the 1720s by Count Nicholas von Zinzendorf at Herrnhut in Saxony with an intensely experiential style of spirituality. They soon carried their vibrant faith across the world—to the Inuit of Greenland, to the slaves of the West Indies, and to the tribes of southern Africa. The reports of their effective missions spurred a number of English Evangelicals to consider the possibility of imitating them: "None of the moderns," according to the Baptist William Carey, "have equalled the Moravian Brethren in this good work."[1] There was therefore an embryonic missionary movement under way even before Carey devised a scheme for a Baptist evangelistic initiative across the world.

William Carey, originally a shoemaker but by 1792 the pastor of a Baptist church in Leicester, was the author in that year of a work entitled *An Enquiry into the Obligations of Christians to Use Means for the Conversion of the Heathens.* The book argued that the commission found at the end of the gospels of Matthew and Mark, in which Jesus

William Carey (1761–1834)
Baptist Missionary

commands his disciples to go and teach all nations, was not, as many had supposed, binding only on the first generation of Christians, but was still in force. Surveying the world's religious statistics, Carey concluded that over half the earth's inhabitants remained "in the most deplorable state of heathen darkness."[2] Christians must therefore bring them the light of the gospel. There was the prospect of success because the Bible promised a "glorious increase of the church, in the latter days."[3] Carey, like many of his own and subsequent generations, was a convinced postmillennialist who held that the knowledge of God would certainly fill the earth before the return of the Savior. In this confidence, he proposed that Christians should pray for the coming of that time. The Particular Baptists of Carey's Northamptonshire Association, inspired by the earlier prayer call by the American theologian Jonathan Edwards, had been holding monthly prayer meetings for the spread of the Christian faith since 1784. The expectations generated by that movement led to a strong response when, in a sermon preached in Nottingham later in the same year, Carey urged his denomination to set up a society to take the gospel to the world. "Expect great things," he famously declared, "Attempt great things."[4] On October 2, 1792, the Baptist Missionary Society (BMS) was formed. The model was the trading company of the day, with private subscribers contributing large or small amounts to a common enterprise. The same pattern was to be adopted later in the decade by the Missionary Society (subsequently the London Missionary Society), supported chiefly by pedobaptist Dissenters, and by the Church Missionary Society, established by Evangelical Anglicans. The Baptists were leading the way in world mission.

The BMS immediately began its work. In 1793 Carey himself was sent as the society's second missionary to India and soon settled at Serampore, near Calcutta. Carey, assisted from 1799 by his two colleagues William Ward and Joshua Marshman, set about laying a foundation for long-term mission. The first convert, Krishna Pal, did not come until seven years after Carey's arrival, but in 1800, as the missionary put it, he had "the happiness to desecrate the Gunga [Ganges] by baptizing the first Hindoo."[5] Thereafter a steady and increasing flow of Indians came forward for baptism. Places of worship were built in the cities and preaching stations opened in the nearby countryside. Literature was a priority. Carey finished translating the New Testament into Bengali as early as 1796. During his lifetime he turned the whole Bible into six Indian tongues and parts of it into as many as twenty-nine other languages. The mission printed these texts of scripture, together with tracts for distribution, grammars, and dictionaries. In order to come to terms with the religious culture of India, Carey and Marshman published one of the Vedas, the sacred texts of the Hindus, and Ward composed a massive *Account of the Writings, Religion and Manners of the Hindoos* (1811). From 1818 the trio issued a periodical called *The Friend of India*, at various times monthly, quarterly, and weekly, in order to disseminate news of the mission but also to promote the welfare of India. As time went on, the missionaries did not scruple to attack social evils such as *sati*, the practice of burning widows alive on their husbands' funeral pyres, which they persuaded the governments of India to ban. Nor were environmental concerns beyond their remit. Carey, who took great interest in botany, collected specimens of Indian flora to ensure their preservation. Altogether the mission showed an engagement with the indigenous culture and secular affairs of India that was astonishing for a pioneer venture.

Carey's efforts kindled enthusiasm for the cause of overseas missions in the United States. The Philadelphia Association, for example, raised substantial funds for Serampore, and as early as 1800 a group of Baptist and Congregational women formed the Boston Female Society for Missionary Purposes with the same primary objective. By 1810 the Congregationalists had set up an American Board of Commissioners for Foreign Missions in order to launch a scheme of their own. One of the first missionaries, however, was Adoniram Judson, a Congregationalist who had formerly studied at Brown University, a Baptist institution. In the course of the voyage out to India, he and his wife, Ann, began to doubt whether he could baptize infants, and on arriving in Calcutta they were immersed by William Ward. Adoniram Judson's colleague Luther Rice, another Congregationalist turned Baptist, returned from India to organize denominational support at home and created the General

Missionary—or Triennial—Convention in 1814. The Judsons themselves set up missionary operations in Burma. Adoniram preached, a small number of converts gathered as a church, and a colleague who joined the mission in 1816 printed books and tracts on a press sent from Serampore. By 1836 Adoniram and his indigenous colleagues had translated the whole Bible into Burmese. Ann Judson produced the first Thai translations of scripture as early as 1819, taught girls, adopted orphans, and wrote the first history of the mission. In 1824, two years before her early death, she negotiated the release of her husband from the hands of Burmese resistance fighters against the British. The couple became missionary icons, inspiring the extension of missionary enterprise into Assam, Siam, southern India, China, and Liberia. When the Southern Baptists began their separate existence in 1845, their earliest fields were Nigeria and China. Even the small Free Will Baptists began their own mission to Orissa in India, sending out their third agent by 1851. Overseas missions had entered the lifeblood of Baptists in America as well as in Britain.

Advantages of the Missions

The missionary enterprise that blossomed over subsequent years enjoyed a range of substantial advantages that help explain its high degree of success. Not all the circumstances, however, were as propitious as historians have sometimes suggested. At least one of the suggested advantages turns out to have been at best a dubious asset. It has been proposed that Christian missions gained from the expansion of Western empires that marked the same epoch. It is true that imperial strategies could sometimes benefit missions. The opening of Chinese ports to Westerners under the unequal treaties signed from 1842 onwards, for example, permitted missionaries to take up residence in the country. In British colonies the administration sometimes offered encouragement and protection to Anglo-American missions, which were valued by the authorities for providing services that they themselves would otherwise have needed to supply. Yet there were also tensions between missionaries and colonial authorities. In 1865, when the governor of Jamaica suppressed a disturbance among the black population with wildly excessive force, leaving 439 people dead, the Baptists protested loudly on behalf of their coreligionists among the victims and created a major debate in British politics. Again, a rising in Nyasaland against British rule in 1915 by John Chilembwe, a Baptist preacher who had been educated in America, made colonial authorities wary of missions that trained African leaders for many years afterwards. Some colonial methods, furthermore, were distinctly unhelpful to missions. In particular, the policy of indirect rule, the administration of territory through indigenous rulers, meant that missionaries were excluded wherever the local authorities were unsympathetic. Vast tracts of land under Muslim government, in northern Nigeria for instance, were effectively closed to Christian missions. And the rivalries of colonial powers could be disastrous for missions. When Cameroon was taken as a German colony in 1884, British Baptist missionaries had to leave, and, though German Baptists took over from 1891, they in turn were expelled by the Allies during the First World War. There was no consistent benefit to missions from colonial rule and sometimes empire was a serious handicap.

The Western civilization that missionaries carried with them was, at the time, more of an advantage. Historians have subsequently argued that the missionaries were engaged in cultural imperialism, and have pointed out that Western values such as the duty of time-keeping were conducive to capitalist enterprise. Indigenous cultures, they contend, were undermined by the alien forces impinging on them. It is true that the Baptist missionaries, like their contemporaries of other denominations, were under the sway of modes of thinking inherited from the Enlightenment that assumed the superiority of Western ways. Human progress, it was generally held, had already made great strides in the West; it remained for the rest of the world to catch up. Christian missions, it was agreed at the Edinburgh World Missionary Conference in 1910, were to spread literature, especially in the Far East, that would illuminate "the moral forces which have been chiefly instrumental in developing Western civilisation."[6] It is also true that it was often believed that missions would bring economic benefits in their wake. The great

Scottish Congregational missionary David Livingstone championed the alliance of Christianity and commerce as an antidote to the slave trade, and many thought like him. Yet missionaries were not merely the tools of capitalism. The peoples of the world, they believed, might ultimately enjoy a higher standard of living as a result of the trade opened up by missions, but they were themselves the agents of a higher cause. At times missionaries were prepared to be outspoken in criticizing the exploitation of indigenous peoples in the name of commercial development. In the years around 1900, for example, the American Baptist missionaries in the Congo provided evidence against the atrocities of the ramshackle administration in collecting the rubber tax. And by and large the local inhabitants welcomed the greater prosperity and novel ways brought by the missionaries. Many took pride, for example, in wearing Western clothes. There was at times a measure of resentment against interference with long-standing customs, but indigenous elites in particular gained prestige from the contacts with the outside world that they gained from the missionaries. Far from being passive victims of cultural imperialism, local notables were generally skillful and selective users of techniques such as literacy and house building introduced by the newcomers to their lands. Baptist missions, though at times guilty of cultural insensitivity, were actually appreciated more because of the Western civilization they represented.

A further advantage of the missions grew up on the field. As missionaries spent more time among peoples overseas, they gained experience and realized how better to go about their work. The result could be difficulties with the home board. When, in 1852, Burma was ravaged by war, the American Baptist Justus Vinton transferred his mission from a rural location to the city of Rangoon in order to help the destitute, but he was censured by his committee in Boston for taking unauthorized action and so resigned to join another society. Missionaries could, in fact, be converted by the country they had come to convert. Timothy Richard, a Welshman serving with the BMS in China from 1870, is a case in point. He began with the conventional methods of street preaching and Bible distribution, but soon recognized that Chinese ways were best. So he began to use wall posters, the traditional local means of spreading news. Richard decided that it was fruitless to engage in indiscriminate evangelism, and so started to concentrate his efforts upon "the worthy," those with a potential interest in the gospel. A serious famine in 1876–1879 prompted him into organizing relief for the hungry and so catering for physical as well as spiritual needs. He hoped that Western knowledge would eventually foster structural change in the country and would also help the Chinese think well of Christianity, and so he accepted a newspaper editorship to spread useful information. He carried the same strategy further by becoming secretary of the Society for the Diffusion of Christian and General Knowledge among the Chinese and eventually advocated a Western type of university that would prepare the way for the gospel. Even his theology changed, and reached a favorable estimate of another religion. He came to believe that Buddhism, far from being a dangerous foe, was a divine means of preparing the people for the reception of the gospel. Richard was unusual in the extent of the changes he adopted during his career, but typical in his flexibility. Missionaries could adapt their methods and their thinking to the needs of the time and place.

The missionaries had a huge asset in the indigenous Christians. From the very start of a mission, even before there were any conversions, local people were essential. They not only provided services for mission stations, but also acted as instructors in the local language. The translations of the Bible were usually prepared by those skilled in the vernacular as much as by the missionaries. Thus, in 1806 Carey recorded that he translated into Sanskrit "with the assistance of the chief Pundit of the College" and then "sat down with a Tilingua Pundit . . . to learn that Language."[7] Once there was a group of local converts, they were put to work in finding more. Men were commissioned as evangelists and women were appointed Bible colporteurs. Thus Krishna Pal, Carey's first convert, became a missionary himself, working in Calcutta, Jessore, and Sylhet. It was these folk, not the missionaries from the West, who did the bulk of the evangelizing. After some time, often of considerable duration, other local men qualified as pastors, though still under missionary supervision. Pastors required institutional training. In Jamaica, for instance, Calabar College was established in 1843 to prepare men for ministry. Some newer Baptist communities even set up missionary societies of their own. Thus, from 1841 to 1853, there was a distinct Jamaica Baptist Missionary Society that sent its agents to Fernando Po and Cameroon in West Africa. From the 1850s the predominant policy of the Western missionary societies was for a time a "three-self" goal: self-government, self-propagation, and self-support. The aim was to place control of church affairs, responsibility for spreading the gospel, and the duty of raising money in the hands of local people. Although these ideals are associated with the American Congregationalist Rufus Anderson and the Evangelical Anglican Henry Venn, they were equally pursued by Edward Bean Underhill, the able secretary of the BMS from 1849 to 1876. Underhill encountered stiff resistance to the implementation of his strategy, but he wanted to end the financial dependence of Christians, especially in India, on the home society. The BMS under Underhill's leadership was seeking its own extinction, knowing that it could rely on the efforts of the Christians in the lands it had evangelized.

Another advantage of the missions was their deployment of women in the cause. Missionary wives, as the instance of Ann Judson has already shown, could play a large part in the venture. Usually they were not allowed to preach to mixed-gender congregations, but Calista Vinton, the wife of Justus Vinton in Burma, acted on the conviction that, according to her daughter, "she had as truly a vocation to preach the gospel as her husband."[8] Sometimes, however, the greatest achievement of the missionary wives was the creation of a Christian home in which the relations of husband and wife were far more equal than in the surrounding society. By contrast with celibate Roman Catholic priests, Protestants could turn the family into a missionary unit. By the middle years of the century, however, the idea of sending out single women was being mooted. The first dispatched by the Foreign Mission Board of the Southern Baptist Convention, Harriet Baker in 1847, did not turn out to be a success in China, and the experiment was abandoned. But a change of policy took place after the publication by Marianne Lewis, wife of the superintendent of the Calcutta Mission Press, of a pamphlet, *A Plea for Zenanas* (1866). Lewis pointed out that all men except close relatives were excluded from the *zenanas*, the private quarters of women of high caste in India, and so their occupants could be reached for the gospel only by other women. The Ladies' Association set up as a result in connection with the BMS paid single female missionaries and Indian Bible women to engage in *zenana* visitation and other pioneer evangelism. The women's organizations formed in North America during the later nineteenth century concentrated on supporting female agents, whether Western or indigenous. Unmarried women became an increasing proportion of the global missionary force. The most celebrated among them was Charlotte (Lottie) Moon, sent out in 1873 from Virginia to China by the Southern Baptist Foreign Mission Board, a redoubtable person who demonstrated conclusively that single women could be effective evangelists. From 1888, at her suggestion, an annual Christmas offering for missions was taken up in her sending denomination, and from 1918, six years after her death, it was named in her honor, becoming one of the chief means of raising money for missions among Southern Baptists. By 1910, 55 percent of missionaries sent by American denominational agencies were female. The whole enterprise depended in the twentieth century more on women than on men.

Much of women's work was in schools, which formed a further strength of the missionary movement. The gift of literacy was one of the most potent weapons in the movement's armory. Education was a priority from the start because of the need to train national Christians to be the primary evangelists. Thus, by 1818, around Serampore there were already ninety-two schools and about ten thousand pupils under instruction. It was not expected that large-scale elementary education would produce great numbers of Christians immediately, but it was hoped that it would prepare the way for an eventual mass movement toward Christian truth. The system was capped from 1818 by an institution, Serampore College, which, although—and partly because—it was designed to produce missionaries, provided advanced learning in science and languages as well as theology. As the scope of the missionary endeavor grew, similar arrangements, though often on a smaller scale, were made elsewhere. In the American Baptist field in East China, for instance, there were, by 1900, five ordinary schools and three boarding schools, all staffed by Chinese teachers but under missionary guidance. Six years later a Shanghai Baptist College, jointly sponsored by Northern and Southern Baptists, was established, and five years on it became a university. More specialist education was also provided. Women's organizations often concentrated on girls' schools, a striking innovation in many parts of the world. There was also industrial education. From 1878 the American Baptist Missionary Union, as the Northern organization was called at the time, agreed to send out "intelligent Christian laymen, practically trained in commerce, farming and the mechanic arts" to give instruction to indigenous people.[9] This type of training was specially favored by the African American Baptist missions, flourishing from the late nineteenth century onwards, which transplanted to Africa the ideals of Booker T. Washington's Tuskegee Institute. By the 1920s so much energy was given to education of various kinds that some missionaries began to fear an eclipse of direct evangelism. Wesley W. Lawton, a Southern Baptist in the Chinese interior, noted with dismay in his diary in 1923 that "there is much more lecturing . . . than preaching the Word of God."[10] But there can be no doubt that Baptist educational efforts did a great deal to advance the missionary cause.

Likewise, health care became a significant benefit to the Baptist missions. Initially missionaries without specialist skills gave basic medical advice and occasionally performed minor surgery, but that was not regarded as their vocation. From the 1870s, however, professional doctors were sent out as medical missionaries. The heavy death-toll among missionary personnel suggested the wisdom of having some medically trained staff on the field, but the emphasis gradually shifted toward the provision of health care for the sick among the indigenous peoples. The welfare of the body, it was slowly but increasingly held, was a Christian concern as well as the welfare of the soul. The BMS dispatched its first trained doctor to China in 1870, though its early medical missionaries were expected to preach as well as to heal. Canadian Baptists sent female medical staff to their Telugu field in eastern India from the 1890s, and over the years they won the warm regard of the Muslim minority and the untouchables. Female doctors and nurses were approachable by women patients who, had the medical staff been male, would have been unable to consult them directly, and so played a significant part in the growth of medical missionary work. Of the American Baptist Missionary Union's twenty-seven physicians in 1902, nine were women. By that date the union also possessed twelve hospitals and many dispensaries in its various fields. Yet when Anna Kay Scott, serving in Swatow, China, requested two further doctors from the union's board to staff the medical mission she was developing, its reply was that resources must be channeled toward graduates of theological seminaries. The hesitation still evident in this response was largely overcome in the interwar period, when medical missions were a strong priority. Colonial administrations particularly valued missions for the health care they provided. By 1938 there were 1,350 doctors, 13,000 nurses, and over 1,000 hospitals supported by Protestant missions worldwide. This battery of institutional compassion helped persuade many people of the benevolent intentions of Christian missions.

A further strength of the missionary movement was that, from the later nineteenth century, it was not confined to denominational channels. Although the Baptist missionary organizations continued, a range of new undenominational bodies arose that included Baptists alongside other fervent Evangelicals in their ranks. These were the faith missions. Their pioneer was James Hudson Taylor, an Englishman with a background in the Brethren movement, one of whose leading figures, George Müller, ran an orphanage based on the faith principle. Müller did not organize the raising of funds, but instead relied on God to provide whatever was needed. Taylor applied the same principle to missions. The members of the China Inland Mission that he founded in 1865 had no assured financial support, but went out in faith. The mission grew, opening up new areas remote from the Chinese coast for the gospel. Other bodies, based in North America as well as in Britain, copied Taylor's example of pioneering. The Sudan Interior Mission (1893), the Africa Inland

Mission (1895), and the Regions Beyond Missionary Union (1899) were among the largest of them. They recruited some of the most dedicated young people of the day to their ranks. They were usually strongly premillennialist, with their expectation of the imminence of the second advent injecting urgency into their endeavors. Educational work and health care were not for them, since the single vital task was the saving of souls in the brief time left. There was a spirit of adventure as, having put their trust in the Lord, they sallied forth into the unknown. The Africa Inland Mission proposed, for example, to evangelize "the darkest spot on Africa's continent of darkness."[11] The faith missions gathered strength as the twentieth century advanced and became bastions of the Fundamentalist side in the controversies of the 1920s. The Bible school run in Minneapolis by William Bell Riley, the leader of Fundamentalism in the Northern Baptist Convention, for instance, had trained 136 missionaries by 1936, and nearly all of them entered a faith mission. The agencies may not have worn the label Baptist, but much of the groundbreaking missionary work of the twentieth century by Baptists was achieved under the banner of the faith missions.

ACHIEVEMENT AND CHANGE

Partly as a result of these various factors, the Baptists achieved a great deal in church planting overseas. Missionary consciousness did not immediately become general, for, as we have seen, it aroused antagonism in America, and, though the outright hostility was less in Britain, only 44 percent of Particular Baptist churches supported the BMS financially as late as 1850–1851. Nor had the impact on the world been huge. Seven years earlier there were only 1,449 members in all the BMS churches in the Indian subcontinent. Later, however, there were some remarkable breakthroughs in specific parts of the world. The American Baptist mission in the Telugu-speaking region of eastern India had 8,691 baptisms in a six-week period in 1878, one of the many mass movements of converts into the Christian faith in modern India. Again, between 1919 and 1924 the BMS in Mizoram in northeastern India enjoyed a wave of revival that made the Baptist membership increase from 1,017 to 3,198. Such remarkable church growth was exceptional, but it did take place. More normal was slower but steady expansion, which accounts for the bulk of the growth on the African fields of the National Baptist Convention and the Lott Carey Baptist Foreign Missionary Convention, the two main African American missionary organizations. They claimed as many as 25,000 overseas converts between 1895 and 1921. The missionary impetus spread far beyond North America and Britain, the heartland of missionary enterprise, to many other Baptist bodies. South Australia established its own missionary society in 1865 and soon other Australian colonies imitated it; New Zealand followed in 1885, Sweden in 1889, South Africa in 1892, Germany in 1898, and Norway in 1915. Many chose to go where existing Baptist missions were functioning. Thus the Norwegians sent their first missionary in 1918 to the Congo, a long-standing BMS field. To the successes in setting up Baptist churches in new lands must be added some more indirect achievements. In the Congo and Angola a prophet movement emerged in 1921, led by Simon Kimbangu, who had been converted through the Baptist mission six years before. Although he was imprisoned for treason by the Belgian colonial authorities from 1921 until his death in 1951, his powerful ministry bore eventual fruit in 1959 in an independent church that has become the largest indigenous denomination in Africa. The Kimbanguists too should be seen as the offspring of the Baptist missionary movement.

The twentieth century witnessed the gradual transfer of authority from missionaries to national church leaders. The process was partly the delayed effect of the earlier three-self philosophy that had aspired to bring autonomy to the newer churches. By 1925 the American Baptist Foreign Mission Society, together with its female equivalent, could note at a joint review meeting that already there was a good deal of devolution of responsibility. In Burma, its first field, for example, the committee of management of the Baptist convention had a majority of national members. Financial difficulties during the Great Depression of the 1930s accelerated the process, with the BMS making explicit the connection between low income and the transfer of authority as early as 1931. The Second World War had a further powerful effect. By raising hopes of freedom for colonized peoples in the political sphere, it encouraged the leaders of the churches to look for greater independence too. "The time seems to have come, or to be dawning," wrote H. R. Williamson, the foreign secretary of the BMS in 1944, "when our African brethren will expect to share with their missionary colleagues in joint Missionary and Church Councils."[12] The expulsion of missionaries from China in the wake of the triumph of the Communist forces in 1949 made missions realize that local leadership must be put in place ready for any similar closing of other countries to foreign personnel. The resulting process can be followed clearly in the BMS work in the Congo. In 1954, when the society's foreign secretary urged strengthening African leadership, most of the missionaries there still thought the policy premature. The first two Congolese, however, were admitted to a missionary field conference two years later and church councils of African leaders started to be set up. Financial responsibility was transferred from mission to church in most districts in 1958. After the Congo became independent of Belgium in 1960, pressure for parallel changes in the mission increased. In the following year missionaries became answerable to one of the three regional Baptist church communities that had been created, and in 1962 control of the BMS hospitals and dispensaries passed to the Central Council of Baptist Churches. Under political pressure from the Congolese government, the three regional communities merged in 1972 as a single Baptist church community, a fully autonomous body. The emergence of the church from the mission, a development closely intertwined with political decolonization, was complete. A similar process took place in most former Baptist missionary fields over roughly the same period.

The subsequent pattern of world mission was summed up by the word partnership. Missions were no longer sent from the West to the rest of the world, but the advance of Christianity across the globe was increasingly conceived as a cooperative venture between equals. An epoch-making event was the International Congress on World Evangelization convened in Lausanne, Switzerland, by Billy Graham in 1974. At the event, the Peruvian Baptist minister Samuel Escobar challenged Western evangelists to incorporate elements of Latin

American liberation theology into their message. If the gospel was to be seen in its totality, he argued, it must be recognized as a force for justice and freedom. Thereafter it was hard to forget that, if partnership was to be a reality, the voice of the underprivileged parts of the world must be heard. There was occasional friction as local aspirations clashed with lingering missionary paternalism. The Baptist Theological Seminary of Zimbabwe is a case in point. Founded and originally wholly funded by Southern Baptist missionaries, the seminary came under the control of a local board with a majority of church representatives in 1986, but twenty years later still could not obtain its trust deeds from the Southern Baptist Convention. The International Mission Board of the Southern Baptists wanted to ensure the orthodoxy of the teaching at the seminary; the principal saw the policy as "a kind of ecclesiastical colonialism."[13] Much theological education, however, was testimony to the effectiveness of partnership as Western sources paid for teaching that aimed to train new generations of church leaders. In the new phase of missions, many older agencies reduced their numbers of career missionaries: by 1982 there were only 203 working with the American Baptist Churches. At the same time, however, there was a mushrooming of short-term mission trips: by 1992 over 10,000 Southern Baptists participated in them each year. The Southern Baptists nevertheless remained strongly committed to encouraging career missionaries, with 3,816 supported by its Foreign Mission Board in 1987. In some formerly receiving countries, long-term missionary service had also become popular. In 2004 the Brazilian Baptists had 540 missionaries in 59 countries. Foreign missions had become a much less one-sided phenomenon.

A review of the Baptist part in the missionary movement has to concede that the denomination was less responsible for its creation than has often been claimed. There were Catholic missions long before William Carey, and there were Protestant missions for almost a century before him. Nevertheless, Carey holds a prominent place in the missionary record. His *Enquiry* and sermon of 1792 led to the creation of the first Anglo-American foreign missionary organization, the Baptist Missionary Society, and his work at Serampore inspired others, including the first Americans, to join in the enterprise. The movement enjoyed great advantages over the next two centuries, though, on balance, the colonial empires were not as significant aids as might be imagined. The Western civilization brought by the missions, though sometimes insensitively introduced, added to their appeal. Once in the field, missionaries gained experience that proved a huge asset, adding to their flexibility and effectiveness. The indigenous helpers were the chief propagators of the faith, while women, both married and single, played a major role in the missionary enterprise. The provision of schools and colleges on the one hand, and of medical care on the other, powerfully reinforced the message of the missions. And undenominational faith missions acted as a vehicle for many twentieth-century Baptists to spread their faith. All these features of the movement helped ensure its impact. The later twentieth century saw the transfer of responsibility for the churches that had been planted to local leaders and a remodeling of foreign mission on new lines of partnership. The overall result was not just a huge growth in the number of Christians, but also a reordering of their distribution. At the start of the period, Baptists existed, with very few exceptions, only in the British Isles and in North America. At its end, there were large and flourishing Baptist communities in India and Burma, China and Brazil, Nigeria and Congo, and in many other lands where missionaries had served. It was the most significant achievement of the Baptists.

FURTHER READING

Estep, William R. *Whole Gospel—Whole World: The Foreign Mission Board of the Southern Baptist Convention, 1845–1995*. Nashville: Broadman & Holman, 1994.

George, Timothy. *Faithful Witness: The Life and Mission of William Carey*. Birmingham, Ala.: New Hope, 1991.

Potts, E. Daniel. *British Baptist Missionaries in India, 1793–1837*. Cambridge: Cambridge University Press, 1967.

Robert, Dana L. *Christian Mission: How Christianity Became a World Religion*. Chichester, West Sussex: Wiley-Blackwell, 2009.

Stanley, Brian. *The History of the Baptist Missionary Society, 1792–1992.* Edinburgh: T&T Clark, 1992.

Torbet, Robert G. *Venture of Faith: The Story of the American Baptist Foreign Mission Society and the Woman's American Baptist Foreign Mission Society, 1814–1954.* Philadelphia: Judson Press, 1955.

Chapter 14

THE GLOBAL SPREAD OF THE BAPTISTS

The growth of Baptists toward becoming a worldwide communion was not only the result of organized missions. By the start of the twenty-first century, it is true, a high proportion of the members of the denomination could be found in churches on the former mission field. The missionary movement discussed in the previous chapter had all but achieved its goal of implanting the Christian faith in every land on earth. But Baptists also spread by other means. During the nineteenth and twentieth centuries migration took place on an unusual scale. New means of transport—railroads and steamships in the nineteenth century, automobiles and airplanes in the twentieth—allowed a great deal more population mobility than in the past. People of Baptist conviction left their homes in Europe in order to seize fresh opportunities in countries that were opening up for settlement. The pioneers of the nineteenth century, who will figure largely in this chapter, laid foundations for much greater growth in the twentieth. Although the main destination was the United States, many moved to other lands. Latvians, Germans, and Swedes, for example, all built up flourishing Baptist communities in Brazil. English, Welsh, and Scottish migrants set up Baptist chapels throughout the British Empire and so established a substantial presence in Australia, Canada, New Zealand, and South Africa. The European diaspora of the period was responsible for a significant proportion of the new Baptist churches throughout the world. At the same time, individuals and organizations, from North America at least as much as Europe, were propagating the faith in territories that were part of the Christian world—among the peoples of their own continents, Latin America, and the Russian Empire. The expansion of the Baptists in these lands is a major dimension of their story.

NATIONAL CONTRIBUTIONS TO THE SPREAD

The countries that already possessed Baptist communities in 1800 naturally took the lead in advancing the Baptist cause. For a long time England held the most prominent position. Charles Haddon Spurgeon, for example, took a detailed interest in the work of Christian missions, of both the denominational and the undenominational kinds, but he also saw the growth of Baptist witness in continental Europe and lands of British settlement as a priority. Spurgeon admired the German work of Johann Gerhard Oncken that was mentioned in chapter 6, and traveled to Hamburg in 1867 to open Oncken's new church building there. Because Spurgeon presided over a flourishing training college for pastors, he was also able to direct able men to appropriate destinations in parts of the British Empire. When, in 1876, a Baptist church first began in Cape Town, at the southern tip of Africa, it wrote to Spurgeon, who duly dispatched one of his trainees, and by the great preacher's death in 1892 Spurgeon's men had filled many of the pulpits in the embryonic Baptist Union of South Africa. The wealth of England, the fruit of extensive trade and early industrialization, enabled the country to do more than send personnel abroad. Repeatedly, English money supported Baptist ventures elsewhere, whether in Europe or the empire. Thus Spurgeon arranged for his London congregation to pay for two of Oncken's home missionaries. Likewise, when numbers of Baptists began to multiply in Quebec, their leaders turned to England for financial assistance. Between 1838 and 1849 the huge sum of 17,000 pounds was raised in England for the support of up to twelve pastors and the erection of a theological college in Montreal. The consequences were not all gain. Not surprisingly, the subsidies sometimes tainted the Baptists as professors of an alien creed. Thus the people of Hamburg stigmatized the faith propagated by Oncken as the "new English religion."[1] This label, though earned in Oncken's pre-Baptist days, also clung to his subsequent efforts. An awareness that English gold lay behind local faces could be a handicap to Baptist work. Yet the support of English Baptists often proved crucial to the growth of a denominational presence in other countries.

Wales, though much smaller than England, had long played a distinctive part in the spread of the Baptists. In the seventeenth century the church at Ilston in Glamorgan had emigrated as a body to Pennsylvania; in the eighteenth, a regular flow of correspondence from Wales helped sustain the vigor of Baptist life in the colony. Fresh bodies of migrants augmented the Welsh settlers in Pennsylvania during the nineteenth century, many of them Baptists. Both at home and abroad the Welsh Baptists almost all used their own Celtic tongue for worship, giving them a special sense of identity. Since the Welsh language resembled the version of Celtic spoken in Brittany, the people of Wales considered that strongly Roman Catholic region of western France their special mission field. In 1834 the Baptist churches of Glamorgan launched an effort to plant Breton-speaking churches. Taken over by the Baptist Missionary Society (BMS) nine years later, the mission became a cause dear to Welsh hearts. When, in 1885, the BMS resolved to withdraw support from the Breton mission, strong Welsh protests ensured that a measure of funding continued. The mission succeeded in establishing a small cluster of enduring Baptist churches. Welsh-language chapels sprang up wherever Baptists from the principality penetrated. Thus, in Australia, gold prospectors erected such places of worship in the diggings of Victoria, and miners did the same in the coalfields round Newcastle, New South Wales. Some of the Welsh remained so attached to their language that, in 1865, a party led by three ministers, two Independent and one Baptist, set off for an unsettled part of South America in order to preserve their tongue from being overwhelmed by the wave of

English sweeping through their homeland. After arriving in the Chubut Valley of Patagonia, they put up chapels where the grand Welsh hymns sounded across the pampas. Soon, however, the other Nonconformists absorbed the Baptists, who ceased to hold distinct denominational services; and in the twentieth century the whole community eventually became Spanish-speaking, resorting to chapel only for occasional Welsh choral concerts. Rarely outside Wales did the language survive in worship down as far as the year 2000. Nevertheless, with their strong sense of cultural identity, the Welsh had helped further the Baptist cause worldwide.

Scotland played an equivalent role in the advance of the gospel in its Baptist guise. A few Scots, chiefly in the Highlands, spoke Gaelic, another Celtic tongue, and carried their faith and language with them to the New World. More Scottish emigrants, however, used English and so evangelized a wider community. They included followers of Robert Haldane, a gentleman of independent means who promoted gospel preaching throughout Scotland and who adopted believer's baptism in 1808. From eight years afterwards a number of Baptists from Haldaneite churches joined the flow of Scottish emigrants to Canada. They took Haldane's energetic style of evangelism with them, and seemed less preoccupied with points of church order than their coreligionists with American roots. In 1828 Haldane's Edinburgh Bible Society gave employment to Johann Gerhard Oncken. The contact with Haldane must have introduced the young German to Baptist principles, and subsequently the National Bible Society of Scotland, the successor of the Edinburgh body, paid for a number of his colporteurs on the continent of Europe. Bristo Place Baptist Church in Edinburgh supported Gottfried Fryderic Alf, who trained under Oncken at Hamburg and became the pioneer of Baptist work in Poland. In a similar way, the Bohemian Baptist Mission, based in Scotland, backed the planting of Baptist churches in his native land by Henry Novotny, a Czech who had trained for the Reformed ministry at a Presbyterian college in Edinburgh and who, in 1885, was baptized as a believer. The most outstanding example of a Scottish Baptist promoting Baptist gospel work abroad, however, was probably William Daniel Thompson MacDonald. Trained by Spurgeon, MacDonald served churches in Scotland, emigrated to the United States in 1880, and eight years later went to Chile as an agent of the American Bible Society. MacDonald became an evangelist of the Christian and Missionary Alliance in southern Chile, but subsequently withdrew to found, in 1908, the Baptist Union of Chile, with himself as superintendent. Called "El Escoces" ("the Scotsman") by the Chileans, he exercised a decisive sway over the early development of Baptist life in his adopted country. The Baptists of Scotland were a molding influence over denominational work in many lands.

The role of the United States in developing Baptist life abroad steadily increased. Whereas in the nineteenth century Britain had normally been more prominent, America replaced it in the twentieth century. A symbolic change took place in 1892, when Norwegian Baptist work ceased to be subsidized by Britain and started to be helped financially from the Northern states of America. The United States did not provide personnel in large numbers since the country was a receiver rather than a giver in the population movements of the era. Indeed, America's welcoming of immigrants with the promise of religious liberty had the effect of sapping the strength of emergent Baptist witness in a number of European countries. "Several members have emigrated to America," ran a report on French affairs in 1857, "including one ordained minister, and others are seriously contemplating a similar step."[2] The constant draining away of key people was profoundly disheartening in France, as elsewhere. Yet individuals from the United States did play important pioneering roles in many lands. In Venezuela, for instance, O. R. Covault, a Baptist pastor from Ohio, went in 1924 as an independent missionary to the English-speaking black immigrants from the Caribbean islands, and was afterwards taken on by a missionary organization and formed a cluster of Baptist churches. And America gave openhandedly. Oncken (once more) received a steady income from the American Baptist Foreign Mission Society from 1835 onwards. Americans funded the first Baptist pastor in Lebanon, who started a church in Beirut in 1895. A Southern Baptist layman who had made a fortune in footwear paid for a new building for the Central

Baptist Church in Caracas, Venezuela, in 1951. Yet giving could create tensions. Southern Baptists generously supported postwar Baptist work in Italy. At one point, only thirty-five national pastors worked alongside as many as twenty-five missionaries. The Italians found the experience stifling, and, after setting up a Baptist Union of their own in 1956, they asserted their independence by claiming, for example, the right to analyze public issues with the help of Marxist philosophy, something the Americans condemned outright. Similar troubles simmered in many Latin American countries. Baptists in other parts of the world could resent financial dependence even while appreciating the generosity of the United States.

The Germans also took a disproportionate part in the spread of the Baptists. In some regions of Europe, Baptist churchmanship seemed as self-evidently German as it did English or American elsewhere. Until unification in 1871 no single German state existed, but instead a mosaic of German-speaking principalities covered central Europe. In addition, a large number of German families had

Johann Gerhard Oncken (1800–1884)
Baptist Pastor and Church Planter

dispersed over territories farther east. Oncken's men did their primary work among these people, in the diaspora as much as in the German-speaking lands. The Germans associated with Oncken's base in Hamburg planted Baptist convictions in successive countries: Denmark (1839), the Netherlands (1845), Austria (1846), Sweden (1847), Switzerland (1847), and so on. Usually, if German was one of the local tongues, German-speakers became Baptists before the users of any other language. In Memel in East Prussia, an epicenter of Baptist work in northeastern Europe, the church, though founded in 1841 amongst the Germans, began to reach the Lithuanians, who formed a high proportion of the local population, only in 1854. The Latvians on the Baltic Sea, particularly unhappy with the degree of German control exercised over their religious life, created a separate Baptist Association in the 1880s. The German image of the Baptists could prove a handicap. Yet Germans carried their Baptist churchmanship beyond the bounds of Europe. Ethnic Germans emigrated in large numbers to the United States and Canada, and set up churches to worship in their own tongue. "We consider it most important and desirable," ran a resolution of their first North American conference in 1851, "that our children be instructed in the German language."[3] Like the Welsh, the Germans wished to preserve their linguistic heritage. Gradually, however, it faded, the two world wars being times when many dropped their inherited language. Baptists who spoke German also found their way in significant numbers to other lands such as South Africa, where, at the first statistical return of the Baptist Union, in 1880, equal numbers of members came from English and German churches. The German part in the global spread of the Baptists must not be underestimated.

REASONS FOR THE SPREAD

Some of the ways in which Baptist convictions spread have already been touched on, but it will be useful to distinguish a number of the chief factors involved in the process. In the first place, there was the migration of groups. In an early instance of this phenomenon, a party of black Baptists departed under the leadership of David George, their pastor, from Halifax, Nova Scotia, to the west coast of Africa in 1792. George, while still a slave, had led a church in South Carolina, but in the aftermath of the War for Independence he went as a free man to Nova Scotia, a remaining British colony to the north. He determined, with most of his flock, to travel to the other side of the Atlantic in order to join the new settlement of Sierra Leone, a place designed to be a haven for the victims of slavery and a beacon of Christianity for the rest of Africa. George set up a Baptist church in the capital, Freetown, the first on the continent. In a similar way, liberated slaves migrated to Liberia, a colony established by Americans as an equivalent of Sierra Leone. Lott Carey, a black Baptist preacher from Richmond, Virginia, founded a church among them in 1822 in Monrovia, the capital, and so inaugurated a strong tradition of Baptist life in the country. In these instances a missionary motive blended with other ambitions in the migrating groups. More often, however, a quest for greater prosperity formed the overriding reason for removal. Large numbers traveled across oceans in order to discover a better life, usually with the intention of remaining permanently in the new home. People of Baptist churchmanship journeyed among them. Thus, in 1877, a group of French-speaking Swiss and Belgians moved to Argentina and settled in the province of Santa Fe. One of them asked his former pastor, Paul Basson, to come out to look after a small but growing congregation. Basson inaugurated Baptist activity in the country, eventually founding the Central Baptist Church in Buenos Aires, but the initiative had come from an ordinary colonist. Mass migration proved to be a fundamental explanation of Baptist growth in the nineteenth and twentieth centuries.

A second reason for Baptist expansion on a global scale was personal mobility. Often individuals without families moved to another land, sometimes intending to return to their homes after a while. The reason, once more, could in some instances be explicitly religious. The man often regarded as the first Baptist missionary, George Liele, falls into this category. A slave and ordained preacher, Liele had been responsible for the conversion of David George in South Carolina. At the end of the American Revolution in 1783, he traveled without any organization behind him to Jamaica in order to evangelize. Within seven years he had gathered a large church in Kingston, had baptized over 500, and had laid the foundations of Baptist work on the island. Later on, others who traveled alone could at times fulfill something like a missionary vocation. Lough Fook, a Chinese Baptist, determined in 1861 to journey to the opposite side of the world as an indentured worker to evangelize the coolies of British Guiana in South America. There, in the capital, Georgetown, he organized a Baptist church that, by 1878, had more than 200 members and had even sent missionaries back to China. It was more common, however, for the reason for individual mobility to be economic. Sailors often figured in this pattern. Prominent individuals in the beginnings of Baptist life in Sweden, Denmark, and Finland around the middle of the nineteenth century had all been baptized in the United States while ashore from their ships. Again, Frederick Crowe, a sailor put off his boat by the captain in Belize, then British Honduras, in Central America, was immersed there before going as a pioneer colporteur into Guatemala in 1841. Although Crowe's work did not last, he did manage to present a copy of the Bible to the Guatemalan president. Often an individual would go to some fresh destination in quest of work and there find opportunities to spread the faith. Martin Kalweit followed this pattern when, in 1862, he moved from Memel in East Prussia to Tiflis, now Tbilisi, the capital of modern Georgia. Five years later he baptized a Russian merchant, Nikita I. Voronin, who was to become a significant leader of Baptists in Tsarist Russia. Travel explains the implanting of Baptist life in many new lands.

Literature, thirdly, played a conspicuous part in the process. The work of the British and Foreign Bible Society (BFBS), founded in London in 1806 to print and distribute Bibles throughout the world, often prepared the way for Baptist penetration. Its editions of the scriptures were translated into many languages and were often extremely cheap. Sometimes BFBS agents themselves fostered the early growth of the denomination. Thus Edward Millard, the BFBS representative in Vienna from 1851, not only organized the distribution of over 3 million copies of the Bible in the Austro-Hungarian Empire, but also held meetings in his home that eventually, in

1869, led to the creation of the first Baptist church in Austria. The American Bible Society, founded in 1816 with a similar remit to that of the BFBS, also began appointing permanent foreign representatives twenty years later. Denominational publications contributed to the process too. Oncken started a printing and publishing firm in Hamburg even before his baptism in 1834 and thereafter used it as an agency for the promotion of Baptist work, bequeathing it after his death to the German Baptist Union. As many as 100,000 tracts were printed annually. Already in 1837, twenty brethren of the Hamburg church acted as distributors of tracts and Bibles. Oncken's trainees, as much colporteurs as preachers, sold and gave away literature wherever they went. When, in 1856, for example, Karl Johann Scharschmidt arrived in Bucharest, then the capital of Wallachia and now of Romania, he soon set up a tract association. In Sweden and Norway the American Baptist Publication Society initially employed the first Baptist leaders for similar distributions of books and tracts. The Swedes naturally made literature a comparable priority when they moved to the United States. In 1871, when the Swedish Baptists of North America numbered fewer than 1,500, they began a monthly magazine; by 1885 they were able to support a flourishing weekly denominational newspaper. The printed word was also a potent influence on Baptist expansion in Latin America during the twentieth century. The Baptist Publishing House at El Paso, Texas, produced in Spanish a church manual, a model covenant, and a periodical called *Nueva Era* ("New Age") that repeatedly helped consolidate fledgling Baptist communities. Literature, which could penetrate where people could not, powerfully assisted Baptist expansion.

Other Christian bodies constituted, fourthly, a major factor in the growth of the Baptists. In New Zealand, for example, Methodism provided inspiration for the start of Baptist work in the Canterbury plains of the South Island. William Pole, long a Primitive Methodist evangelist in England, was baptized and served as a Baptist pastor in Huntingdonshire before emigrating to New Zealand in 1867, but did not drop his Methodist techniques in his new country. He organized, on the model of a Methodist circuit, a team of lay preachers who set up a network of small rural Baptist causes. Methodists rather than Baptists sometimes did the pioneering work in parts of Latin America. In Peru, for instance, a Methodist became the agent of the American Bible Society from 1884. His mission paved the way for the subsequent Baptist presence, not least by securing fuller civil rights for Protestants. The legacy of other denominations could be clearly seen on the continent of Europe. The Moravians, the pioneers of modern missions, had shaped the spirituality of Gottfried Wilhelm Lehmann, who became one of Oncken's right-hand men; he introduced among Baptists their love-feasts, occasions when believers spoke of their experience over a simple meal of bread and water. The Lutherans, who predominated in northern Europe, often prepared the ground for the Baptists. In Estonia, for example, a Lutheran revival in 1877 gave birth to free churches, including most of the early Baptists. Tsarist Russia, which then included Estonia, in fact provides several clear instances of indigenous movements that stirred spiritual aspirations subsequently fulfilled by the Baptists. The Molokans, beginning in modern Ukraine in the eighteenth century, reacted against the formalism of the Orthodox Church by establishing small prayer groups and rebelling against the sacraments. The Stundists, also emerging in Ukraine, adopted a form of revivalism and turned to careful Bible study. Both groups, which sometimes interacted with each other, prepared the ground for Baptist growth in the same region. Mennonites, who continued to exist in many parts of the Russian dominions, fed into the emergence of the Baptists. Even the Orthodox authorities, by providing a new translation of the scriptures in 1862, contributed to the rise of the new denomination. Around St. Petersburg, by contrast, the development of the Evangelical Christians, who later merged with the Baptists, took place as a result of evangelism in fashionable circles during the 1870s by Lord Radstock, an aristocratic British evangelist with a background in the so-called Plymouth Brethren. The debt of the Baptists to other Christian denominations is well illustrated by their eclectic origins in the Russian Empire.

A fifth reason for Baptist growth, paradoxically, was the opposition that they encountered. In many countries they faced fierce

resistance from the authorities in church and state, which often led
to the containment or even extinction of their witness. In Guatemala,
for example, the earliest Baptist work, by the sailor Frederick Crowe,
ended abruptly, in 1845, with his expulsion from the country at the
request of the Catholic clergy. In Rome itself the Baptist church had
to be erected behind the building line so as to be hidden by adjacent
structures. And the regime of General Franco in Spain, according
to a decree of 1945, allowed non-Catholic "cults" to practice their
faith only in "the interior of the respective temples, without mani-
festation or outward show in the public street."[4] In Muslim lands
restrictions could be even tighter, with Saudi Arabia allowing no
Christian places of worship at all. Sometimes, however, restrictions on Baptists actually helped their spread. The earliest Swedish
Baptists, for example, took a collective decision in 1853 to migrate
to America so as to escape the Lutheran monopoly in their native
land. The endurance of Baptists under persecution often gained
the respect of their neighbors. In the Russian Empire the bonding
between the Orthodox Church and the tsarist state provided particularly difficult circumstances. The head of the Holy Synod in Russia,
Konstantin Pobedonostsev, declared in 1881 that "there are and
must be no Russian Baptists."[5] The authorities condoned beatings
of members of Baptist churches and the dissolution of their meetings. But the sufferings of the believers raised the question of why
they were willing to undergo so much adversity for the sake of the
gospel. Stalin's anti-religious campaign of the 1930s, which entailed
the exile of many Baptists to Siberia and the execution of their leaders, though devastating for the churches, had similar effects. The
exiled Christians, thrown back on their faith, increased in numbers
in several places where they were sent. The same results flowed
from the repression of Christianity in Maoist China in the second
half of the twentieth century. Although the state-approved Chinese
Protestant church usually extinguished Baptist identity, the number
of Christians mushroomed in the post-missionary era. Often by the
twenty-first century only the choice of hymns indicated the denominational origins of a congregation, but the faith itself flourished. The
repression of the churches could promote their growth.

Often the repression did not lead to extinction because of the sixth factor, international action in favor of religious liberty. Sometimes the voices raised came from Baptists themselves, but at times leaders of the denomination could persuade their governments to intercede with foreign rulers on behalf of the persecuted. Because Britain and the United States long considered themselves Protestant powers, at times they exerted their influence on behalf of Protestants abroad. Thus, in 1849, the small Central American country of Costa Rica signed a treaty with Britain guaranteeing the right of worship to non-Catholic foreigners. Baptists sometimes intervened on behalf of their coreligionists on the European continent. Thus, in 1840, shortly after the formation of the Hamburg church, the police broke up a service and Oncken was sentenced to four weeks in prison with a heavy fine. A petition bearing 6,000 English and American signatures reached the Hamburg Senate, urging it to ensure the security of the congregation, and the persecution withered away. In 1858 John Howard Hinton and Edward Steane, the secretaries of the Baptist Union of Great Britain and Ireland, traveled to Sweden to try to obtain greater liberties for Baptists in that land. They rallied the Evangelical Alliance, an international body based in London that Hinton and Steane also ran, to the same cause. In 1852 the American Baptists persuaded the United States to urge the king of Prussia to protect the Baptists in his territories from harassment. In the twentieth century the same defense of religious liberties remained a significant concern of governments—indeed of a wider number, organized in the League of Nations and then the United Nations. The chief beneficiaries turned out to be the Romanian Baptists, who in the interwar years suffered active repression by the state, often at the instigation of the Orthodox clergy. In a repeated pattern, persecution would break out and James Henry Rushbrooke, as general secretary, would protest on behalf of the Baptist World Alliance, the global confessional body. The oppression would ease but then return. Rushbrooke and his fellow denominational leaders would then call on political leaders for action, international public opinion would demand protection for the Baptists, and—for a while—harassment would cease. Without the help from outside the country, Romanian Baptist growth might have been stunted. In the twentieth century, as in the nineteenth, the defense of religious liberty contributed to the spread of the Baptists.

RESULTS OF THE SPREAD

The advance of Baptists, by means of migration to nominally Christian countries as well as missions to non-Christian lands, meant that, by the early years of the twenty-first century, the denomination had a global spread. Something of its varying character can be indicated by a series of three case studies of contrasting national Baptist communities. The first is Australia, where Baptists have never been numerous. A peak of 2.37 percent of the population identified themselves as Baptists in 1901, and by 2001 the proportion had dropped to 1.6 percent. The nation began as separate British colonies around the coast of the vast island, and the British identity persisted long into the twentieth century. When, in 1918, H. Estcourt Hughes, a Baptist minister born in Australia, preached in Adelaide on "Our own Church in our own Land," what stood out was the extent of the continuing affiliation to the "mother country." "God," he declared, "had kept this land for England and for Protestantism."[6] The Roman Catholics, a strong element in Australia, were regarded as outsiders; so were the Aborigines, the native peoples of the land who held no citizenship and whom Hughes does not mention. During the twentieth century, in consequence of the failure of Britain to defend Australia during the Second World War and the subsequent arrival of continental European and Asian immigrants, the British links slowly slackened. In Evangelical circles including the Baptists, American influence gradually supplanted the British dominance. Christian literature, music, and teaching materials came increasingly from the United States. The American sway, however, did not eliminate local characteristics. Although Australia became a single Commonwealth in 1901, its states, which had begun as distinct colonies, retained their individuality, not least among Baptists. The Baptists of South Australia, described in 1901 as "broad, liberal and modern," had a tradition of open communion.[7] The denomination in Tasmania, by contrast, had a conservative theological bent as a result of all its pulpits' being filled by Spurgeon's men in the late nineteenth century. Queensland and New South Wales also leaned toward conservatism, while Victoria and Western Australia, though diverse, were more centrist in their Evangelicalism. The Baptist Union of Australia, which did not emerge until 1926, was a fading force by the end of the twentieth century. In a country of vast distances, local variety prevailed. Canada and other countries of original British settlement showed very similar characteristics. So, in two major respects Australian Baptists displayed typical features of this type of nation: early British affinities gave way to American cultural domination, and regions revealed markedly different tones.

A second case study is Russia and Ukraine, until the breakup of the Soviet Union a single state. There again variety has been a salient feature of Baptist life. The influence of different Christian bodies on the formation of the Baptists left its legacy. In the far south, in Transcaucasia, the orderly German Baptist tradition predominated, but in Ukraine it collided with the indigenous Molokan preference for a freer style. The Germans wanted adherence to the Calvinistic confession drawn up at Hamburg; many of the locals preferred to cultivate an unconstrained spirituality, fearing a fresh lapse into formalism. The Baptist leader Vasilii Ivanov, himself of Molokan stock, observed that the Russians liked to keep Molokan practices, but the Germans hoped to get rid of them and "set up everything in the German manner."[8] Other tensions were injected by the group of believers that arose from Lord Radstock's evangelism in St. Petersburg, the Evangelical Christians, who, though observing believer's baptism, did not maintain an ordained ministry and upheld open communion. At the first congress of the Union of Evangelical Christians–Baptists, shortly after the 1905 revolution allowed such a general meeting, a delegate asked if all the members were required to call themselves "Baptists." It was a term that he regarded as "non-Biblical and non-Russian."[9] In these circumstances a unified sense of Baptist identity was hard to achieve. Yet the warm spiritual theology of Ivan Kargel and the firm organizing ability of Ivan Prokhanov did weld the Evangelical Christians into an enduring entity, and one that, as Prokhanov's vice presidency of the Baptist World Alliance in 1911 showed, was willing to align itself with wider Baptist life. The common suffering of the Stalinist era merged the different streams more fully, and in 1944 the state required the formation of the All-Union Council of Evangelical Christians–Baptists. Disunity, however, broke out again. Friction over subservience to the Communist authorities led, in 1961, to the harsh repudiation of the All-Union Council by the more radical spirits. The congregations that formed the resulting Reform Baptists, or "underground church," suffered persecution for refusing to register with the state. Although the All-Union Council dissolved at the collapse of the Soviet state, the two traditions of Baptists persisted in both Russia and Ukraine. Both had a strong Baptist presence at the opening of the twenty-first century: there were some 100,000 church members in Russia, and about twice that number in Ukraine. They illustrate, in an acute way, features common to lands with a Christian heritage where Baptist faith and order were introduced in the nineteenth century: marked differences of ethos that arose from the external Christian traditions playing on them, and enduring differences of opinion over the proper attitude to the authorities in church and state.

The third case study is of the most Baptist land on earth. It is not a whole country, but a part of northeastern India, the remote, hilly, and forest-clad state of Nagaland. The Naga people are roughly 90 percent Christian and, though Roman Catholicism arrived after the Second World War, perhaps 80 percent (estimates vary) of the whole people have a Baptist allegiance. The Christian faith came into the territory through Godhula, a local evangelist working with the American Baptist missionaries of Assam. Godhula encountered a Naga tribesman when he came down to trade in a river valley, led him to Christian faith, and learned his version of the Naga language. Despite the reputation of the hill-dwellers for violence and beheadings, Godhula set off in 1871 to preach the gospel to the Naga people. Nine were baptized in the following year. Edward Winter Clark, an American missionary, and his wife, Mary, lived among the Ao Nagas, settling disputes, fostering literacy, and producing a dictionary and grammar. Steadily, the Christian message spread from village to village and from tribe to tribe. Churches were organized and associations, beginning with the Ao Baptist Association in 1897, sprang up to coordinate them. There were different reactions in various parts of Nagaland. The Ao Nagas were notable for sending out missionaries. The warlike Angami Nagas were slow to convert. The Sema Nagas turned Christian with hardly any missionary contact. By around 1970, however, most of the Nagas had adopted Christianity. The effects were marked. Educated young men developed a Naga consciousness, which, through the Naga National Council, demanded independence from India. Since 1956, away from the gaze of the world's media, there has been a sporadic freedom struggle, supported by some Baptists but not by others, that has sometimes been marked by Naga atrocities (a revival of their violent traditions) and by stern repression on the part of the Indian army. Baptist freedom fighters held armed prayer meetings. A non-Western form of Baptist Christianity emerged, much given to dreams as a means of communication with the Almighty. "I don't have to be like Anglicans and Catholics," a Baptist Naga was reported in 1986 as saying, "and go through all those rituals. . . . What I am talking about is Naga Christianity—an indigenous Naga Christianity."[10] The aversion to ceremonial is discernibly Baptist, but the assertion of distinctiveness is emphatic. When the gospel spread to the Nagas, it took on the lineaments of local culture. The Christians of this territory were not just Baptists, but were Naga Baptists.

The global spread of the Baptists during the nineteenth and twentieth centuries was therefore a more complex process than is sometimes suggested. Although, as the previous chapter demonstrated, it was partly a missionary achievement, it was also a consequence of the wealth of England, the language of Wales, and the energy of Scotland being deployed in lands with a nominal Christian allegiance. The Americans and the Germans played distinctive parts, though, as in the case of England, their role could be resented and so inhibit church growth. Several mechanisms of the transfer of Baptist convictions can be identified. There were group movements, sometimes amounting to migration *en masse*; individuals traveled to new lands; literature was deployed on a large scale; and other Christian bodies assisted the process. The repression that

Baptists encountered could actually benefit their diffusion, and yet the protection they enjoyed helped prevent their extinction. The result of the whole process, formal missions included, was the planting of Baptist churches throughout most of the world, but not with a uniform set of characteristics. Australian Baptists, though molded first by Britain and then by America, showed diversity in the different states. In Russia and Ukraine the Baptists were varied in origin, often unsure of their Baptist allegiance, and in recent years bitterly divided. Naga Baptists were Naga. Baptists naturally interacted with their cultural settings and so emerged differently. It was not that they adopted a set of qualities unique to their own land, for many of the influences were international. The British, American, and German influences were pervasive. It was not that groups simply moved from one part of the world to another, taking their whole cultural baggage with them, for other forces were at work. Individuals, literature, and other Christian bodies impinged on the groups, and persecution and protection could have different effects. Nor were the characteristics uniform across the nations: South Australian Baptists, St. Petersburg Evangelical Christians, and Ao Nagas held attitudes different from those of their neighbors. Rather, the features of Baptist life in various lands were the fruit of their people's specific experiences, the interplay of a whole range of factors. Baptist identity was, in practice, multiform.

FURTHER READING

Anderson, Justice C. *An Evangelical Saga: Baptists and Their Predecessors in Latin America*. N.p.: Xulon, 2005.

Briggs, John H. Y., ed. *A Dictionary of European Baptist Life and Thought*. Milton Keynes: Paternoster, 2009.

Coleman, Heather J. *Russian Baptists and Spiritual Revolution, 1905–1929*. Bloomington: Indiana University Press, 2005.

Manley, Ken R. *From Woolloomooloo to "Eternity": A History of Australian Baptists*. 2 vols. Milton Keynes: Paternoster, 2006.

Pierard, Richard V. *Baptists Together in Christ, 1905–2005: A Hundred-Year History of the Baptist World Alliance*. Falls Church, Va.: Baptist World Alliance, 2005.

Randall, Ian M. *Communities of Conviction: Baptist Beginnings in Europe.* Schwarzenfeld, Germany: Neufeld, 2009.

Randall, Ian M., Toivo Pilli, and Anthony R. Cross, eds. *Baptist Identities: International Studies from the Seventeenth to the Twentieth Centuries.* Milton Keynes: Paternoster, 2006.

Wardin, Albert W., ed. *Baptists around the World: A Comprehensive Handbook.* Nashville: Broadman & Holman, 1995.

Chapter 15

BAPTIST IDENTITY

The identity of Baptists became a major subject of discussion in the last quarter of the twentieth century. The question of what characteristics were distinctive to members of the denomination, and therefore worth prizing, turned into a lively issue, for two main reasons. On the one hand, the global expansion of the denomination that has been the subject of the last two chapters created a fresh scenario. When, in earlier times, British and American voices dominated conversation about Baptist principles, they had their own long traditions to guide them. Although there was sometimes a measure of discrepancy between the views taken on the two sides of the Atlantic, there was sufficient common ground for the question of Baptist identity to be a matter of consensus. When voices from other nations joined in the discussion, however, there was more scope for disagreement. International diversity meant that the Baptist Heritage Commission of the Baptist World Alliance needed to address the question. In 1989 it produced a document, tentatively entitled "Towards a Baptist Identity," which expounded the core distinctive beliefs of the denomination, including, for example, the authority of scripture and religious liberty. On the other hand, a controversy that, from 1979, tore apart the Southern Baptist Convention, by far the largest single Baptist denominational body, raised the question of which side upheld authentic Baptist convictions. The conservatives claimed to represent the convention's inherited view of the Bible; the moderates insisted that they stood for the traditional Baptist priority of freedom. The Baptist identity was at issue. This chapter will review the origins and course of the Southern Baptist debate, consider the main variations among Baptists during and after that tumultuous time, and note the significance of national divergences from Baptist norms. What did Baptist identity turn out to be?

Baptists had often tried to explain to outsiders who they were. They wanted to explain their identity so that they would not be misrepresented. This was the primary aim of the Particular Baptist London Confession of 1644: it was designed "for the cleering of the truth we professe."[1] On many occasions, too, they debated among themselves what the proper opinions of Baptists are—a contentious business because there is no obvious court of appeal. For Methodists, the teaching of John Wesley can help determine the authentic denominational position; for Presbyterians, the Westminster Confession can be used as a guide to what members should believe and practice. There is no agreed equivalent among Baptists. Their normal treatment of the Bible alone as authoritative in religion means that they have often refused to accept other documents as carrying any weight. In any case, they have been divided. Particular Baptists sometimes saw the 1689 London Confession as their equivalent of the Westminster Confession, but General Baptists self-consciously differed. During the seventeenth and eighteenth centuries, despite one or two attempts, it was impossible to formulate a declaration of faith that would satisfy both sides. The independence of each congregation has further complicated matters. Each local church was able to determine its own corporate beliefs or lack of them. Sometimes associations adopted confessions of faith, as many American Baptist associations accepted the New Hampshire Confession of 1833, but, as the nineteenth century advanced, many individual churches more or less consciously moved away from the practice. There was great and increasing scope for diversity. Baptist apologists had an increasingly difficult task.

There was, in fact, a significant shift in the expression of Baptist principles shortly after the opening of the twentieth century. The standard method of defending the distinctive features of Baptist identity during the nineteenth century had been an appeal to the Bible. That approach had not been universal in America. The widely respected Francis Wayland had argued in 1859 that the New Testament gave no enduring instructions about the form of church government, so that communities of Christians were free to be guided by expediency. Wayland, however, had not been widely heeded on this subject. Far more influential was Edward T. Hiscox, who, in the same year, published *The Baptist Directory*, in which he set out approved denominational practice with scripture proofs for each point. The normal standpoint was that of John Quincy Adams (not the former president), who, in 1876, wrote confidently of the position of the Baptists. "They follow the New Testament model of a church," he declared, "and invite all to test them by it."[2] This conviction was as common in Britain as in the United States. It appeared, for example, in Charles Williams' *The Principles and Practices of the Baptists* (1903), an official handbook issued with the authority of the Baptist Union, which still contained a page listing passages of scripture quoted as proof texts. In 1908, however, a book adopting a revolutionary method appeared: Edgar Y. Mullins, president of Southern Baptist Theological Seminary, published *The Axioms of Religion*. Mullins did not wish to abandon the Bible as the authority for ecclesiastical matters. "The Scriptures," he wrote, "are the rule of faith and practice." Yet he was taking fresh ground. He concluded the same sentence by adding "and the omnipresent Spirit the interpreter."[3] The Holy Spirit, he believed, guided the church's understanding of the Bible through Christian experience. The category of experience was elevated to a much higher place than it had hitherto occupied. The authority for Baptist faith and practice moved significantly from the written text of the Bible to the personal experience of Christians.

Edgar Young Mullins (1860–1928)
Baptist Theologian and Statesman

It seems evident that Mullins, though working out a new approach, was not intending to abandon older positions. His book was a sophisticated text, not simply setting out to restate Baptist views but attempting to show that they were philosophically defensible. Mullins, who had studied at The Johns Hopkins University, one of the foremost centers of American scholarship, was adjusting to the intellectual currents of the day. The high prestige of Immanuel Kant at the time meant that the philosopher's supreme valuation of the human individual was in vogue. It seemed to offer a defense against contemporary contentions that human beings were simply part of the material order. Like Borden Parker Bowne, the leading Methodist theologian at Boston University, Mullins adopted a form of personalism, a highlighting of the significance of the person who experiences the world. Unlike Bowne, however, Mullins was unwilling to sacrifice anything of the Evangelical heritage he had received. He therefore tried to fuse the personalist's stress on experience with the Evangelical's emphasis on coming to know Christ for oneself. The two seemed to mesh closely: the core of authentic Evangelical experience, he believed, marks out the dignity of each human person in the sight of God. The result was the case propounded in *The Axioms of Religion*. The primary axiom of Baptist faith and practice is "soul competency," the principle that religion is "a personal matter between the soul and God."[4] From that all else flows—the right of a holy and loving God to be sovereign, the equal right of human beings to access to God, the right of believers to equal privileges in the church, and so on. Instead of appealing to the Bible for each separate Baptist principle, Mullins suggested with great ingenuity that they all could be derived from that single axiom. Baptists therefore possessed an intellectually coherent position. In setting out this view, Mullins was not abandoning the possibility of referring to the Bible in order to vindicate denominational beliefs. Rather, he was restating Baptist convictions in a form that he hoped would be more convincing from a philosophical point of view.

The book proved extraordinarily influential. Other Baptists began to see soul competency as their prized possession. Mullins, as president of Southern Seminary, exercised a predominant sway over generations of pastors training for the ministry of the Southern Baptist Convention. He was also the central figure in the denominational structures, the man behind the first *Baptist Faith and Message* (1925), a document setting out the convention's beliefs. This statement disclaimed being a creed, but it was based on the New Hampshire Confession and subsequently formed an anchor of Southern Baptist Convention identity. Mullins' stance, however, was adopted far beyond his own denomination. His *Axioms of Religion* was issued by the Judson Press, the official publisher to the

Northern Baptist Convention, and so exerted sway among his coreligionists of the North. Mullins was also a speaker at the 1905 Baptist World Congress that inaugurated the Baptist World Alliance, and he immediately gained a world reputation for an exposition of the six axioms he was to restate in his book three years later. He went on to serve as president of the alliance from 1923 to 1928, and became the unquestioned bearer of Baptist identity at a global level. James H. Rushbrooke, the English minister who was the other leading figure in the alliance in the 1920s, echoed Mullins when, in an address to the Baptist Union of Great Britain and Ireland in 1926, he called soul competency the "unifying principle" for all that was distinctive about Baptist theology.[5] Although the American's phrase never gained widespread currency in the British Isles, it made its impact on Baptist leaders there. Mullins' views were responsible, as we have seen, for confirming a low estimate of the doctrine of the church, and they were equally powerful in providing a rationale for the principle of a free church in a free state. Although the Bible was far from forgotten, soul competency became the supreme Baptist value. Mullins drastically reoriented the way in which Baptist principles were presented.

The synthesis forged by Mullins remained a satisfying account of their identity for the Southern Baptists during much of the twentieth century. It was the intellectual counterpart of the practical arrangement whereby a vast denominational body of many millions stayed together. The broader-minded elites of denominational bureaucrats and faculty members were allowed to direct the affairs of the convention at the price of restraining their views for fear of provoking anxieties among the more theologically conservative grassroots. There were occasional expressions of suspicion about the willingness of the convention's educational institutions to teach biblical criticism, but the sheer success of the denomination in achieving massive growth stifled discontent. In 1935 total membership numbered some 4,480,000; by 1965 it was about 10,780,000. In the 1960s, however, the underlying worries about critical views of the Bible surfaced. In 1961 there was alarm over the publication by Ralph Elliott, of Midwestern Theological Seminary, Kansas, of *The*

Message of Genesis, which argued that much of the Old Testament was to be taken not literally but symbolically. Anxieties were strengthened because the authorities refused to instruct the convention's Broadman Press to withdraw the book, even though the press did take the book off the market and Elliott was dismissed by his seminary. The remedy adopted by the convention was the revision of the *Baptist Faith and Message* so as to strengthen the obligation of denominational teachers to be loyal to the authority of scripture. A second controversy was sparked in 1970 by the appearance of the first volume of a new series of Broadman Bible Commentaries, on Genesis, by G. Henton Davies, a Welsh Baptist who was principal of Regent's Park College, Oxford. Again the offense was the historical-critical method, and again the book was withdrawn by the press. Two other publications prepared the way for a more serious conflagration. Harold Lindsell's *The Battle for the Bible* (1976) warned that the Southern Baptists were in danger of slipping their biblical moorings, and two years later the Chicago Statement on Biblical Inerrancy provided a rallying cry in the contention that the scriptures are free from error. In 1979 controversy burst into flame.

The initial spark was the dismay of Paul Pressler, a Texas appeals court judge, when he found that former members of a boys' club that he ran in Houston were being taught to doubt the Bible once they began attending Baylor University, a Baptist institution. Pressler took his concern to his friend Paige Patterson, then president of Criswell Bible College in Dallas. Together they planned to demand that the higher education institutions of the Southern Baptist Convention should be made to toe the line on biblical inerrancy. At first the authorities in the denomination judged that, as on previous occasions, the issue could be contained, but that was a serious mistake. The president of the convention, elected annually by the representatives of the churches, nominated members of the committee on committees, which in turn selected recruits for the boards that ran the institutions of Southern Baptist life. By ensuring that the president chose only those willing to appoint inerrantists, critics could change the whole direction of the denomination. Pressler and Patterson pursued this policy with thorough efficiency, encouraging the conservative churches to ensure that their messengers voted only for conservatives. From the election of Adrian Rogers in 1979 onwards, only those willing to implement this strategy were chosen as presidents of the convention. By 1984 the apparently relentless pursuit of power by the conservatives was alarming the moderates who had previously controlled affairs. Roy L. Honeycutt, president of Southern Seminary, declared a "holy war" against the conservatives. In 1985 the moderate candidate for the presidency, Winfred Moore, was indistinguishable from the conservatives in theological opinion, and yet was defeated because he opposed limiting Baptist leadership to inerrantists. Thereafter the issue was virtually decided. In 1986 the first denominational agency, the Home Mission Board, fell to the conservatives, and gradually the rest followed. By 1990 it remained only to work out the consequences of the conservative victory.

In this fierce struggle over Baptist identity the synthesis created by Mullins fell apart. The conservatives ("Fundamentalists" to their opponents) insisted on one side of what Baptists in the Mullins era had stressed; the moderates ("liberals" to their opponents) insisted on another. The Bible was pitted against freedom. That is not to say that there were only two parties, for it would be truer to describe the range of opinion as a continuum, ranging from actual Fundamentalists on the right to actual liberals on the left. Most stood nearer the center, being conservative in their theological views but moderate in their denominational allegiance. Yet, in the heat of battle, there was a real polarization that meant that the two sides believed that different issues were at stake. The conservatives, on the one hand, held that the sole fundamental issue was the Bible. They could quote the first clause of the 1925 *Baptist Faith and Message*, framed by Mullins, affirming that scripture "has truth, without any mixture of error, for its matter."[6] Hence, they argued, the denomination was committed to biblical inerrancy. According to Pressler, the word "conservative" applied to "a belief that the original text of the Bible was written by God in such a way that it is free from error or mistakes."[7] Whether that principle was to be reaffirmed, they claimed, was the single question before them, though implications flowed from it. For one thing, the denomination could be called "Evangelical." The conservative leaders were much influenced by Northern Evangelicals, particularly Carl Henry and Francis Schaeffer, who asserted the cruciality of insisting on an inerrant text of the scriptures as originally given. The Southern Baptists, according to the conservatives, should align with this point of view. Another implication was that moral stances apparently validated by the Bible were obligatory. Thus, in 1986, Patterson warned that the convention would, in the future, no longer employ people who failed to resist abortion or euthanasia. Moderates might see this policy as falling under the sway of the New Christian Right, but for conservatives the question was one of defending biblical principles. In their eyes, the one ultimate question under debate was the nature of the Bible.

For moderates, on the other hand, the priority was the Baptist commitment to freedom. As one of their leaders, Alan Neely, put it in the title of his book, "being Baptist means freedom."[8] It followed that believers possessed the liberty to interpret the Bible for themselves. Against the conservatives, moderates held that different ways of understanding scripture, unshackled by inerrancy, were permissible. They did not discard their allegiance to the authority of scripture. Indeed, in a celebrated summary of moderate principles, first forged in 1985 but issued in revised form eight years later as *The Baptist Identity: Four Fragile Freedoms*, Walter B. Shurden placed "Bible Freedom" before "Soul Freedom." The latter principle, however, showed the strength of the debt to Mullins: soul freedom is treated as equivalent to "the competency of the soul before God."[9] The experiential side of Mullins' synthesis came into its own, validating the individual's conscience. Those who stressed freedom in this manner were horrified by the way in which conservatives were willing to emphasize authority, by asserting, for example, the duty of church members to obey their pastors. The whole conservative enterprise was, in the estimation of moderates, utterly unbaptist, an expression of an "urge for power."[10] An implication of the claim to be maintaining the Baptist heritage of freedom was the common repudiation of the label "Evangelical." Baptists, it was stressed, were different from Northern Evangelicals precisely because, unlike them, they valued liberty so highly. There were also implications that touched on national politics. Since freedom was the priority, moderates argued, Baptists should insist on liberty of conscience for all and so adhere to the strict separation of church and state. There should be no toying with school prayers or grants from public money for religious purposes. The consequence was that moderates often felt distant from Republican overtures to the Religious Right on such issues, finding more affinity with the Democratic Party, which many had, in any case, supported from their youth. To the ecclesiastical struggle, therefore, was added a party-political dimension. The partisan edge helps explain the vitriolic nature of the combat.

The outworking of the Southern Baptist battles continued long after the 1980s. Within the denomination, the process of determining the fate of institutions steadily proceeded. The previous presidents of the Sunday School Board and of the Foreign Mission Board left office in 1991 and 1992, respectively, and were replaced by conservatives. Some of the universities associated with the denomination, because they enjoyed a much greater degree of autonomy than its agencies, were able to end their control by state conventions: Baylor in 1990, Mercer in 2005. The seminaries, falling under the aegis of convention appointees, turned into conservative institutions. Southern Seminary, for instance, appointed R. Albert Mohler Jr. as its president in 1993, and, in the next two years, encouraged several faculty members to resign, including Molly T. Marshall, a critic of exclusively male language about God, and Diana Garland, dean of Church Social Work, in a dispute over how strict the criteria for new faculty should be. Sections of the denomination split off. The Alliance of Baptists and the Cooperative Baptist Fellowship, representing different shades of moderate opinion, became more or less independent bodies. In Virginia, the state where moderates had shown the greatest strength, a group calling itself the Southern Baptist Conservatives of Virginia broke away from the state convention in 1996, the first outright schism that arose from the dispute. Texas and North Carolina Baptists reached a compromise allowing churches of conservative and moderate complexion to coexist, but this measure did not prevent the founding of a separate Southern Baptists of Texas Convention for loyalists to the national body.

Perhaps most crucially, the division spread to the rest of the world. When, in 2003, the Baptist World Alliance decided to accept the Cooperative Baptist Fellowship as a member body, the Southern Baptist Convention decided to sever its links with the world organization. Soon, amidst charges that the alliance was liberal, the convention took steps to foster likeminded conservative Baptists throughout the world. The outcome was schism on a global scale.

In the years surrounding the controversy, seven fairly distinct strands of Baptist life could be identified. The tendencies in the United States, which normally had equivalents elsewhere, had existed before the struggle of the 1980s, but they were, in part, accentuated by the disputes. In the first place were those who were not ashamed to call themselves liberals. In a 1985 representative survey of Southern Baptists, only 1 percent chose liberal as a self-description, but there was a higher proportion among the American Baptists of the North and the members of the denomination in Britain. The Alliance of Baptists, begun among Southern Baptists in 1988, catered to churches of liberal loyalties. Among the American Baptists were eminent figures who could be labeled liberal or even radical. The theologian Harvey Cox, an American Baptist minister who taught at Harvard from 1965 to 2009, was the author of *The Secular City* (1965), a classic statement of the view that God is as present in secular developments as in religion. In Britain, Michael Taylor, principal of the Northern Baptist College, delivered an address to the Baptist Union in 1971 in which he declared that he must stop short of saying that Jesus is God. This drastic abandonment of accepted christological belief created a sharp controversy in which conservative churches left the union. Although the denomination resolved its commitment to orthodoxy in the following year, it was evident that radical theology existed in its ranks. In other world bodies, and most obviously the Anglican communion, the most acute debates in the early twenty-first century focused on the acceptability of homosexual behavior. Was a committed partnership between people of homosexual orientation legitimate for Christians? A few Baptists said yes. In 1992 there was formed an Association of Welcoming and Affirming Baptists, which urged the full inclusion of lesbian, gay, bisexual, and transgender persons in church life. The Baptist Peace Fellowship, formed in the North in 1940 but reconstituted as a nationwide body in 1984, broadened its stance to embrace environmentalism and gender issues as well as peacemaking. Most of its members would probably have identified with a liberal theological position.

There were, secondly, the classic Evangelicals. These were Baptists endorsing the emphases on the Bible, the cross, conversion, and activism that had been displayed over the centuries by Evangelicals, but without any strong additional allegiance to charismatic renewal or Calvinist theology. There was a certain breadth to their approach, for they were normally willing to tolerate diversity within their churches. Although the term "Evangelical" was often understood to imply a commitment to inerrancy, this was often not the case, especially outside the United States. Paradoxically, those in this tendency might not, especially in the American South, avow the name "Evangelical," but that term best describes them. The Cooperative Baptist Fellowship, founded in 1991 to cater to Southern Baptist moderates, included many of this stamp. They generally had a high regard for evangelism, though typically they would not sever it from social action and called the combination "mission." Thus, in 2005, the minister of spiritual formation at First Baptist Church, Winston-Salem, North Carolina, a Cooperative Baptist Fellowship congregation, could praise the idea of a missional church that was "about being on mission 24/7."[11] Many of those who remained inside the Southern Baptist Convention would not have differed. One of the most influential texts about mission in global Evangelicalism at the end of the twentieth century, *The Purpose-Driven Church* (1995), was by Rick Warren, the pastor of Saddleback Valley Community Church in Orange County, California, a megachurch that was also a Southern Baptist congregation. The American Baptists, the African American denominations, and the Baptists of Australia, Britain, and Canada all had many churches that avowed a similar point of view. Rarely restricted in their fellowship to Baptists, their members often played a prominent part in interdenominational initiatives, such as local missions or student work. Although they were Evangelical, they also had a dash of catholicity.

A third strand was the premillennial point of view. These Baptists were Evangelicals who added to the characteristics they shared with others in this camp their own belief in the imminent second advent. They favored, it was sometimes said, "the Book, the Blood, and the Blessed Hope." The General Convention of Regular Baptists, a denomination formed in 1932 as a result of the Modernist controversy in the Northern Baptist Convention, had articles of faith that committed it to premillennialism, but the belief was far more widespread. In 1985 as many as 59 percent of Southern Baptist respondents surveyed agreed with a premillennial view of history and the future. In Oklahoma during the 1970s there was a Baptist Premillennial Fellowship, strongly faithful to the Southern Baptist Convention. The loyalist policy had to be maintained because adventism was commonly associated with separation from denominational affiliations. It was one of the hallmarks of independents throughout the world. In 1971 in Australia, there were twenty-one such churches, all militantly Fundamentalist. Some such congregations, especially in America, grew to huge proportions, drawing tens of thousands of worshipers each Sunday. These megachurches often functioned effectively as denominations in themselves, with elaborate educational facilities, training schools, and commercial operations. Most of the televangelists such as Pat Robertson also belonged to this school of thought, and they were partly responsible for its vigor. In Britain, where broadcasting was closed to preachers of this kind, premillennial teaching faded away in the late twentieth century. The greatest reinforcement of adventist teaching in America and in some other lands, however, came from the immensely popular "Left Behind" series of novels by the Baptist Tim LaHaye and his coauthor Jerry Jenkins. By 2006 they had sold no fewer than 63 million copies worldwide; the associated PC game *Left Behind: Eternal Forces* was advertised as allowing players to join "the ultimate fight of good versus evil, commanding Tribulation Forces or the Global Community Peacekeepers."[12] The premillennial current still flowed strongly wherever these novels were read.

In the fourth place, there was charismatic renewal. From the 1960s the Pentecostal experience of speaking in tongues spilled over into other Protestant churches throughout the English-speaking world and beyond. A whole new style of Christian life welled up, open to signs and wonders, eager to see divine healing, and dedicated to contemporary idioms of worship. There was much initial resistance among Baptists, who often saw the development as an unhealthy immersion in experience, to the neglect of the word. Yet, as successive pastors and congregations were affected by the movement, renewal became a growing force in many lands. New Zealand Baptists were particularly strongly affected at an early stage. In 1971 an American Baptist Charismatic Fellowship was formed. By the same year Southern Baptists, though they normally rejected the development, included in their ranks some who were holding Preachers' Renewal Conferences. An Australian Baptist pastor who attended such a conference at Lake Windermere, Missouri, received an experience there that rid him of his former Fundamentalist hostility. "I got killed," as he put it, "and Filled."[13] In the 1970s the "Effataa" revival at a Baptist church in Tallinn, the capital of Estonia, was marked by healing services and charismatic signs. So popular were the Russian-language services that they were banned in 1981, following pressure from the Soviet authorities. Gradually, the new ethos spread to churches that did not wholly avow its theological premises. Young people were drawn by its music, which typically discarded organs and hymn books in favor of guitars, keyboards, and drums. Contemporary songs and raised hands, a charismatic hallmark, invigorated the experience of worship. By the end of the twentieth century, over half the churches of the Baptist Union of Great Britain had been more or less drastically altered by renewal. Some churches were so transformed that they left the union altogether in order to forge links with new connections of charismatic congregations. In France, although the more conservative of the two main Baptist bodies and the independent Baptists set their faces against the charismatic style, the largest of the denominations, the Baptist Federation, was open to its influence. By the early twenty-first century, nearly half the Baptists of France were synthesizing Baptist ways with charismatic practices and a few were no longer emphasizing Baptist distinctives at all. Charismatic renewal was a vast and growing global phenomenon.

There was, fifthly, the Calvinist strand. The Reformed expression of the faith had never disappeared from Baptist life. Primitive Baptists in America and Strict Baptists in England existed in order to bear witness to Calvinism in a robust form. African American churches were also predominantly Calvinist, though they espoused a more moderate type of Calvinism and sometimes displayed a version of the New Hampshire Confession in their buildings. A survey of black Baptist churches in Oklahoma taken in 1989 showed that only a single congregation rejected Calvinism. But among most white Baptists of North America and elsewhere the Reformed tradition was in decay around the middle of the twentieth century. In its later years, however, Calvinism enjoyed a revival. Martyn Lloyd-Jones, a Welsh minister of the Congregational Westminster Chapel in the heart of London, promoted Calvinist teaching in his influential sermons, and from 1957 the Banner of Truth Trust, associated with Lloyd-Jones, republished Reformed classics that enjoyed a worldwide circulation. Already in 1960, under the influence of Banner of Truth publications, a Baptist Reformation Alliance was formed in Tasmania, and Calvinism, a powerful force among Sydney Anglicans, spread elsewhere in Australia. Baptist preachers in America, such as John Piper of Minneapolis, took up the cause of the doctrines of grace, as Calvinists delighted in calling their distinctive position. Among Southern Baptists, an annual Founders' Conference was set up to propagate, as its title indicated, the views of the denomination's original leaders in 1845. Only a small minority of the conservative victors in the struggle of the 1980s avowed Calvinism, and often their successors were ambivalent about it. Russell D. Moore, Dean of Theology at the Southern Baptist Theological Seminary, for instance, confessed himself in 2009 to be "a weird hybrid," who believed with Calvinists in personal election but with Arminians in a universal atonement.[14] Yet many at Southern, including its president, R. Albert Mohler Jr., were exponents of Reformed teaching. Calvinism, like charismatic renewal but rarely in combination with it, was making marked advances in the early years of the twenty-first century.

In the sixth place, there was an affinity for the Anabaptists. Over the centuries, Baptists had sometimes wanted to bridge the gap between themselves and the body that had preceded them in adopting believer's baptism. In the 1790s John Rippon, in his *Baptist Annual Register*, treated Mennonites as the continental branch of the Baptists. In the United States the peace witness of the Mennonites was attractive to American Baptists who championed pacifism during and after the Second World War. In the middle years of the twentieth century, Ernest Payne, general secretary of the Baptist Union of Great Britain and Ireland, pursued scholarly studies of the Anabaptists, stressing their interaction with the Baptists over the years. But more active borrowing of Anabaptist ideals in England was fostered by Alan and Ellie Kreider, Mennonite representatives based in London in the 1970s and 1980s. Charismatic renewal generated interest in radical Christianity, and a charismatic Baptist leader, Nigel Wright, cooperated with Alan Kreider in launching a network of Anabaptist study groups. Wright, who published *The Radical Kingdom* (1986) as a restatement of Anabaptist ideas for modern consumption, went on to serve as principal of Spurgeon's College, which became a center for their dissemination. In an age when Christendom was past, the views of its earliest critics seemed especially relevant to mission. The International Baptist Theological Seminary in Prague, set amid lands where Anabaptists had flourished, promoted study of their legacy alongside that of the Baptists. In the United States, as we have seen, the Anabaptists were treated as the progenitors of the Baptists by William R. Estep. His institution, Southwestern Baptist Theological Seminary, became even more of a center for the recovery of the Anabaptist heritage under the presidency of Paige Patterson from 2003. Although Patterson conceded that there was no indisputable connection between Baptists and continental Anabaptists, he held that there was much to learn from them, not least their sheer courage in the face of martyrdom. The Anabaptists were alternatives to the Calvinists as exemplars of the faith.

A seventh strand of Baptist life was High Church in orientation. Its most eloquent expression was a manifesto called "Re-Envisioning Baptist Identity" issued in 1997 by a group of Baptists including Curtis W. Freeman, later director of the Baptist House of Studies at Duke University Divinity School. Freeman expounded the manifesto as a critique of the Enlightenment captivity of Baptist theology. The individualism of the Enlightenment was the central target because, as Freeman argued, it was ultimately responsible for the Baptist battles of the 1980s since it equally underlay the positions of the two sides. Against individualism the manifesto set the principle of community. The manifesto urged Baptists to see the freedom that they prized as a gift received "through the divine community of the triune God and with the Christian fellowship that shares in this holy communion." Although part of the inspiration for the communitarian ideal came from the Anabaptists, the document also celebrated "the church catholic" and retrieved, the authors believed, the early Baptists' exalted doctrine of the church. There were affinities, as we have seen in chapter 11, with the sacramental revival in Britain. The manifesto described the sacraments as "powerful signs" rather than as "mere symbols."[15] In Britain, Paul Fiddes, principal of Regent's Park College, Oxford, urged Baptists to think of themselves as bound together by covenant, a concept he derived from early Baptist sources. Fiddes, like the authors of the manifesto, drew on denominational tradition and arrived at a higher churchmanship than had been customary. The same impulse toward more exalted churchmanship was seen in the growing number of congregations where liturgy was elaborated. None was more striking than South Yarra Community Baptist Church in Melbourne, Australia, where, by 2009, the arrangements, deeply influenced by Eastern Orthodox practice, included the use of a censer to disperse drops of water over the congregation and the display of a beam of wood—an iconostasis—bearing portraits of assorted saints, including John Bunyan. There were striking High Church elements in Baptist life.

The seven strands of Baptist life all appeared in many parts of the world. Often, however, they were drastically modified by local conditions. As the previous chapter has suggested, there were innumerable national variations that defy analysis. Yet something of their character can be illustrated by a case study of Latvia, one of the small republics on the Baltic Sea that once formed part of the Soviet Union. Because Soviet law permitted only singing as a congregational activity, choirs played a significant part in services. The Lutheran traditions of the country made "altar paintings" acceptable, and the sectarian image of Baptists led some churches to downplay their distinctive identity to the extent of avoiding the denominational title in their names. The Baptist denomination, however, was one of eight that were officially recognized by the state and so could provide religious instruction in state schools. The leaders of the denomination, as had been customary for senior Lutheran, Catholic, and Orthodox clergy, were consulted by the government and took part in Independence Day ceremonies. Here was a degree of state involvement that would be frowned on by many Baptists elsewhere. Most remarkably, the Baptists had a bishop. Their leader around 1870 used the title unselfconsciously, and after the Second World War, when the Russians took over the country, leadership by a Latvian bishop was convenient for Baptists to ensure control over their own affairs. The bishop signed all official documents first, represented the Baptist Union in discussions with bishops of other churches, and, after the collapse of the Soviet system, even wore a purple shirt, the international sign of episcopal dignity. The standing of the Baptist bishops, however, was circumscribed because they were elected for only a limited term of years and normally continued to act as local pastors. Nor was Latvia unique in possessing Baptist bishops. Moldova and Georgia in the Caucasus did so too; the latter even had an archbishop. Baptist practice in Latvia, as in these other countries, was constructed out of its own particular experience. "Baptist faith," declared one of their pastors in 1912, "is faith found by Latvians themselves."[16] The Latvian cameo illustrates the extent to which specific national circumstances could affect the patterns of denominational life.

The attitude of Baptists to their identity became a highly contentious matter in the later twentieth century. In earlier times there had been divergence between different Baptist groupings, but at the start of the twentieth century a unifying axiom was proposed by Edgar Y. Mullins. The idea of soul competency became the key to Baptist principles, opening the door to an understanding that combined convictions derived from the Bible with a rationale framed in terms of Christian experience. Baptists in the United States had discovered a banner under which to march. In the Southern Baptist Convention there were rumblings when the Bible seemed to be called into question, and from 1979 they turned into a cacophony of conflict. Conservatives proclaimed the inerrancy of scripture to be the one thing needful; moderates insisted, on the contrary, that freedom was the Baptists' birthright. The sustained ideological struggle terminated in conservative control of the denomination, but at the expense of losing moderates to other groupings and of creating a fissure among Baptists across the world. In the wake of the controversy there were seven main strands of Baptist life. A liberal section of opinion upheld liberty in theology and tolerance in practice as the cardinal virtues. Classic Evangelicals pursued holistic mission without qualms about interdenominational cooperation. Premillennialists, on the other hand, objected to anything savoring of compromise with error, often to the extent of separating from denominational organizations. Charismatic renewal, where it was tolerated, induced a revolution in worship that offered powerful attractions to the young. Although it was of long standing, Calvinism was another force with markedly growing appeal, and the Anabaptists formed a further pattern for imitation from the past. Finally, High Church views were beginning to spread, in a few local churches as well as among intellectuals. Nor were the variations all created by schools of theology. Factors arising from local conditions impinged on national practice, leading to unusual phenomena such as Baptist bishops. So Baptist identity in the early twenty-first century was diverse. Although the sharpest Baptist battles were over, the consensus of the Mullins epoch was past.

FURTHER READING

Ammerman, Nancy Tatom. *Baptist Battles: Social Change and Religious Conflict in the Southern Baptist Convention.* New Brunswick, N.J.: Rutgers University Press, 1990.

Dockery, David S., ed. *Southern Baptist Identity: An Evangelical Denomination Faces the Future.* Wheaton, Ill.: Crossway Books, 2009.

Ellis, William E. *A Man of Books and a Man of the People: E. Y. Mullins and the Crisis of Moderate Southern Baptist Leadership.* Macon, Ga.: Mercer Universtiy Press, 2003.

Hankins, Barry. *Uneasy in Babylon: Southern Baptist Conservatives and American Culture.* Tuscaloosa: University of Alabama Press, 2002.

Mullins, Edgar Y. *The Axioms of Religion.* Philadelphia: Judson Press, 1908.

Shurden, Walter B. *The Baptist Identity: Four Fragile Freedoms.* Macon, Ga.: Smyth & Helwys, 1993.

Chapter 16

CONCLUSION

The issues examined in this book have yielded a number of conclusions that can usefully be drawn together. The treatment of the various topics has been long and broad, covering four centuries and touching on most parts of the world. There has been discussion of a wide range of subjects that historians have explored sufficiently to make analysis worthwhile. In chapter 10 on the role of women, though, it was noted that, because too little research has so far been done, it is at present impractical to review the place of gender as a whole in Baptist life. The same is true of a large number of other themes, including several near the heart of Baptist life. Up to now, for instance, there has been far too little written on aspects of Baptist spirituality such as conversion and revivals. Even the conduct of worship services is a very opaque subject, and still awaits its chroniclers. But several questions of great moment for understanding Baptists have been addressed. There has been consideration of a number of political themes, ranging from the rebuke administered by one of the earliest Baptists to their king, to the close identification of twentieth-century Baptists with American civil religion. Social issues have been addressed, for there has been scrutiny of

Baptist involvement in the social gospel movement, of their vary-ing attitudes toward racial problems, and of the place they made for women. And cultural developments have not been ignored, because the Enlightenment and Romanticism have emerged as cru-cial remolding forces that impinged on Baptist life. The main focus, however, has normally been on essentially religious matters such as theology and missions. Theological divisions of different kinds were salient in each of the centuries, and the spread of the gospel became a central preoccupation of most Baptists from the later eighteenth century onwards. In this complex story, what has most obviously emerged?

THE FINDINGS OF THE BOOK

The chapter on the Reformation showed that Baptists pursued its main principles with great thoroughness. They were the inheritors of continental protests against developments in medieval Christendom and of English Puritan objections to the half-reformed Church of England. The separatists determined to cast off all connection with Catholic practice and Anglican compromise, and it was from their ranks that Baptists emerged. John Smyth, as the next chapter men-tioned, was so concerned to flee from all idolatry that he refused to have the Bible in a worship service. The case for seeing continu-ity between continental Anabaptists and English Baptists was care-fully evaluated. Although there were Anabaptists in Amsterdam when Smyth baptized himself in 1609, and although they appear to have transmitted Arminian teaching to Smyth and his friends, the Anabaptists seem to have had no direct influence on his decision to perform the act of baptism. Nevertheless, as a later chapter showed, the inspiration of the Anabaptist example remained a potent force in the twenty-first century. In seventeenth-century England and the other lands to which they spread, the Baptists were united by their belief in a gathered church, their endorsement of the kingship of all believers, and their practice of believer's baptism. Yet once the confused period of the earlier 1640s was over, they crystallized out into the Particular Baptists, who were Calvinists and close to the Independents, and the General Baptists, who were Arminians and nearer to the Quakers. Although both bodies were sections of Protestant Dissent, suffering together from persecution in the later seventeenth century, they were two separate denominations.

The eighteenth century witnessed a transformation in Baptist life. Toleration made conditions easier and the Enlightenment initially made theology more rationalist, but the biggest change was made by the Evangelical Awakening. Baptists at first looked askance at a movement that ignored the questions of church order that they held dear, but they were subsequently infiltrated by the converts and theology of the revival. The effect was immense. Most Baptists ceased to be introspective, their numbers exploded, and they launched new missionary ventures at home and abroad. In the nineteenth century they remained, for the most part, fervent Evangelicals, and organized a host of new agencies for the spread of the gospel. Some objected to the innovations, but many, especially in England, were so convinced of the priority of fellowship with other Evangelicals that they ceased to make baptism a condition of participation in the Lord's supper. American Baptists divided over sectional allegiance, Alexander Campbell's Reform proposals, and, in some measure, over Landmarkism. Language and race were enduring lines of separation, but the old contrast between Calvinists and Arminians faded. A new tendency toward theological polarization, however, arose among Baptists, as among all Evangelicals, toward the end of the century. Broader theological views molded by Romantic ways of thinking coupled with biblical criticism came into vogue. Charles Haddon Spurgeon protested in the Downgrade Controversy, and, in the wake of the First World War, conflict broke out between Fundamentalists and Modernists. Most Baptists, however, remained moderate Evangelicals, cautiously embracing new perspectives while at the same time maintaining evangelistic priorities. In the twentieth century the legacy of the Evangelical Awakening was still the most potent factor shaping Baptist life.

The broader issues facing Baptists included their attitude toward the ills of modern society. In the mid-nineteenth century they had felt inhibitions about addressing questions requiring social change, but they long expected improvement through postmillennial hopes and practical philanthropy. Their own temperance and social purity activism, together with a range of external influences, pushed them toward greater corporate engagement with social problems. The social gospel, especially as promoted by Walter Rauschenbusch and John Clifford, was the result, though from the 1920s it became the target of severe criticism by theological conservatives. Perhaps the most serious social issue was the racial question. Although Baptists joined in the pressure against the slave trade and many of them subsequently denounced American slavery, they included in their ranks many slaveholders as well as many slaves. Native Americans and other indigenous peoples were often treated shamefully. Even after the slaves were freed, racial oppression continued in the American South. African Americans found in their churches a haven from the ills of a segregated society and in their ministers their leading champions. After the Second World War black churches provided the impetus for the civil rights movement that eventually changed white Baptist attitudes and banished the most outrageous aspects of racial inequality. The place of women in church and society has formed another issue among Baptists. There was usually a female majority in their churches, but early Baptists were insistent on following the limitations on women's speech that they found in the Bible. Nevertheless, women played a far larger part in Baptist life than has normally been recognized—through their spirituality, literature, childcare, charitable work, and missionary support. Reform pressure actually took them into public affairs, but women were still rarely found in church leadership until the twentieth century. The rise of feminism led to women entering the ministry, but that development was resisted by those who saw it as breach of the clear teaching of scripture. So the role of women, like the social gospel and the racial question, was sometimes a hotly contested topic amongst Baptists.

Baptists were concerned over the long term with religious liberty. At their origins they made a decisive break with the long-standing Christian tradition of expecting the state to promote the interests of the church, and argued for something approaching total freedom of conscience. Later on they were normally content to defend the toleration the English authorities gave to Dissent, but in the ferment of the creation of the American republic, the Baptists argued for the separation of church and state. A full-blooded defense of liberty of conscience for all, however, was qualified for much of the nineteenth and twentieth centuries by a desire to maintain the Protestant values of the English-speaking world. In the more recent past Baptists have divided over the meaning of their historic defense of liberty, with some favoring the strict separation of church and state but others believing that a public preference for religion is legitimate. There have also been differences over the proper denominational stance toward the church, ministry, and sacraments. It is plain that the Baptists have consistently defended the principles of the gathered church and believer's baptism but have rejected priestly understandings of ministry and any physical presence of Christ at the Lord's supper. But there have been changes over time in their understanding of these ecclesiological matters. In their early years they professed a High Churchmanship that steadily declined during the debates of the eighteenth and nineteenth centuries. By the twentieth century they were low in their churchmanship, often seeing that position as essential to their identity. A sacramental revival, however, challenged that assumption in the later twentieth century, and asserted in particular that baptism is a distinct means of grace. It would be as mistaken, therefore, to hold that there has been a single Baptist attitude on questions surrounding the nature of the church as it would be to claim that there has been unanimity on issues of church and state.

The expansion of Baptists on a global scale is a phenomenon of the nineteenth and subsequent centuries. The process was accomplished by two means, the foreign missionary movement to non-Christian lands and the less formal migration of Baptists to fresh parts of the Christian world. Although other church bodies had already promoted missionary work, the creation of the Baptist Missionary Society in 1792 was a landmark in the history of missions. It inaugurated the era of Anglo-American organizations spreading the faith outside Christendom. Colonial empires did less for missions than historians sometimes suppose, but the missionaries brought features of Western civilization that were much appreciated. The missions were also helped by experience in the field, by indigenous workers and women activists, and by the schools, colleges, hospitals, and dispensaries they provided. Undenominational societies supplemented Baptist organizations and national leaders gradually took over from missionaries. The effect was the planting of Baptist churches in many new regions. The same result came from the transfer of personnel to regions of the world that, though predominantly Christian, had lacked a Baptist presence. The United Kingdom, the United States, and Germany were the countries most responsible for this spread. Groups and individuals, literature, and other Christian bodies all played their part in the process. Sometimes repression could help the cause, but Baptists under persecution also received help from their coreligionists and from government intervention. As a consequence of the processes of expansion, Baptists became a feature of most lands under the sun, and greater variety in Baptist life has been the outcome. The growth of the Baptists has accentuated their diversity.

THE IMPLICATIONS OF THE SURVEY

What inferences can be drawn from this analysis? In the first place, it is evident that Baptist history can best be understood internationally. Not only were there movements of missionaries and groups from one land to another, but the main themes of denominational history were long played out in roughly similar ways on the two sides of the Atlantic. The Baptists who began the churches of America originally came from Britain, but links, influences, and intertwinings also continued over the long term. The revival of the eighteenth century affected Baptists in England and America in the same manner; there was a schism among Calvinists over whether faith was a duty on both sides of the Atlantic in the nineteenth century; and the social gospel was advocated in similar terms by Clifford and Rauschenbusch at the opening of the twentieth century. It has sometimes been supposed that the Baptists of America were in some sense separate from their coreligionists in Britain. "The Baptist movement of New England," according to its distinguished historian William G. McLoughlin, "was essentially an indigenous, parallel movement to that in England, and not an offshoot or extension of it."[1] The evidence, however, does not support the notion that Baptists in America were a distinct people. William H. Brackney has shown that the early churches of the New and Old Worlds, New England included, interacted extensively with each other.[2] It is true that the Separate Baptists were a distinctive product of America, but the Regular Baptists with whom they merged were not. Representatives of the Philadelphia Association wrote in 1762 to the Baptist Board of Ministers in London that they wished to correspond because they were part of the Baptist community in the British dominions "whereof you have in some sort the superintendence."[3] Nor did independence end the borrowing of ideas. When a trio of enterprising New York ministers reprinted standard Baptist works in 1846, the collection was full of English authors: John Bunyan, Andrew Fuller, Robert Hall, and so on.[4] Spurgeon's sermons were devoured in the United States at least as much as the tales of Charles Dickens. American Baptists were long aware that their community was essentially transatlantic.

Subsequently there were a number of alterations in the pattern of Baptist relationships, but the international dimension persisted. One change was that the direction of the dominant flow of influence reversed. Whereas in the centuries down to the nineteenth, the British contribution to America by way of personnel, ideas, and practices was preponderant, in the twentieth and twenty-first centuries the American sway over Britain was in the ascendant. The impact of Billy Graham, the international American evangelist, on Britain from the 1950s onwards had no equivalent in the opposite direction. A second new development was the extension during the nineteenth and twentieth centuries of the range of countries affected by the Baptists of Britain and America. In the years after the Second World War the American influence became pervasive. Even in Romania under Communism, the systematic theology taught at the Bucharest Baptist Seminary was inspired by Augustus H. Strong and Edgar Y. Mullins. A third development was the creation of an organization to foster and coordinate bonds between global Baptists. The Baptist World Alliance (BWA), begun in London in 1905,

Billy Graham (b. 1918)
Baptist Evangelist

was late in starting, for the Anglicans, Lutherans, Presbyterians, Methodists, and Congregationalists had all begun their world confessional bodies during the previous century. But the BWA subsequently acted as a significant vehicle for mutual support and the exchange of ideas. Initially it was dominated by people from Britain and the United States, but the main theme of its history was the widening of international participation. Its third congress, in 1923, was in Stockholm, signaling an awareness of the growing strength of continental European Baptist life; its tenth, in 1960, met outside North America or Europe for the first time, in Rio de Janeiro, symbolizing the growth of the denomination in the southern hemisphere. Regional organizations were gradually set up and the staff internationalized from the 1980s. Voices from newer Baptist lands were heard with greater frequency at congresses, councils, and commissions, and attendance grew from those regions. By the eighteenth congress in Melbourne in 2000, there were as many as 452 delegates from India, once the first field of the denomination's missions. The BWA formed an institutional expression of the internationalism of Baptist life.

A second inference from the findings concerns the relations between gospel and culture. The review has demonstrated that repeatedly the Baptists, in wanting to spread the Christian message, have been molded by the contexts in which they have operated. There has been a constant adjustment to political forces. Thus Baptists became much less concerned to assert that religious liberty should be conceded to all when they gained toleration. Equally, they have accommodated themselves to their social settings. The social gospel, though theologically inspired, was also a response to new circumstances thrown up by the rise of industrialism. Perhaps most powerful as molding influences in the West have been successive broad movements of taste and intellect. Enlightenment ways of thought had a decisive effect on the way in which the Baptists formulated their version of Calvinism, their attitude to religious liberty, and even their doctrine of the church. Romanticism, in turn, reshaped their theology and practice in drastic ways. Both inside and outside the West, national characteristics have asserted themselves too. Americans cast Baptist apologetic in terms acceptable to the nation's civil religion, and Australians developed distinct theological balances in different states. In Russia and Ukraine there was friction between Baptists because of feelings that indigenous preferences were being flouted. In Nagaland Baptists displayed different local characteristics in the various parts of the land. And in Latvia Baptists had bishops. So national and sub-national customs have drastically affected the way Baptists have expressed their faith. The gospel has been adapted to the various forces playing on their lives.

Yet the gospel the Baptists believed has also been a shaper of culture. Because the focus of this book has been on the Baptists themselves, this aspect of their role has received less attention than is its due. There have been glimpses of the impact of Baptists on their wider societies in such matters as the translation of the social gospel into welfare policies and the demand of African American church members for their civil rights. Their influence on the way of life around them has sometimes been highly significant. In many countries their role has been essentially countercultural. In Italy after the Second World War, Baptists were often active in the Socialist and Communist Parties because they formed the effective opposition to the Christian Democrats who represented the traditional Catholic dominance of their country. In Russia during the 1960s and 1970s Baptists were willing to starve themselves so as to extract Bibles and paper from the Soviet authorities. Often in the West, where a countercultural role came less naturally, an influence has been exerted through artistic creativity. Thomas A. Dorsey, the son of a Georgia country preacher, composed gospel songs while based in Chicago. Bringing elements of the blues tradition into his repertoire, from the 1920s onwards Dorsey forged a new idiom and became "The Father of Gospel." The 1950s rock 'n' roll singer Buddy Holly, of Lubbock, Texas, was a pioneer of musical effects that inspired the Beatles. Although Holly is not normally thought of as a Baptist, a letter written by his family after the singer's early death in 1959 reveals his allegiance: "Ours was a christian home and Buddy knew that he was a christian as he had taken care of that important matter early in life. He was a member of the Baptist Church, where he had attended Sunday School and church since babyhood, and he had strong convictions regarding his faith."[5] The gospel songs of Holly's Baptist congregation helped form his style as a composer, which in turn remolded the popular culture of the day. The phenomenally successful novelist John Grisham, who during the 1990s sold over 60 million copies of his books, is another example of a Baptist creative artist whose work is discernibly affected by his religious formation. In many and various ways, both overt and unexpressed, both deliberate and unintentional, members of the denomination have transmitted the influence of the gospel to their culture.

Consequently, Baptists have a multifaceted identity. They originated as radical repudiators of medieval idolatry but went through many subsequent convolutions. They turned into Evangelicals and remain overwhelmingly so. They held contrasting and often conflicting views on social questions. They developed diverse understandings of the church and of the ideal relations of church and state. Their global spread generated far more variety. Hence it is not surprising that, in the twentieth century, as chapter 15 showed, their heritage became a contested area in the largest of the national denominations, the Southern Baptists. Nor should it be unexpected that there were at least seven identifiable streams of life in the worldwide Baptist community at the opening of the twenty-first century. In this multiplicity of identities, believer's baptism continued to be a bond of fellowship among the various Baptist groups, and yet that mode of initiation is now the possession of millions of baptistic congregations beyond the Baptist fold. The practice of immersing on profession of faith is no longer a mark that distinguishes Baptists from other Christians. The belief that all church members should be conscious believers has also been seen as a basic Baptist principle, but again that does not mark them off from many other Evangelicals. A third conviction, the responsibility of members to share in the rule of their own church, was memorably expressed by the first Baptist in the principle of the kingship of all believers. Once more, however, this belief was historically shared with the Congregationalists. Taken together, these three convictions—believer's baptism, a regenerate church membership, and the kingship of all believers—do seem fundamental to Baptist life, but even when taken together they do not form a characterization that includes all Baptists while excluding all others. Some of the most broad-minded Baptists might be unhappy with requiring evidence of conversion as a requirement for membership, while many Pentecostals would happily embrace all three convictions. In the end, therefore, the Baptist identity, a phenomenon of the flux of history, may elude definition. It is perhaps enough that, over the generations, Baptists have conscientiously attempted, with varying degrees of success, to embody the gospel in their cultures.

NOTES

Chapter 1

1   Castle Donington [misspelled "Donnington"] Baptist Church Book 6,
    17 November 1864; quoted by Frank W. Rinaldi, *The Tribe of Dan: The
    New Connexion of General Baptists, 1770–1891: A Study in the Transition
    from Revival Movement to Established Denomination* (Milton Keynes:
    Paternoster, 2008), 85–86.

Chapter 2

1   Eamon Duffy, *The Voices of Morebath: Reformation and Rebellion in an
    English Village* (New Haven, Conn.: Yale University Press, 2001).
2   J. Ayre, ed., *The Works of John Jewel*, 4 vols. (Cambridge: Parker Society,
    1845–1849), 3:106; quoted by Felicity Heal, *Reformation in Britain and
    Ireland* (Oxford: Oxford University Press, 2003), 387.
3   Patrick Collinson, *The Elizabethan Puritan Movement* (London: Cape,
    1967); and idem, *The Religion of Protestants: The Church in English Society,
    1559–1625* (Oxford: Clarendon, 1982).
4   Commonplace book of Abdias Ashton, MSS Mun. A/2/78, p. 87, Chetham
    Library, Manchester; quoted by Peter Lake, *Moderate Puritans and the
    Elizabethan Church* (Cambridge: Cambridge University Press, 1982), 147–
    48.

5   "The Separatist Covenant of Richard Fitz's Congregation," in *The Early English Dissenters in the Light of Recent Research (1550–1641)*, ed. Champlin Burrage (Cambridge: Cambridge University Press, 1912), 2:15.

6   Peter Marshall, *Reformation England, 1480–1642* (London: Arnold, 2003), 121.

7   Henry Jacob, *A Defence of the Churches and Ministery of Englande* (Middelburg, 1599), 11; quoted by Stephen Brachlow, *The Communion of Saints: Radical Puritan and Separatist Ecclesiology, 1570–1625* (Oxford: Oxford University Press, 1988), 56.

8   Roger Hayden, ed., *The Records of a Church of Christ in Bristol, 1640–1687* (Bristol: Bristol Record Society, 1974), 92.

9   Hayden, ed., *Church of Christ in Bristol*, 93.

Chapter 3

1   Ernest A. Payne, "Contacts between Mennonites and Baptists," *Foundations* 4 (1961): 39–55; William R. Estep, *The Anabaptist Story* (Nashville: Broadman, 1963).

2   Barrington R. White, *The English Separatist Tradition: From the Marian Martyrs to the Pilgrim Fathers* (London: Oxford University Press, 1971); Winthrop S. Hudson, "Baptists were not Anabaptists," *Chronicle* 16 (1953): 171–79.

3   Estep, *Anabaptist Story*, 202–9, following Irvin B. Horst, *The Radical Brethren: Anabaptism and the English Reformation to 1588* (Nieuwkoop: De Graaf, 1972).

4   Glen H. Stassen, "Anabaptist Influence in the Origin of the Particular Baptists," *Mennonite Quarterly Review* 36 (1962): 322–48. The argument is restated in Glen H. Stassen, "Opening Menno Simons' *Foundation-Book* and Finding the Father of Baptist Origins alongside the Mother—Calvinist Congregationalism"; and "Revisioning Baptist Identity by Naming our Origin and Character Rightly," *Baptist History and Heritage* 33 (1998): 34–44, 45–54.

5   Stanley A. Nelson, "Reflecting on Baptist Origins: The London Confession of Faith of 1644," *Baptist History and Heritage* 29 (1994): 34–35.

6   "The First London Confession, 1644," Article XL, in H. Leon McBeth, *A Sourcebook for Baptist Heritage* (Nashville: Broadman, 1990), 50.

7   Stephen Wright, *The Early English Baptists, 1603–1649* (Woodbridge, Suffolk: Boydell, 2006), 13.

8   John Smyth, "The Differences of the Churches of the Seperation" (1608), in *The Works of John Smyth*, ed. William T. Whitley, 2 vols. (Cambridge: Cambridge University Press, 1915), 1:282.

9 Smyth, "Differences of the Churches," 1:273, 274.

10 *The Works of John Robinson, Pastor of the Pilgrim Fathers*, 3 vols. (Boston: Doctrinal Tract and Book Society, 1851), 3:168.

11 Wright, *Early English Baptists*, 33 n. 92, shows that the traditional date (which had been questioned by Stephen Brachlow, *The Communion of Saints: Radical Puritans and Separatist Ecclesiology, 1570–1625* [Oxford: Oxford University Press, 1988], 150 n. 1) is correct.

12 Albert H. Newman, *A History of Anti-Pedobaptism* (Philadelphia: American Baptist Publication Society, 1902), 387.

13 *Corde Credimus*, Article 2; quoted in Benjamin Evans, *The Early English Baptists*, 2 vols. (London: J. Heaton, 1862–1864), 1:253.

14 Jason K. Lee, "Smyth's View of Christ," *The Theology of John Smyth: Puritan, Separatist, Baptist, Mennonite* (Macon, Ga.: Mercer University Press, 2003), 209–43.

15 Champlin Burrage, *The Early English Dissenters in the Light of Recent Research (1550–1641)* (Cambridge: Cambridge University Press, 1912), 1:230.

16 John Smyth, "The Character of the Beast" (1609), in *Works of John Smyth*, ed. Whitley, 2:757.

17 Wright, *Early English Baptists*, 99–102.

Chapter 4

1 Henry Jacob, *A Declaration and Plainer Opening of Certain Points* (Middelburg, 1612), 5–6; quoted by Patrick Collinson, "Sects and the Evolution of Protestantism," in *Puritanism: Transatlantic Perspectives on a Seventeenth-Century Anglo-American Faith*, ed. Francis J. Bremer (Boston: Massachusetts Historical Society, 1993), 162.

2 This is to follow the case made out by Stephen Wright, *The Early English Baptists, 1603–1649* (Woodbridge, Suffolk: Boydell, 2006), 75–89.

3 "The First London Confession, 1644," Article XXI, in H. Leon McBeth, *A Sourcebook for Baptist Heritage* (Nashville: Broadman, 1990), 48.

4 Benjamin Coxe, *An Appendix to a Confession of Faith* (London, 1646), 11; quoted by Barrington R. White, "The Frontiers of Fellowship between British Baptists, 1609–1660," *Foundations* 11 (1968): 253.

5 Thomas Edwards, *Gangraena*, pt. 1 (London, 1646), 55 (*bis*); quoted by Murray Tolmie, *The Triumph of the Saints: The Separate Churches of London, 1616–1649* (Cambridge: Cambridge University Press, 1977), 133.

6 Quoted by D. Mervyn Himbury, *British Baptists: A Short History* (London: Carey Kingsgate, 1962), 61.

7 Quoted by H. Leon McBeth, *The Baptist Heritage* (Nashville: Broadman, 1987), 82.

8   Barrington R. White, *Association Records of the Particular Baptists of England, Wales and Ireland to 1660*, pt. 3 (London: Baptist Historical Society, n.d.), 176.

9   J[ames] O[ckford], *The Doctrine of the Fourth Commandment, Deformed by Popery, Reformed & Restored to its Primitive Purity* (London, 1650), 58; quoted by Don A. Sandford, *A Choosing People: The History of the Seventh Day Baptists* (Nashville: Broadman, 1992), 59.

10 "The First London Confession, 1644," Articles XXIV and XXIII, in McBeth, *Sourcebook*, 49.

11 "First London Confession," in McBeth, *Sourcebook*, 46.

12 "A Brief Confession or Declaration of Faith," Article IV, in William L. Lumpkin, *Baptist Confessions of Faith*, rev. ed. (Valley Forge, Pa.: Judson Press, 1969), 225–26.

13 Benjamin Coxe, "To the Reader," in *God's Ordinance, the Saints Priviledge*, by John Spilsbury (London, 1646); quoted by Tolmie, *Triumph of the Saints*, 72.

14 Luke Howard, *A Looking Glass for Baptists* ([London], 1672), 5; quoted by White, "Frontiers of Fellowship," 250; emphasis original.

15 John Griffiths, *God's Oracle and Christ's Doctrine* (1655), 92; quoted by White, "Frontiers of Fellowship," 254.

16 "The First London Confession, 1644," Article XLVII, in McBeth, *Sourcebook*, 51.

17 "Orthodox Creed," Article XXXIX, in Lumpkin, *Baptist Confessions*, 327.

18 Edward Barber, *A True Discovery of the Ministry of the Gospell* (London, 1645), 1; quoted by Barrington R. White, *The English Baptists of the Seventeenth Century* (London: Baptist Historical Society, 1983), 35.

19 Edward B. Underhill, *Records of the Churches of Christ Gathered at Fenstanton, Warboys and Hexham, 1644–1720* (London, 1854), 5–6; quoted by White, *Baptists of the Seventeenth Century*, 46.

20 "Brief Confession," Article XXIV, in Lumpkin, *Baptist Confessions*, 233.

21 *A Declaration by Congregational Societies in and about the City of London, as well as Those Commonly Called Anabaptists, as Others* (1647), 9; quoted by Tolmie, *Triumph of the Saints*, 170.

22 White, *Association Records*, pt. 2, 61.

23 White, *Association Records*, pt. 2, 56.

24 Thomas Grantham, *Christianismus Primitivus* (London, 1678); quoted by Ted L. Underwood, *Primitivism, Radicalism and the Lamb's War: The Baptist-Quaker Conflict in Seventeenth-Century England* (New York: Oxford University Press, 1997), 84.

25 Christopher Blackwood, *The Storming of Antichrist*, part 2; quoted by McBeth, *Sourcebook*, 43.

26 William Kiffin, preface to Thomas Goodwin, *A Glimpse of Syons Glory* (London, 1641); quoted by Tolmie, *Triumph of the Saints*, 85.

27 Thomas Collier, *The Exaltation of Christ in the Dayes of the Gospel* (London: Giles Calvert, 1646), 234; quoted by Barrington R. White, "Thomas Collier and Gangraena Edwards," *Baptist Quarterly* 24 (1971): 106.

Chapter 5

1 James Foster, *An Essay on Fundamentals with a Particular Regard to the Doctrine of the Ever-Blessed Trinity* (London: For J. Clarke, 1720), 4; quoted by Stephen Copson, "Stogdon, Foster, and Bulkeley: Variations on an Eighteenth-Century Theme," in *Pulpit and People: Studies in Eighteenth Century Baptist Life and Thought*, ed. John H. Y. Briggs (Milton Keynes: Paternoster, 2009), 50.

2 John Gill, *The Watchman's Answer to the Question, "What of the Night?"* (1750), 25; quoted by Timothy George, "Controversy and Communion: The Limits of Baptist Fellowship from Bunyan to Spurgeon," in *The Gospel in the World: International Baptist Studies*, ed. David W. Bebbington (Carlisle: Paternoster, 2002), 48.

3 Abram D. Gillette, ed., *Minutes of the Philadelphia Baptist Association, 1707 to 1807* (1851; repr., Springfield, Mo.: Particular Baptist Press, 2002), 47.

4 *Christian History*, August 27, 1743; quoted by Thomas S. Kidd, *The Great Awakening: The Roots of Evangelical Christianity in Colonial America* (New Haven, Conn.: Yale University Press, 2007), 111.

5 Raymond Brown, *The English Baptists of the Eighteenth Century* (London: Baptist Historical Society, 1986), 78.

6 Thomas S. Kidd, "'Do the Holy Scriptures Countenance Such Wild Disorder?': Baptist Growth in the Eighteenth-Century American South," in *Baptists and Mission: Papers from the Fourth International Conference on Baptist Studies*, ed. Ian M. Randall and Anthony R. Cross (Milton Keynes: Paternoster, 2007), 109.

7 Minutes, May 27, 1792; quoted by Damon C. Dodd, *The Free Will Baptist Story* (Nashville: Executive Department of the National Association of Free Will Baptists, 1956), 84.

8 Dan Taylor, *A Dissertation on Singing in the Worship of God* (London, 1786); quoted by H. Leon McBeth, *A Sourcebook for Baptist Heritage* (Nashville: Broadman, 1990), 110.

Chapter 6

1   William M. Tryon to editor, *Baptist Banner*, October 14, 1841.
2   Nathan O. Hatch, *The Democratization of American Religion* (New Haven, Conn.: Yale University Press, 1989).
3   W. J. Berry, comp., *The Kehukee Declaration and Black Rock Address* (n.p., n.d.), 25.
4   Joshua Lawrence, "Declaration of the Reformed Baptist Churches in the State of North Carolina [1827]," *Primitive Baptist* 7 (May 14, 1842), 130; quoted by John G. Crowley, *Primitive Baptists of the Wiregrass South: 1815 to the Present* (Gainesville: University Press of Florida, 1998), 60.
5   John Taylor, *Thoughts on Missions* (n.p., 1819), 22; quoted by William W. Sweet, *Religion on the American Frontier: The Baptists, 1780–1830* (New York: Henry Holt, 1931), 72.
6   William P. Throgmorton and Lemuel Potter, *Who Are the Primitive Baptists? The Throgmorton-Potter Debate* (St. Louis, Mo.: Nixon-Jones, 1888), 2; quoted by Howard Dorgan, *In the Hands of a Happy God: The "No-Hellers" of Central Appalachia* (Knoxville: University of Tennessee Press, 1997), 24.
7   Lawrence, "Declaration," 130; quoted by Crowley, *Primitive Baptists*, 60.
8   "Constitution of the Apple Creek Association," Article 19, in Sweet, *Religion on the American Frontier: The Baptists*, 64.
9   Quoted by Robert W. Oliver, "John Collett Ryland, Daniel Turner and Robert Robinson and the Communion Controversy, 1772–1781," *Baptist Quarterly* 29 (1981–1982): 78.
10 Olinthus Gregory, ed., *The Works of Robert Hall, A. M.*, 6 vols. (London, 1832), 2:14; quoted by Michael Walker, *Baptists at the Table: The Theology of the Lord's Supper amongst English Baptists in the Nineteenth Century* (Didcot, Oxfordshire: Baptist Historical Society, 1992), 46.
11 Thomas Edwards, "Our Privileges and Duties," *Circular Letter to the Churches of the Radnorshire and Montgomery Baptist Association* (1897). I am grateful to the Rev. Dr. Michael Collis for this reference.
12 Quoted by John McCardell, *The Idea of a Southern Nation: Southern Nationalists and Southern Nationalism, 1830–1860* (New York: Norton, 1979), 183.
13 *Proceedings of the Fifth Annual Meeting of the Baptist State Convention of North Carolina* (Newborn, N.C.: Recorder Office, 1835), 8; quoted by Mitchell Snay, *Gospel of Disunion: Religion and Separatism in the Antebellum South* (Cambridge: Cambridge University Press, 1993), 31.
14 Aldexander Campbell in *Christian Baptist* 1 (1823): 21–22; quoted by Robert F. West, *Alexander Campbell and Natural Religion* (New Haven, Conn.: Yale University Press, 1948), 31.

15 *Tennessee Baptist,* October 6, 1857; quoted by H. Leon McBeth, *A Sourcebook for Baptist Heritage* (Nashville: Broadman, 1990), 318, 319.

Chapter 7

1 William Medley, *Rawdon Baptist College: Centenary Memorial* (London: Kingsgate, 1904), 26.

2 *General Baptist Magazine,* February 1859, 46–49; quoted by John H. Y. Briggs, *The English Baptists of the Nineteenth Century* (Didcot, Oxfordshire: Baptist Historical Society, 1994), 109–10.

3 John Howard Hinton, "Strictures on Some Passages in the Rev. J. B. Brown's 'Divine Life in Man,'" *Baptist Magazine,* April 1860, 226.

4 Crawford H. Toy, *Quotations in the New Testament* (New York: Scribner's, 1884), xxix; quoted by Gregory A. Wills, *Southern Baptist Theological Seminary, 1859–2009* (New York: Oxford University Press, 2009), 147.

5 Archibald Fergusson in *Annual Paper concerning the Lord's Work in Connection with the Pastors' College, Newington, London, 1881–82* (London: Alabaster, Passmore & Sons, 1882), 17.

6 C. H. Spurgeon in *Outline of the Lord's Work by the Pastor's College and its Kindred Organisations at the Metropolitan Tabernacle* (London: Passmore & Alabaster, 1867), 14.

7 Patricia S. Kruppa, *Charles Haddon Spurgeon: A Preacher's Progress* (New York: Garland, 1982), 424.

8 William Newton Clarke, *An Outline of Christian Theology* (New York: Scribner's, 1898), 1.

9 Shailer Mathews, *The Gospel and the Modern Man* (New York: Macmillan, 1910), 235.

10 Edgar Y. Mullins, "Southern Baptists and the Changing Viewpoint," *Biblical Reporter* 22 (April 1903): 2; quoted by Wills, *Southern Baptist Theological Seminary,* 237.

11 William B. Riley, *The Menace of Modernism* (New York: Christian Alliance, 1917); quoted by William Vance Trollinger Jr., *God's Empire: William Bell Riley and Midwestern Fundamentalism* (Madison: University of Wisconsin Press, 1990), 34.

12 *Watchman-Examiner,* July 1, 1920; quoted by George M. Marsden, *Fundamentalism and American Culture: The Shaping of Twentieth-Century Evangelicalism, 1870–1925* (New York: Oxford University Press, 1980), 159.

13 William B. Riley, "Modernism in Baptist Schools," *School and Church* (October–December 1920): 407–22; quoted by Trollinger, *God's Empire,* 54.

14 *Watchman-Examiner,* June 29, 1922; quoted by Trollinger, *God's Empire,* 56.

15 B. I. Greenwood reported in *Record*, June 14, 1923.

Chapter 8

1 Walter Rauschenbusch, *Christianity and the Social Crisis* (New York: Macmillan, 1907), 65.

2 Russell H. Conwell, *Acres of Diamonds* (1890; repr., New York, 1915); quoted by Henry F. May, *Protestant Churches and Industrial America* (New York: Harper & Brothers, 1949), 199.

3 *The Church* (1854), 308; quoted by David W. Bebbington, "The Baptist Conscience in the Nineteenth Century," *Baptist Quarterly* 24 (1991): 17.

4 [No author] "The Millennium: Its Nature and Blessings," *General Baptist Magazine*, July 1854, 308.

5 *Watchman and Reflector*, March 26, 1857; quoted by Timothy L. Smith, *Revivalism and Social Reform: American Protestantism on the Eve of the Civil War* (Nashville: Abingdon, 1957), 152–53.

6 Walter Rauschenbusch, *A Theology for the Social Gospel* (1917; repr., Nashville: Abingdon, 1945), 131.

7 Ronald C. White Jr. and C. Howard Hopkins, *The Social Gospel: Religion and Reform in Changing America* (Philadelphia: Temple University Press, 1976), 73.

8 Shailer Mathews, *The Social Gospel* (Philadelphia: Griffith & Rowland, 1910), 107.

9 Charles F. Aked, *Calvin and Calvinism* (London: James Clarke, [1891]), 7.

10 Mathews, *Social Gospel*, 11.

11 Mathews, *Social Gospel*, 151.

12 Augustus H. Strong to Walter Rauschenbusch, 28 December 1917; quoted by Christopher H. Evans, *The Kingdom is Always but Coming: A Life of Walter Rauschenbusch* (Grand Rapids: Eerdmans, 2004), 299.

13 Walter Rauschenbusch, "The New Evangelism," *Independent*, May 12, 1904; quoted by Evans, *Kingdom is Always but Coming*, 168.

14 Mathews, *Social Gospel*, 107.

15 John Clifford, *The Effect of Socialism on Personal Character* (n.p., 1893), 2.

16 John Clifford in *Christian World*, January 20, 1898.

17 Walter Rauschenbusch, "The Welsh Revival and Primitive Christianity," in *Walter Rauschenbusch: Selected Writings*, ed. Winthrop S. Hudson (New York: Paulist Press, 1984), 111. (Originally published in *The Watchman*, June 15, 1905.)

18 Isaac M. Haldeman, *Professor Rauschenbusch's "Christianity and the Social Crisis"* (New York: Charles C. Cook, 1911), 42, 40; quoted by Evans, *Kingdom is Always but Coming*, 225.

Chapter 9

1 Randy J. Sparks, "Religion in Amite County, Mississippi, 1800–1861," in *Masters and Slaves in the House of the Lord: Race and Religion in the American South, 1740–1870*, ed. John B. Boles (Lexington: University Press of Kentucky, 1988), 63.

2 Richard Furman, *Exposition of the Views of the Baptists relative to the Coloured Population of the United States* (Charleston, S.C.: A. E. Miller, 1823); quoted by H. Leon McBeth, *A Sourcebook for Baptist Heritage* (Nashville: Broadman, 1990), 253.

3 William McLoughlin, *Cherokees and Missionaries, 1789–1839* (New Haven, Conn.: Yale University Press, 1984), 155.

4 Records of the Academy Baptist Church, Mississippi (n.d.); quoted by Randy J. Sparks, *On Jordan's Stormy Banks: Evangelicalism in Mississippi, 1773–1876* (Athens: University of Georgia Press, 1994), 198.

5 Tishomingo Baptist Association, *Proceedings of the Ninth Annual Session* (1869), Memphis, 8; quoted by Sparks, *Jordan's Stormy Banks*, 192.

6 *Christian Index*, March 22, 1883; quoted by McBeth, *Sourcebook*, 282.

7 Southern Baptist Convention, "Report of the Home Mission Board," *Annual* (1891): xxxvi; quoted by McBeth, *Sourcebook*, 287.

8 Paul Harvey, *Freedom's Coming: Religious Culture and the Shaping of the American South from the Civil War through the Civil Rights Era* (Chapel Hill: University of North Carolina Press, 2005), 39.

9 Paul Harvey, *Redeeming the South: Religious Cultures and Racial Identities among Southern Baptists, 1865–1925* (Chapel Hill: University of North Carolina Press, 1997), 231 (original source unidentifiable).

10 Elias Camp Morris, *Sermons, Addresses, Reminiscences and Important Correspondence* (Nashville: National Baptist Publishing Board, 1901); quoted by Harvey, *Redeeming the South*, 189.

11 Sutton E. Griggs, *Imperium in Imperio* (Cincinnati: Editor Publishing, 1899); quoted by Harvey, *Redeeming the South*, 234.

12 George D. Kelsey, undated MS, Drew University Library, Madison, N.J.; quoted by Dennis C. Dickerson, "African American Religious Intellectuals and the Theological Foundations of the Civil Rights Movement, 1930–55," *Church History* 74 (2005): 227.

13 Quoted without source by Harvey, *Freedom's Coming*, 94.

14 Andrew M. Manis, "'Dying from the Neck Up': Southern Baptist Resistance to the Civil Rights Movement," *Baptist History and Heritage* 34 (1999): 33.

15 Billy G. Pierce in *Arkansas Baptist Newsmagazine*, August 8, 1963, quoted by Mark Newman, *Getting Right with God: Southern Baptists and*

Desegregation, 1945–1995 (Tuscaloosa: University of Alabama Press, 2001), 61.

16 Thomas B. Maston, *Segregation and Desegregation: A Christian Approach* (New York: Macmillan, 1959), 163; quoted by Newman, *Getting Right with God*, 67.

17 Southern Baptist Convention, *Annual* (1960); 273; quoted by Newman, *Getting Right with God*, 81.

18 Fannie Lou Hamer, "Sick and Tired of Being Sick and Tired," *Katallagete* (Fall 1968): 26; quoted by Harvey, *Freedom's Coming*, 198.

19 Quoted by Leroy Fitts, *A History of Black Baptists* (Nashville: Broadman, 1985), 287.

20 *Baptist Times*, June 28, 1956, 9; quoted by Ian M. Randall, *The English Baptists of the Twentieth Century* (Didcot, Oxfordshire: Baptist Historical Society, 2005), 306–7.

21 Southern Baptist Convention, *Annual* (1995): 81; quoted by Newman, *Getting Right with God*, 202.

Chapter 10

1 John Smyth, "Paralleles, Censures, Observations" (1609), in *The Works of John Smyth*, ed. William T. Whitley, 2 vols. (Cambridge: Cambridge University Press, 1915), 2:430.

2 Maze Pond Baptist Church Book (1691–1745), 109; quoted by Michael R. Watts, *The Dissenters: From the Reformation to the French Revolution* (Oxford: Clarendon, 1978), 320.

3 Abram D. Gillette, ed., *Minutes of the Philadelphia Baptist Association, 1707 to 1807* (1851; repr., Springfield, Mo.: Particular Baptist Press, 2002), 53.

4 *General Baptist Repository* (April 1850): 188–89; quoted by David W. Bebbington, Kenneth Dix, and Alan Ruston, eds., *Protestant Nonconformist Texts*, vol. 3: *The Nineteenth Century* (Aldershot, Hampshire: Ashgate, 2006), 249–50.

5 Abigail Harris Papers, 1801–1827, Cumberland County Historical Society, Greenwich, N.J.; quoted by Janet Moore Lindman, "Beyond the Meetinghouse: Women and Protestant Spirituality in Early America," in *The Religious History of American Women: Reimagining the Past*, ed. Catherine A. Brekus (Chapel Hill: University of North Carolina Press, 2007), 151.

6 *Baptist Magazine*, 1852, 698; quoted by Linda Wilson, *Constrained by Zeal: Female Spirituality amongst Nonconformists, 1825–75* (Carlisle: Paternoster, 2000), 109.

7   Abigail Harris Papers, Miscellaneous Items, 24 May 1808; quoted by Lindman, "Beyond the Meetinghouse," 151.

8   [E. Macpherson], *A Mother's Legacy to her Children* (Bristol, n.d.), 57; quoted by Bebbington, Dix, and Ruston, *Protestant Nonconformist Texts*, 245.

9   Frank K. Prochaska, *Women and Philanthropy in Victorian England* (Oxford: Clarendon, 1980), 147.

10 *Baptist Magazine*, 1852, 698; quoted by Wilson, *Constrained by Zeal*, 57.

11 Alma Hunt, *History of Woman's Missionary Union* (Nashville: Convention Press, [1964]), 49.

12 Southern Baptist Convention, *Annual* (1917): 90; quoted by Paul Harvey, "Saints but Not Subordinates: The Woman's Missionary Union of the Southern Baptist Convention," in *Women and Twentieth-Century Protestantism*, ed. Margaret Lamberts Bendroth and Virginia Lieson Brereton (Urbana: University of Illinois Press, 2002), 15.

13 William T. Whitley, ed., *Third Baptist World Congress, Stockholm, July 21–27, 1923* (London: Kingsgate, 1923), 99; quoted by Kendal P. Mobley, *Helen Barrett Montgomery: The Global Mission of Domestic Feminism* (Waco, Tex.: Baylor University Press, 2009), 1.

14 National Baptist Convention, *Journal of the Twentieth Annual Session of the National Baptist Convention, Held in Richmond, Virginia, September 12–17, 1900* (Nashville: National Baptist Publishing Board, 1900), 68; quoted by Evelyn Brooks Higginbotham, *Righteous Discontent: The Women's Movement in the Black Baptist Church, 1880–1920* (Cambridge, Mass.: Harvard University Press, 1993), 150.

15 "Women and Men as Partners in Church and Society" (December 1985); quoted by "American Baptist Policy Statements," *American Baptist Quarterly* 5 (1986): 160.

16 "Resolution on the Place of Women in Christian Service" (June 1973); quoted by Bill J. Leonard, *Baptists in America* (New York: Columbia University Press, 2005), 217.

Chapter 11

1   John Smyth, "The Differences of the Churches of the Seperation" (1608), in *The Works of John Smyth*, ed. William T. Whitley, 2 vols. (Cambridge: Cambridge University Press, 1915), 1:269.

2   Edward Barber, *A Small Treatise on Baptisme, or Dipping* (n.p., 1641); quoted by H. Leon McBeth, *A Sourcebook for Baptist Heritage* (Nashville: Broadman, 1990), 42.

3   John Fawcett, *Christ Precious to Those That Believe* (1799; repr., Minneapolis: Klock & Klock Christian Publishers, 1979), 230; quoted by Michael

A. G. Haykin, "'His Soul-Refreshing Presence': The Lord's Supper in Calvinistic Baptist Thought and Experience in the 'Long' Eighteenth Century," in *Baptist Sacramentalism*, ed. Anthony R. Cross and Philip E. Thompson (Carlisle: Paternoster, 2003), 188.

4   Charles H. Spurgeon, *Till He Come* (London: Passmore & Alabaster, 1894), 7.

5   "Orthodox Creed," Article XXX, in W. L. Lumpkin, *Baptist Confessions of Faith*, rev. ed. (Valley Forge, Pa.: Judson Press, 1969), 319.

6   Morgan Edwards, *The Customs of Primitive Churches* (Philadelphia, 1774), 9–10; quoted by Philip E. Thompson, "Re-Envisioning Baptist Identity: Historical, Theological and Liturgical Analysis," *Perspectives in Religious Studies* 27 (2000): 294 n. 33.

7   Henry Lawrence, *Of Baptism*, 3rd ed. (London: F. Macock, 1659), 10; quoted by Stanley K. Fowler, *More Than a Symbol: The British Baptist Recovery of Baptismal Sacramentalism* (Carlisle: Paternoster, 2002), 25.

8   "Orthodox Creed," Article XXVII, in Lumpkin, *Baptist Confessions*, 317.

9   Hercules Collins, *An Orthodox Catechism* (London, 1680), 41–42; quoted by E. P. Winter, "Calvinist and Zwinglian Views of the Lord's Supper among the Baptists of the Seventeenth Century," *Baptist Quarterly* 15 (1954): 327.

10   Spurgeon, *Till He Come*, 69.

11   Andrew Fuller, "The Practical Uses of Christian Baptism," in *The Works of Andrew Fuller*, ed. Thomas Belcher (Philadelphia, 1845), 3:341; quoted by Barry Vaughn, "The Transition from the Sacramental to the Ordinal View of Baptism in Baptist Historical Documents," *Oklahoma Baptist Chronicle* 29 (1986): 60.

12   Francis Wayland, *Salvation by Christ* (Boston, 1859), 321; quoted by Norman H. Waring, "The Individualism of Francis Wayland," in *Baptist Concepts of the Church*, ed. Winthrop S. Hudson (Philadelphia: Judson Press, 1959), 152.

13   John Clifford, *The Ordinances of Jesus and the Sacraments of the Church* (London, 1888), 4; quoted by Anthony R. Cross, *Baptism and the Baptists: Theology and Practice in Twentieth-Century Britain* (Carlisle: Paternoster, 2000), 13.

14   L. F. Greene, ed., *The Writings of John Leland* (1845; repr., New York: Arno, 1969), 58; quoted by Edwin S. Gaustad, "The Backus-Leland Tradition," in Hudson, *Baptist Concepts*, 119.

15   Francis Wayland, *Notes on the Principles and Practices of Baptist Churches* (New York: Sheldon, Blakeman, 1857), 132.

16   Charles Stovel, *The Baptismal Regeneration Controversy Considered* (London, 1843), 141; quoted by John H. Y. Briggs, *The English Baptists of*

the Nineteenth Century (Didcot, Oxfordshire: Baptist Historical Society, 1994), 46.

17 Edgar Y. Mullins, *The Axioms of Religion* (Philadelphia: Judson Press, 1908), 53.

18 William R. McNutt, *Polity and Practice in Baptist Churches* (Philadelphia: Judson Press, 1935), 22.

19 Herschel H. Hobbs, *The Baptist Faith and Message* (Nashville: Convention Press, 1971), 83.

20 Augustus H. Strong, *Systematic Theology* (Philadelphia: Judson Press, 1907), 964.

21 H. Wheeler Robinson, "The Place of Baptism in Baptist Churches To-Day," *Baptist Quarterly* 1 (1922–1923): 210.

22 Curtis W. Freeman, "Can Baptist Theology Be Re-envisioned?" *Perspectives in Religious Studies* 26 (1999): 306.

Chapter 12

1 George Truett, "Baptists and Religious Liberty"; quoted by H. Leon McBeth, *A Sourcebook for Baptist Heritage* (Nashville: Broadman, 1990), 469.

2 John Smyth, "A Paterne of true Prayer" (1605), in *The Works of John Smyth*, ed. William T. Whitley, 2 vols. (Cambridge: Cambridge University Press, 1915), 1:166.

3 Thomas Helwys, *A Short Declaration of the Mistery of Iniquity* (1612; repr., London: Kingsgate Press for the Baptist Historical Society, 1935), 69.

4 Helwys, *Mistery of Iniquity*, 46.

5 John Murton, *Persecution for Religion Judged and Condemned* (1620); in *Tracts on Liberty of Conscience and Persecution, 1614–1661*, ed. Edward B. Underhill (London: J. Haddon, 1846), 192.

6 Edward Barber, *To the Kings Most Excellent Majesty* (1641); quoted by John Coffey, "From Helwys to Leland: Baptists and Religious Toleration in England and America, 1612–1791," in *The Gospel in the World: International Baptist Studies*, ed. David W. Bebbington (Carlisle: Paternoster, 2002), 16–17.

7 Samuel Richardson, *The Necessity of Toleration in Matters of Religion* (1647), in Underhill, *Tracts*, 274.

8 Roger Williams, *The Bloudy Tenent of Persecution* [1644], ed. Edward B. Underhill (London: J. Haddon, 1848), 193–94.

9 Alvah Hovey, *A Memoir of the Life and Times of the Rev. Isaac Backus* (Boston: Gould & Lincoln, 1859), 210.

10 John Williams, Journal, May 12, 1771, Virginia Baptist Historical Society,

Richmond, Va.; quoted by Rhys Isaac, "'The Rage and Malice of the Old Serpent Devil': The Dissenters and the Making and Remaking of the Virginia Statute for Religious Freedom," in *The Virginia Statute for Religious Freedom: Its Evolution and Consequences in American History*, ed. Merrill D. Peterson and Robert C. Vaughan (Cambridge: Cambridge University Press, 1988), 142.

11 John Leland, "The Rights of Conscience Inalienable" [1791], in *The Writings of John Leland*, ed. L. F. Greene (1845; repr., New York: Arno, 1969), 188.

12 Minutes of the Baptist Union of Great Britain and Ireland (1833–1842), May 3, 1838, 147, Angus Library, Regent's Park College, Oxford.

13 Minutes of the Philadelphia Baptist Association (1815), p. 7, Philadelphia Baptist Association, Philadelphia, Pa.

14 *Proceedings of the Baptist General Convention of Texas* (1912): 133; quoted by C. C. Goen, "Baptists and Church-State Issues in the Twentieth Century," *American Baptist Quarterly* 6 (1987): 228.

15 *Proceedings of the Baptist General Convention of Texas* (1905): 82; quoted by Goen, "Baptists and Church-State Issues," 228 n. 3.

16 *New York Baptist Annual* (1921): 29; quoted by Goen, "Baptists and Church-State Issues," 229.

17 Truett, "Baptists and Religious Liberty," in McBeth, *Sourcebook*, 469.

18 Joseph M. Dawson, "The Church and Religious Liberty," *Review and Expositor* 50 (1953): 156–58; quoted by Goen, "Baptists and Church-State Issues," 241.

19 W. A. Criswell reported in *Church and State* 37 (1984): 23.

Chapter 13

1 William Carey, *An Enquiry into the Obligations of Christians to Use Means for the Conversion of the Heathens*, ed. Ernest A. Payne (1792; repr., London: Carey Kingsgate, 1961), 37.

2 Carey, *Enquiry*, 62.

3 Carey, *Enquiry*, 68.

4 Brian Stanley, *The History of the Baptist Missionary Society, 1792–1992* (Edinburgh: T&T Clark, 1992), 14.

5 William Carey to John Sutcliffe, December 29, 1800, Baptist Missionary Society MSS, Angus Library, Regent's Park College, Oxford; quoted by E. Daniel Potts, *British Baptist Missionaries in India, 1793–1837* (Cambridge: Cambridge University Press, 1967), 35.

6 "The Relation of Various Missionary Methods to Carrying the Gospel to All the Non-Christian World," *World Missionary Conference, 1910:*

Report of Commission I: Carrying the Gospel to the Non-Christian World (Edinburgh: Oliphant, Anderson & Ferrier, [1910]), 315.

7   William Carey to John Ryland, June 12, 1806, College Street Baptist Church, Northampton, MSS; quoted by Potts, *British Baptist Missionaries*, 19.

8   Calista V. Luther, *The Vintons and the Karens* (Boston: W. G. Corthell, 1880), 25; quoted by Aileen Sutherland Collins, "Calista Holman Vinton: Not Just a Missionary's Wife," *American Baptist Quarterly* 12 (1993): 213.

9   Dr. M. B. Anderson's resolution to the Executive Committee, quoted by Robert G. Torbet, *The Story of the American Baptist Foreign Mission Society and the Woman's American Baptist Foreign Mission Society, 1814–1954* (Philadelphia: Judson Press, 1955), 152.

10   Wesley W. Lawton, Diary, 18 November 1923; quoted by Paul Harvey, "The Politicization of White and Black Southern Baptist Missionaries, 1880–1930," *American Baptist Quarterly* 13 (1994): 213.

11   "The African Inland Mission," *Hearing and Doing* 1 (1896): 4; quoted by Dana L. Robert, *American Women in Mission: A Social History of Their Thought and Practice* (Macon, Ga.: Mercer University Press, 1996), 208.

12   Henry R. Williamson, *Fresh Ventures in Fellowship* (London: Baptist Missionary Society, 1944), 32; quoted by Stanley, *Baptist Missionary Society*, 364.

13   Henry Mugabe, "Theological Education and the Quest for Identity in the Baptist Convention of Zimbabwe," in *Baptist Identities: International Studies from the Seventeenth to the Twentieth Centuries*, ed. Ian M. Randall, Toivo Pilli, and Anthony R. Cross (Milton Keynes: Paternoster, 2006), 304.

Chapter 14

1   Quoted by Ian M. Randall, *Communities of Conviction: Baptist Beginnings in Europe* (Schwarzenfeld, Germany: Neufeld, 2009), 51.

2   Quoted by Randall, *Communities of Conviction*, 45.

3   "Verhandlungen," First Conference (1851), 8; quoted by Ernest K. Pasiciel, "The Sociocultural Transformation of the North American Baptist Conference," in *Memory and Hope: Strands of Canadian Baptist History*, ed. David T. Priestley (Waterloo, Ontario: Wilfrid Laurier University Press, 1996), 72–73.

4   Quoted by George W. Sadler et al., *Europe—Whither Bound?* (Nashville: Broadman, 1951), 80.

5   Robert F. Byrnes, *Pobedonostsev: His Life and Thought* (Bloomington: Indiana University Press, 1968), 182; quoted by Heather J. Coleman,

"Baptist Beginnings in Russia and Ukraine," *Baptist History and Heritage* 42 (2007): 29.

6   H. Estcourt Hughes in *Australian Baptist*, September 24, 1918, 2; quoted by Ken R. Manley, "'Our own Church in our own Land': The Shaping of Baptist Identity in Australia," in *Baptist Identities: International Studies from the Seventeenth to the Twentieth Centuries*, ed. Ian M. Randall, Toivo Pilli, and Anthony R. Cross (Milton Keynes: Paternoster, 2006), 276.

7   J. H. Sexton in *Australian Baptist* (July 3, 1901): 170; quoted by Manley, "'Our Own Church,'" 291.

8   Vasilii Ivanov, quoted by Coleman, "Baptist Beginnings in Russia and Ukraine," 32.

9   Quoted by Coleman, "Baptist Beginnings in Russia and Ukraine," 31.

10 International Work Group for Indigenous Affairs, *The Naga Nation and its Struggle against Genocide* (Copenhagen: International Work Group for Indigenous Affairs, 1986), 107; quoted by Robert Eric Frykenberg, "Naga Baptists: A Brief Narrative of Their Genesis," in Randall, Pilli, and Cross, *Baptist Identities*, 236.

Chapter 15

1   "The First London Confession, 1644," quoted in H. Leon McBeth, *A Sourcebook for Baptist Heritage* (Nashville: Broadman, 1990), 44.

2   John Quincy Adams, *Baptists the Only thorough Religious Reformers*, rev. ed. (New York: Sheldon, 1876), 176

3   Edgar Y. Mullins, *The Axioms of Religion* (Philadelphia: Judson Press, 1908), 131.

4   Mullins, *Axioms*, 54.

5   James H. Rushbrooke, *Protestant of the Protestants: The Baptist Churches, Their Progress, and Their Spiritual Principle* (London: Kingsgate, 1926), 70.

6   "Baptist Faith and Message" (1925), http://www.sbc.net/bfm/bfmcomparison.asp (accessed November 16, 2009).

7   Paul Pressler, *A Hill on Which to Die* (Nashville, Tenn.: Broadman & Holman, 1999), x.

8   Alan Neely, ed., *Being Baptist Means Freedom* (Atlanta: Southern Baptist Alliance, 1988).

9   Walter B. Shurden, *The Baptist Identity: Four Fragile Freedoms* (Macon, Ga.: Smyth & Helwys, 1993), 23.

10 Charles W. Deweese, ed., *Defining Baptist Convictions: Guidelines for the Twenty-First Century* (Franklin, Tenn.: Providence House, 1996), 32.

11 Brent Greene, in "Moderates asked to embrace 'missional church' move-

ment." *The Biblical Recorder,* March 2005; quoted by Ed Stetzer, "Toward a Missional Convention," in *Southern Baptist Identity,* ed. David S. Dockery (Wheaton, Ill.: Crossway Books, 2009), 179.

12 http://www.leftbehind.com/ (accessed November 29, 2006).

13 Robert Payne MSS, Baptist Union of Victoria Archives; quoted by Ken R. Manley, *From Woolloomooloo to "Eternity": A History of Australian Baptists,* 2 vols. (Milton Keynes: Paternoster, 2006), 2:712.

14 Russell D. Moore, "Learning from Nineteenth-Century Baptists," in Dockery, *Southern Baptist Identity,* 112.

15 "Re-Envisioning Baptist Identity: A Manifesto for Baptist Communities in North America," in Curtis W. Freeman, "Can Baptist Theology be Re-Envisioned?" *Perspectives in Religious Studies* 26 (1999): 303, 306.

16 Janis Inkis, "Jubilejas vienpadsmita diena—Puraciema," *Avots* 30 (1912): 353; quoted by Valdis Teraudkalns, "Leaving Behind Imagined Uniformity: Changing Identities of Latvian Baptist Churches," in *Baptist Identities: International Studies from the Seventeenth to the Twentieth Centuries,* ed. Ian M. Randall, Toivo Pilli, and Anthony R. Cross (Milton Keynes: Paternoster, 2006), 112.

Chapter 16

1 William G. McLoughlin, *New England Dissent, 1603–1833: The Baptists and the Separation of Church and State,* 2 vols. (Cambridge, Mass.: Harvard University Press, 1971), 1:6.

2 William H. Brackney, "Transatlantic Relationships: The Making of an International Baptist Community," in *The Gospel in the World: International Baptist Studies,* ed. David W. Bebbington (Carlisle: Paternoster, 2002), 59–79.

3 Abram D. Gillette, ed., *Minutes of the Philadelphia Baptist Association, 1701 to 1807* (1851; repr., Springfield, Mo.: Particular Baptist Press, 2002), 84.

4 Charles G. Sommers, William R. Williams, and Levi L. Hill, eds., *The Baptist Library: A Republication of Standard Baptist Works,* 3 vols. (New York: Lewis Colby, 1846).

5 The Family of Buddy Holly to Andy Gray, 2 April 1960, Buddy Holly Center, Lubbock, Texas.

INDEX